a
New Yorker
in Egypt

Also by Hans Koning

The Affair
An American Romance
A Walk with Love and Death
I Know What I'm Doing
The Revolutionary
Death of a Schoolboy
The Petersburg-Cannes Express

Love and Hate in China
Along the Roads of Russia
The Almost World
Columbus: His Enterprise

a
New Yorker
in Egypt

HANS KONING
[Hans Koningsberger]

A HELEN AND KURT WOLFF BOOK

HARCOURT BRACE JOVANOVICH

NEW YORK AND LONDON

916.2
K

Copyright © 1976 by Hans Koning

All rights reserved. No part of this publication
may be reproduced or transmitted in any form or
by any means, electronic or mechanical, including
photocopy, recording, or any information storage
and retrieval system, without permission in
writing from the publisher.

Printed in the United States of America

The quotes from Mahmoud Hussein's *Class Conflict in Egypt,*
© 1973 by the Monthly Review Press, are reprinted by
permission of the Monthly Review Press. The quote from
James Aldridge's *Cairo* is reprinted by permission of
Little, Brown and Company.

Library of Congress Cataloging in Publication Data
Koningsberger, Hans.
  A New Yorker in Egypt.
  "A Helen and Kurt Wolff book."
    1. Egypt—Description and travel—1945–
2. Koningsberger, Hans. I. Title.
DT56.K62   916.2'04'50924   76-20535
ISBN 0-15-165520-0

First edition

B C D E

a
New Yorker
in Egypt

Jan. 77   B+T.   7.06

It was mid-September and the sun on the deck of the ship was scorching. The Mediterranean was even bluer than in the travel ads: a chemical blue, like Quink ink, clashing with instead of reflecting the soft blue of the sky. The ship was an Italian car-ferry, only a year old but already falling apart like a slummy apartment building. You had to stand in line for the bad food and pay for it in lire they changed at 620 to the dollar, which was mini-robbery, and my fellow passengers had demonstrated at the chaotic boarding in Mestre (off Venice) that they'd sooner stick a knife in you than take their turns.

But I wasn't sorry I was traveling this way. I was going to Egypt, and I was decided to get there not by being plunked down at an international airport two hundred miles inland, but in the traditional and historical way of the traveler, by coming ashore in Alexandria, where Herodotus arrived (when Alexandria was only a fishing village called Rhakotis), and Strabo, Napoleon, and Flaubert.

This may sound quaint or literary, but to me it was natural. When I left New York, the September 1975 Sinai agreement hadn't yet been signed, and whenever I mentioned my planned journey, the discussion had been of confrontation, Egypt versus Israel, war or peace. That was the permanent crisis that has kept Egypt, off and on, in the news. It wasn't what I meant to write about.

I meant to get away from that brittle and perpetually rehashed actuality, the actuality of the diplomats and the political correspondents who when they say, "Egypt this," "Israel that," "America thus," really refer to about fifty people in each of those countries. I wanted to get away from the communiqués and editorials, out into the streets and on the country roads; and I wanted to go backward in time and away from the morning's headlines. Of course there's no country where you can move farther backward in time than Egypt, and this is one reason, but not the only one, why it has haunted and pulled toward it so many traveling writers and writing travelers. Through history, the Nile Valley has been stupendous in its concentration of terror and beauty, mystery and magic, and if some of the mystery and magic existed only in the imagination of the visitors, it was still Egypt that inspired them. I read many of all the books and diaries earlier travelers produced, but they didn't make me shy about adding another. They made me long to see for myself and write down my own thoughts.

I had been in Cairo on my way through to the Far East quite some years ago, in the last winter of King Farouk, just before the great arson that burned down the old Shepheard's Hotel and made the break with the colonial past. But this journey was to be different, and the boat to Alexandria was but the beginning. I had taken only one bag, easy to carry, and in it were Sterotabs, Flypel, Atebrin, and all the other chemicals and articles people now think they need if they're to survive in Africa outside the Hilton and Sheraton world.

There was an intense excitement on the ferry decks that last afternoon at sea. The odd pale German Mercedes- or Volkswagenbus-owner was lost amidst the Egyptians, Sudanese, and Levantines of all classes, with wives, children, and carryalls bearing the names of unknown airlines; a crowd seeded with transistors loudly giving out the plaintive Arab music of Radio Alexandria. The mood wasn't gay but, rather, nervous, as if no one quite knew what to expect from this homecoming. An occasional Italian crew member would push his way through without looking at anyone, and the lame crew-dog would piss unhindered all over the deck. That scene seemed an added advantage to me of traveling by boat. I once flew the nonstop ten hours from New York to Buenos Aires, and as we were landing, the man next to me woke up and said listlessly, "Which place is this?" From a ship, one place is still *not* precisely like another.

The first sight of land was as I had imagined it would be: a hazy white circle on the horizon just barely visible in the glare, a desert view. After a long time, indefinable yellow elevations stood out, stone towers maybe, or high dunes, or, who knows, mirages. It was the precise spectacle described by the men who accompanied Napoleon when he landed here on July 1, 1798, to give this country the shattering shock (a hundred times Commander Perry's to Japan) that tore it out of its medieval Turkish limbo into the modern age.

Then, suddenly, the haze went, and a half-circle of high rises stood out sharply, with the low sun glittering in the rows of windows. It got cold, the wind rose, and clouds filled the sky. The sea stood hollow and turned black. Anchored ships appeared everywhere, for nowadays ports are so congested and harbor dues so high that ships spend days and weeks way out riding at anchor, to the misery of their crews.

Our ship's engines stopped for the pilot boat, which also emitted a whole string of officials to look into our health, papers, plans, and cargoes. At this contact with the land, or at least with its laws, everyone on deck except the pale car-owners stampeded down the various staircases to disembarkation stations, as if we were about to sink. Docking was still an hour off, though, and by the time we lay fast and I had struggled across a gangway into a high hangar, it was dark. Here another bevy of officials awaited us, but all they asked of me was to sign forms, and five minutes later I sat in a taxi and rode out of the dockyard gate into town. I fished a hidden Egyptian ten-pound note out from my papers and put it in my pocket (bringing it in is forbidden, but I wasn't going to show up waving dollars), and then felt I was no longer distinguishable from a resident of Alexandria; I was no longer in the process of arriving.

But how strange it looked, how different from what I had thought! Alexandria is a Mediterranean town and the Egyptian tourist brochures call it "the pearl of the Mediterranean," but Cannes, Marseilles, and even Piraeus seemed remote indeed. We drove at breakneck speed through wide, empty, dirty streets, bumping and jumping through holes. Only an occasional street lamp penetrated the inky evening. In its cone of light, dust whirled through the air. At a corner I could just barely make out a boy dashing across the front of the taxi like a matador. Alongside, apartment buildings, most of their windows unlit, alternated with shanties and piles of rubble.

We rounded a corner and stopped in front of the hotel I had picked from a list, the Cecil. A strong breeze from the sea blew in my face; beyond the boulevard at the end of the block, the street lights picked out the glimmer of the waves rolling in without sound or surf. On the once-famous boulevard, a few cars went by, and carts pulled by tired men and tired donkeys.

Presently I sat all alone in a hotel dining room which smelled of disinfectant, with gilded mirrors and dusty, motionless ceiling fans above me, and two Nubian waiters, each in a far corner, somberly staring into space.

TWO

I knew I had arrived in the middle of the month of Ramadan, but I hadn't realized that it was Ramadan that had emptied the streets. It is the month when Moslems fast from sunrise to sunset, or more precisely, from the moment "you can tell a white thread from a black one in the light of the coming dawn" (Koran, "The Cow," verse 183), which may be an hour or more before sunrise. As soon as the cannon gave the signal that the sun was back below the horizon, about every person in Alexandria repaired indoors to eat and drink as much as he or she could afford and hold. Everything came to a halt, phones went dead, shops were boarded up.

From that first evening on, I was struck by this unascetic aspect of the great Islamic fast. Every day seemed one long wait for a feast after dark, the way people in England work up a thirst waiting for the pubs to open. Of course, for the poor it is something else again, especially when Ramadan falls in summer—tied to the lunar year, it shifts backward through all the seasons every thirty-three years—and they have to do their work under the Arab sun without a drink of water. But since it helps save one's soul, I felt no need as an outsider and onlooker to sympathize with their plight, any more than I would with saints on pillars or monks in bare cells. Islam, now in its fourteenth century, has much in common with the serious intensity, and the self-righteousness, of medieval Christianity.

The streets of Alexandria filled later that evening with a dense throng of men, women, and children, cars all honking nonstop, horse-drawn carriages (no tourist conveyance here, but a serious means of transport), donkey carts, pushcarts, vendors, dogs, cats, and one man with a performing baboon muzzled with pieces of string. I walked and drove around in a carriage, from one end of the center to the other, and from the canal in its southern section back to the seashore. It didn't seem then, and it has never come to look to me since, like a big city, in spite of its alleged two million inhabitants. The number may be exaggerated; it is a guess anyway, and many of those inhabitants play but a miserable fringe role at the edge of the town's life. Alexandria is a town more than a city: even in my first days I didn't feel overwhelmed by it, or lost. But a far place it surely was, African, though not in any familiar meaning of that word, not like any other part of Africa I knew.

Its Europeanism had vanished. It must be added that much of that Europeanism was in the minds of Western beholders and didn't penetrate very deep. It was a veneer, if an important and glittering one. (Egypt's best-known literary critic —I met him in Cairo, and more about him later—assured me that the *Alexandria Quartet* novels were locally unknown and had no connection with the reality of Alexandria at any time.)

But whatever there had been of Europe, it was gone, together with the thousands of merchants and businessmen who, right up to the Suez Canal war of 1956, had had things pretty much their own way. The street signs used to be bilingual, Arabic and French. Now the French had been taken away, though an odd name here and there had been forgotten and left behind. As many Arabic street names had been changed, some two or three times, whenever the fortunes and perspective of history turned heroes into scoundrels or vice versa, it was pretty tricky to find one's way about. Shops and offices once Greek, Italian, Jewish, or Lebanese had become Egyptian, but few of the new owners had been willing or had bothered to scrape or hew the old names from window glass or marble façade. Thus turbaned heads and galabias, the kaftan-type overdress of the Arab, appeared from under a gilded "Ephtime Ephtimios" or a copperplate "Eli Leon." And the technical structures and pattern of the Western layer—its services, mails, phones, hospitals—had been stirred through the entire Alexandria stew, in which of course they had vanished well-nigh without a trace.

Now the post offices of Alexandria looked like bombed-out London bookmakers' shops or, if you will, like New Haven Railroad depots. That is precisely because the old smoothness of life had been by and for Westerners only (the French even had their own private post office in this town), and they had made little effort to spread the blessings of their civilization. In eighty years, the British had not built one native school or dug one village well.

To me, it was not an unfamiliar sight, Western buildings and offices taken over by a local population who still camped rather than lived in them and who, to the scorn or amusement of the former owners, set a very low priority on keeping up the gimmicks and trimmings that were part of it all. You could see it in Jakarta after the war with the Dutch, in Havana after the revolution, in the big cities of China. In Alexandria there was nothing revolutionary or socialistic about it: new and somewhat sloppy tuans had taken the places of the old ones. In fact, it was during my stay in Alexandria that the first ex-tuans from the old days made their reappearance. Greek businessmen who had once worked here returned, if only on brief visits of reconnaissance: swallows harbingering the Sadat open-door summer.

My Hotel Cecil looked just like that, a place "taken over." Apart from a very old man who spoke beautiful French but who rarely showed up, none of the staff spoke much of any foreign language. They were not friendly, but later their grim aloofness began to appear a bit of a show, hiding uncertainty and, maybe, the hand-clasping, body-touching friendliness of these latitudes, which they must have thought unfitting to their new posts.

After my first evening I had dinner there only one more time, when I was too tired to go anywhere. On that occasion, as I was spooning my celeryless celery soup and reading a paperback, the stern headwaiter in tails came over to me and asked what language my book was in. Upon being told, he said, "Ah, you like such books?" and then went off and returned with a very battered Cronin and an equally battered Somerset Maugham which he offered to me for sale over the soup. At the reception desk a heavy man was in charge, even sterner and more formidable looking than that headwaiter. From the frowns he threw at me, I assumed he disliked me intensely. But late one afternoon, as I was going through my third day of waiting for a long-distance call to London to go through, his phone rang, and he jumped from his chair and shouted at me through the lobby, "London!," looking as happy as he knew he made me. It was a mistake and it wasn't London after all, but I thought then I had been terribly wrong about him. There seemed to be a touching innocence about these men, or perhaps it was just that behind their white and black ties they were still as poor as church mice. That same reception man kept a tray with commemorative coins and stamps, which he tried to sell, but only in a feeble way; and every day he spent an hour polishing the tray and spraying it with a Flitgun against insects or germs.

I may give the impression, with all this Hotel Cecil stuff (even if it did smell of Lysol there), that I was already in the beaten tourist track after all. Not so. The Cecil, with its faded gentility, was an Egyptian businessmen's hotel, with perhaps a couple of tourists; the fact that it provided hot water and towels and toilets that worked simply made it a good bridgehead to get one's bearings from without too much struggle. In fact, I never met a foreign tourist in all of Alexandria, although I realize they're around; their standard itinerary is straight to Cairo and thence up the Nile. But Alexandria has so little hotel space that even while I was there, way past its summer season for Cairenes, rooms were hard to find, and it had been pure chance they took me in at the Cecil.

If I used their Kipling dining room only twice, I spent many hours sitting beside their switchboard, because I had to phone my family and I didn't know yet that in Egypt that's a lost cause. The switchboard was in an alcove, operated until three in the afternoon by a very vague and tired lady but thereafter by one of two bellboys—or, rather, bellmen—who, while dressed in Nubian coffee-pourer outfits, were as sharp as tacks. They had the secret of cranking the handle in some mysterious way that raised Radio Cairo, through which all calls abroad were relayed. Not that it did any good to raise Cairo. Cairo was always optimistic and would say "soon," or "in one hour precisely," but the connection didn't come. I sat there cursing the operators as if I were the typical indignant Victorian Traveler, though I didn't get nasty and didn't start drawing loud comparisons with less benighted nations. A Greek lady who, trying to get Athens, sat through these wakes with me, did just that; snorting and drumming her fingers, she told me and everyone in various languages that in Greece the phones worked and the hotels were clean. "They sure didn't and weren't not so long ago, lady," I answered, but she was not interested in people's answers. Often all the lights went out as I sat there, and someone brought a little piece of candle, which the Nubian would carefully wax to the edge of the switchboard.

One day, presumably, Egypt, too, will have its satellite and all-digit dialing all over the world, and I hope (but doubt) that by that time the Nubian bellboys will have shorter workdays and the waiters won't have to sell paperbacks between courses. I am thinking back with a certain pleasure and nostalgia now to those candle-lit hours, filled with waiting for the line to London and conversations in very broken Arabic with the Nubians about family affairs and how many sons a man should wish for.

THREE

The heart of Alexandria has the shape of a fat *T* standing on its head. In the nineteenth century, the crossbar was called *Place des Consuls,* and that was where the mighty lived. Consuls then and there were very powerful indeed. The square sits in the old photographs, its solid mansions shimmering under that harsh sun: you can almost feel the heat. In the center, there are rows of shade trees, and invariably under one of them an old carriage, the skinny horse head down, the coachman head up and looking at the camera—both turned to dust a hundred years now. On the roofs of the houses, wooden structures look like chicken coops or little water towers, but these were the servants' quarters.

In yellow and sepia, the square and its era look romantic enough, and for some of the men in those houses it must have been a romantic adventure. It was of course foremost a dog-eat-dog struggle of fortunes and bankruptcies, including the final bankruptcy of the country itself, which led to the abdication of its Khedive Ismail and then to the British occupation; a time also of choleras, wives refusing to come back from Paris or London, children's graves in the cemetery, the Cotton Panic and a string of other panics. Few of those stately homes survived the wrath of war and rebellion. One of the buildings is the French Consulate-General, a lovely house facing the sea, flying the tricolor and looking untouched by a century of battle. The French state has finely developed the art of surviving liberation wars and reappearing as friend of the selfsame new nations it once exploited.

When the time came for Alexandria to want a more Egyptian image, the Place des Consuls was renamed Muhammad Ali Square. That was in honor of the Turkish commander (of Albanian birth) who came here in 1801, defeated and murdered all his rivals after Napoleon had left, and ended up as pasha of Egypt, virtually independent of his nominal master in Istanbul, the Sultan of the Ottoman Empire. Ali started a ruling house that lasted precisely a century and a half. His grandson Ismail was the man who announced to the world that Egypt was no longer in Africa but in Europe, who lent peasants to de Lesseps, for free, to dig the Suez Canal, and who commemorated its opening by commissioning Verdi to write *Aida* for his guests (it wasn't finished in time) and serving them, among other courses, truffles in champagne, venison thighs à la Saint-Hubert, and capons garnished with quails. The last of the line was Ali's great-grandson's nephew, King Farouk, who misspelled his own name in Arabic when he signed his abdication here in Alexandria and then left his realm with three hundred trunks and a yacht, to live and die obesely in the gardens of Naples and Monte Carlo.

All these men from Ali on down treated their subject fellahin (peasants) not as slaves, but worse, for they hadn't cost them anything. Ali had Alexandria's Mahmudiya Canal to the Nile dug in such haste that twenty thousand fellahin died of it—many of hunger, as they were supposed to feed themselves. And at Ismail's Suez Canal banquet, the guests, as a local saying expresses it, were eating the flesh of the people rather than those venison thighs. You can read in Lady Duff-Gordon's *Letters from Egypt* of the 1860's what it meant to a village when half its men were commandeered on punishment of death to show up with their own bread and camels for Canal *corvée,* leaving wives, children, harvests. In Farouk's days things had become more modern, that is, more subtle, but basically not very different.

Unjustifiedly, Ali is still sitting on his stone horse in the square. Ismail, who, shaped in Italian marble and bronze, used to look out over the sea, was finally removed. The square was then renamed Midan el Tahrir, Liberation Square, and Ismail's place was taken up by a forbidding kind of cenotaph from which you're kept away by chain fences and soldiers with sky-blue helmets and fixed bayonets. The people of the town have always called the square and the area around it "El Manshiya," but neither that name, which I probably pronounced very badly, nor "Tahrir" got me there; the man on the streetcar who showed me where to get off for it still called it "Muhammad Ali."

There was no mistaking it, but only because its open space was as in the old photographs. The trees were gone, and most of the houses. The center square was now taken up by a parallel series of bus stops, and the east side of the square was a field of rubble and stones. The built-up sides were unmitigated slums, a scene of dust, dirt, fumes, broken pavements, holes filled with debris; and the hot sun stood over it all. There were lots of people around, but it was a depressing sight. The ground floors of the houses were used as little shops, bakeries, and an absolute surfeit of photographers with those old tripods and black cloths, some in front of their doors, some inside. But there weren't any wedding pictures on view, or those photos where you stick your head through a back cloth and look like an aviator. It was only identity-papers pictures they did and exhibited in their windows.

Not just the poverty made it all wretched; I was to see much worse. It was the merciless lack of shade, sun beating on stone without a blade of grass or a leaf, that set you to wonder about the officials who do these things, who take their maps and erase the trees. The south side, along which the streetcar ran, wasn't in better shape, but the coolness along the house fronts made it more human. Here, near noontime, the street was packed with people, on foot, on carts, and hanging from the doors of the streetcars, while automobiles dashed through the crowds, horns screaming and never stopping or even slowing down for anyone, and the people, before or after saving their lives with jumps and runs, screamed back at the drivers.

I walked south from the square—this was in one of my early Alexandria days—down Saba Banat, once called Rue des Soeurs, past the cotton warehouses and through the oldest part of town; this street, with its extension, reaches all the way to the Mahmudiya Canal. On that first walk (and later ones were similar) I began by being shaken by the slums on both sides of the street; then by the slums in the second degree in the side streets, and so on, until beyond the canal I came upon what is called a *bidonville* around Paris—a town built of *bidons,* or oil cans. But just as the slums were worse than our worst slums, this shantytown was worse than anything I had seen, including the *villas miserias* of Brazil. The climate is a mitigating factor, I suppose, but Alexandria's winters are too chilly (fifty degrees is the average minimum in December), and its summers too hot, for any native "carefree outdoor life."

Boys in filthy pajamas and nothing else were pulling carts, heavy ones; tailors were ironing in open shacks, keeping their charcoal-filled irons out on the sidewalk in order to suffer less from the heat; there were blacksmiths working with medieval tools on modern articles, as for instance a bicycle frame needing repair. Junk shops displayed broken-down remnants from the four corners of the earth; a man with a cart collected, not bottles, but broken pieces of bottles and window glass; another man was whipping a horse that tottered on its bones; even smaller boys carried coffees on trays; water carriers filled their sheepskin waterbags at a street hydrant; mountain sheep, in clouds of flies, were tethered in front of black and dark hangars; ironmongers sorted through scraps and rust; men and women descended staircases out of "apartment houses" so unbelievably filthy and dark that I would have thought no one had lived that way since Nero burned down proletarian Rome. The men who were just sitting around in the shade surely didn't seem to be dreaming or loafing; they looked in a state of disrepair, like Bowery bums. Some, half-naked, were asleep or maybe unconscious in doorways. Whole streets were filled to knee-level with garbage, stones, and dust.

There were real stores, too, like for instance suddenly a modern electricity shop with many customers waiting; there were huge piles of fruit for sale—mangoes, figs, pears, dates, nuts—and the never-to-be-forgotten Indian smell of half-rotting mangoes over everything; coffees and a kind of tortilla cake were made and sold in the street. Children were in charge of stands with thousands of yellow and blue junky ballpoints, all the same. There was nothing picturesque about it, unless you think Watts and Bedford-Stuyvesant are picturesque, too. It was misery, and I thought at the time that the only living creatures in sight that were neither visibly suffering nor working themselves sick were the dogs and cats. They were thin all right, but they didn't have to carry or pull anything.

I made it to the canal, crossed its bridge into that shantytown on the other side, and turned right around. The canal, muddy, full of floating debris and derelict houseboats, didn't look as if it still carried any shipping or could provide drinking water that wouldn't kill an ox. I hastily climbed aboard a streetcar, escaping from a horde of children asking for money. We clanged and crept back into town, pressed together like anchovies. My neighbors eyed me, but mostly in a friendly way: you don't see any foreigners on Egypt's streetcars, or in fact much anyone who wears shoes and socks. (An English journalist in Cairo wouldn't believe that I rode streetcars.) At one point we got stuck in an insoluble traffic jam in a narrow road running alongside the slaughterhouse, and I got off. I walked north and was very happy when I caught a glimpse of the sea and felt, or imagined I felt, a breeze.

The oldest part of town as it stands now is Arab, but Alexandria is sitting on top of its own classical past, which will probably never come to light again. Bits and pieces are in museums or on view in their original places, such as Pompey's Pillar. The obelisk once carried here from Heliopolis by the Roman legions now stands shivering in Central Park. Alexandria was 2,307 years old in 1976, one of the rare examples of the successful founding of a town as a deliberate piece of planning (Alexander the Great's) and, even rarer, a town thus created that kept its original personality-cult name through twenty-three centuries of human to's and fro's.

He must have been an amazing man, that twenty-five-year-old Macedonian officer who picked this site for his town. It is opposite the island of Pharos, where later the lighthouse, one of the Seven Wonders of the World, was built, and at the far western tip of the Delta and thus safe from the Nile mud which was always bedeviling the harbors of Rosetta and Damietta. Alexandria is El Iskanderieh in Arabic but that is simply the Arab habit of appropriating any *l*'s and fusing them into the article; Iskander is Alexander, and no general's name has been remembered longer by so many nations. There was no one in that league till Napoleon, who consciously and self-consciously tried to emulate Alexander's moves and policies while in Egypt.

A town plan of Alexandria of two thousand years ago still

exists, with its streets running as neatly east-west and north-south as those of Manhattan (more neatly, actually). To the west was the Gate of the Moon, to the east the Gate of the Sun, which led into a countryside famous for its erotic religious services and for what in Westchester used to be called "swinging parties." Alexandria itself was the setting of Antony and Cleopatra's best years and Antony's "orgiastic society," but there is as little left of that mood as of the Library, which once housed all the learning of the Western world and which was (of course) eventually burned down by some military man.

What changed Alexandria's fate, though, in a deeper and less chancy way, once it was Arab, was its location: the Arab world was oriented away from the sea and Christian sea power, and it faced inland.

Now Alexandria is a busy port for the second time in its long existence, though the prosperity surely hasn't trickled down to the ex-Rue des Soeurs.

FOUR

But I would learn during my stay there that Alexandria was a functioning community, from its hidden millionaires to the men collecting broken glass. The unbelievable poverty of "the people" was part of the machine. The place of the virtually absent infrastructure was taken by a million hands doing things the way they were done a thousand years ago, and—relatively—for even less pay.

This society may be less inhuman than Engels's Manchester in the sense that it is less organized, more loose and haphazard; it seems worse to me in the sense that it is not going anywhere.

Still, I do not want to give the impression that everywhere south of the sea boulevard, town life was a nightmare. There were, contrary to what you'd expect, few beggars. Only small children asked for baksheesh, that is, a tip or handout. "I don't know where all the beggars have gone," an Egyptian (left-wing) journalist was to tell me later, "maybe they've all been shot." And he laughed. Here as elsewhere in Egypt, I rarely saw anyone with trachoma or the other eye afflictions that were once the scourge of this country.

All the colors and variety of types of dress helped make it more cheerful. There was everything from suits and ties to Bedouin robes, with those robes and galabias the large majority. Some few women wore black veils, but mostly they just had black scarves. Black shapeless dresses and scarves were the uniform of the poor, as they are in Sicily, and as incomprehensible to me here as there under an equally burning sun. On their feet, people wore anything from shoes with socks or stockings (rare), to just old shoes, to sandals (the rule), to nothing. Children wore prissy Lord & Taylor type dresses on one end of the scale, and nothing at all on the other.

Physically, you saw everything from New York pallors to the blue-black faces of the southern Sudan. Light skin did, not automatically but more often than not, go with the better clothes and the shoes instead of the sandals. I was very far indeed from being among the well-dressed men in those streets, but as soon as I was out of the main shopping center where the bourgeoisie saunters, I was universally stared at. In very poor sections I created a real stir. I'd learn later that the Egyptian middle classes dream as little of walking through a poor street or through a village as a Central Park Wester of going for a stroll on Lenox Avenue. But when people stared in a way to make me feel my presence was not considered a good idea, I'd go up to someone and ask him the way to somewhere, or if possible I'd buy something at a stall, or just sort of greet everyone in Indian style with folded hands. It established a kind of contact, and they couldn't go on staring as if they wondered whether I was human. This worked in China usually, and it worked here.

The very worst homes were the shacks and huts made from cans, cardboard, and mud; the better ones were in what must once have been decent buildings, like those around Muhammad Ali Square. The tenants didn't live in these as if they were *their* houses; they nested in them in the fashion of the peasants of Dubrovnik who squatted in the ruins of Diocletian's castle. I would often come upon housing construction stopped at an early stage, and here squatters—or, who knows, rent payers—had roofed the concrete piles with wood or tin or canvas, built little walls from old bricks, and thus sort of filled in the concrete skeletons.

Across from the Cecil stood a row of houses of a yellowish stone, of that precise tint and architectural design you see in the nicest old streets of Paris. I used to sit on one of the chairs outside the café on the corner there in the early evening, waiting for the sunset, when they'd serve cups of coffee (Turkish, five cents). The low sun stood right on those buildings and made the yellow almost colorless. They had closed green shutters, and balconies with wrought-iron railings in curlicues. As did so much in Egypt, it looked pure eighteenth century, like those old prints you buy out of wooden boxes in New York bookshops.

Then, as twilight fell, the shutters opened, and people appeared on the balconies. The buildings came to life, and at the same time you realized the terrible decay they were in. Rooms were filled with children, old beds, cardboard boxes; that housing block was as packed as the streetcar in the Rue des Soeurs. And in the windows, here in the center of the second city of Egypt, men and women lit their oil lamps.

FIVE

Alexandria lies farther west than any other town in Egypt; it is the last settlement of any size between the Nile and Libya, twenty-four hours away by train. Its eccentricity stems from the peculiar shape of the country.

Egypt is more than four times the size of England. But just three and a half percent of its surface supports life, is lived on. As Herodotus wrote in one sentence not to be improved upon, "Egypt is a gift of the River Nile."

Egypt is but a very long and very thin river valley plus the triangle of the Nile Delta, a kite with a crinkly tail. There is nothing else. Without the Nile, there would be nothing, period (if I may leave out a few oases). From its darkest beginnings, Egypt thought of the Nile as specially created, coming up out of the underworld to keep the country alive. The river returned to the underworld through the sky. That Nile in the sky gave foreign countries their rain.

Whether you have a cup of tea in Egypt, a glass of beer, or a Pepsi, the water in the end always comes from the Nile. There is no other. And it is at the westernmost tip of the Delta, at the very end of the link with the river that gives life, that Alexandria was built. You don't think of it that way in Muhammad Ali Square, but the city is really an outpost at the edge of the great desert.

Thus Alexandria's attackers, despoilers, and conquerors had always come from the east, or from across the sea—until the year 1942, that is, when tanks made the desert like a sea for modern armies, and when the approaching German general, Rommel, already had the spot for his headquarters in Alexandria picked out. Egyptian high-school boys were chanting his name in the streets, but Rommel didn't quite make it, and from El Alamein his road went all the way back again to the Reich. I am old enough to have known the drama of those days. As numbers go, the battle of El Alamein wasn't in the big league: Stalingrad saw more casualties on both sides in one daylight hour of fighting. But at the time it was the hinge of the entire war. Before, nothing went right with us; afterward, little went wrong. Until some ten years ago, "When I was at El Alamein" were words to shut up everyone else in a British pub. We live in harsher days now in a sense, though it's peacetime; and I guess the drama of those days can't seem so very dramatic to new generations. It doesn't to me either, but I had to go and take a look at El Alamein, if only because it was part of my early youth.

There are two or three trains a day from Alexandria to El Alamein and on to Mersa Matruh (there is only one train a week from Mersa Matruh to Sollum at the Libyan border). One of the daily trains leaves at dawn; the one I picked leaves just after ten in the morning. You'll be told that "foreigners don't take those trains," and I admit that the railroad station was pretty daunting. It had come a long way since the days of Lord Cecil (after whom, maybe, my hotel was once named) and Lord Cromer and the red carpets rolled out for them. People, chickens, sheep, baskets, boxes—a milling mass was vaguely lining up at dark windows with half-effaced signs in an italicized Arabic I couldn't read anyway. But as would happen more often, I was helped by the looseness of this scene. I just opened an office door, which is what other people did without raising anyone's eyebrows, and found a man at a table who wrote me out a ticket for El Alamein, by hand, and took my money then and there. I wondered about the tip for such service, but he firmly counted out the last piaster of change and wished me a good journey. Then I went to my platform, where there was a buffet with wooden chairs set out and coffee for the usual four or five cents. The train ride was supposed to take some three hours for the nearly seventy miles, and I had bought a first-class ticket for less than a dollar. I love trains, and there was a special excitement about waiting there for something that seemed much more "un-known" to me than the longest journey most anywhere in our part of the world.

Our train came in, and the travelers took it by assault. An iron will and constitution got the vanguard a seat in third or second class, but there was no cause for hurry beyond that. We stayed at the platform for a long time while vast amounts of merchandise—crates, birds and rabbits in wicker cages, mail sacks, racks with bottles of beer—were loaded aboard. The first-class coach had its corridors packed, too, but here some seats remained empty. In my compartment with six places, there were three soldiers and I. The seats had loose pillows, as old as the hills of Egypt but in worse shape, and everything else was equally hanging by its nails. There was no glass in the windows. It looked and probably was a train that had survived several wars. It was a nice train all the same.

A few minutes before we pulled out, an officer joined us, a full colonel with red staff tabs. He had rows of service ribbons on his chest and was pretty impressive. The soldiers, who were the shabbiest kind of privates, ignored him, al-though they stopped laughing and talked more softly. He ignored them and me, too, and opened a newspaper. Then at the last moment a ticket collector appeared and the sol-diers had to leave. ("First class" was respected until about one in the afternoon. From then on, people from the corridor came in and sat down, first a man with one leg, and after him everyone else who could fit. They sat in one another's laps and there was much joking. The train was running an hour late by then.)

Whistles whistled, and we were off. We turned east instead of west, as my good old 1929 Baedeker had warned me we would, thus saving me from jumping up and asking foolish questions. In the Hadra district of the city, the Cairo branch line continued east, and the Mersa Matruh line made a 180-degree turn, crossed the Mahmudiya Canal, and started its run west toward the desert. Modern streets lay to the north of the line between the tracks and the sea: Alexandria was up to date in having its good houses in its suburbs only. South of the track an industrial zone sat in swampy fields, with many small factories and oil reservoirs not of metal but of brick. The train used to run here on an embankment along and through Lake Mariut, a lowland filled with Nile water. Mariut had been dry since the Middle Ages, till the British army flooded it again in 1801 to help their siege of the French troops in Alexandria. It still hasn't been completely reclaimed but no longer reaches the railroad. The glitter of its surface could be seen behind and at times under the low smoke from the chimneys. We passed the level crossing of the road to Agami, the beach where rich Alexandrians and Cairenes go for their summer weekends, though assuredly not in this train but by car (most fashionable: a Mercedes with German plates still on it). Then all houses and workshops fell behind. We ran through a sandy plain on which sparse, low bushes grew, green and prickly-looking stuff, like heather. Suddenly the landscape was empty.

Writing now on a cold New York winter's day, I find it impossible to recall—with my senses, that is—the physical onslaught of that enormous sunlight, the enormous glare of a shell of blue over a shell of yellow. This was Alexandria latitude only, a long way from the big sun of Upper Egypt, the *shems el kebir,* and it was not deadly but wonderful. We entered an intense, clean heat, and the wind through the glassless windows dried the sweat running down our necks and cooled us perfectly. With the wind came many flies and a constant whirl of fine sand, which bothered some of my fellow passengers more than it did me, but then they didn't have as much to occupy them as I did. They, in turn, might have been fascinated by a first ride on the Long Island Railroad.

I was put back in the one precise era that has these two ingredients: a train ride in a ruined coach through a fierce countryside no one had yet tried to change, and men for company to whom I was such an absolute stranger that this actually made a link of interest between us. That "precise era" is the turn of the nineteenth century, which I've always thought the greatest for real traveling. The world was still mysterious then but no longer secret and out of reach. I have driven through wild country, but there is a difference between car travel and trains. Cars are so essentially modern, they dominate, they come with paved roads and gas stations and billboards and all the rest. And even bumping along in a jeep or a Land Rover, you are part of the landscape; the train, on the other hand, stays outside it all. A train somehow combines the close contact of a car with the aloofness of a plane ride.

Now each stop looked alike: to the south of the track, only shadeless desert; on the other side of the train, a little station, a few stone huts forming a village, and that was all. I hung out of the window blinking in the hot light; the train tracks dissolved in a haze before reaching the horizon ahead of and behind us. Miserable late-twentieth-century person that I am, I could only think of movie images for comparison, the Hedjaz railway line in *Lawrence of Arabia* but more so, and a movie set in British India with a train full of corpses and flies—I'd forgotten the film's name. At each stop, a crowd of local people had assembled on the north side to await our arrival, and in a precise turnabout of what used to happen on our countryside local lines, the commerce at each stop was selling wares *from* the train, *to* the platform.

Vegetables, chickens, eggs, and beers were sold by the people in the train corridors to the men and women of the village, who were pushing for strategic spots under the windows. That was what those passengers had been about who had come aboard in Alexandria staggering under crates of cabbages: they were selling them along the railroad. They were all shouting their wares through the windows and there was intense bargaining over each little tin piaster, while the conductor seemed to wait for all transactions either to succeed or to flop. Then we'd be off again, and the sandy wind would start blowing through. It made me feel dry and tough, like tanned leather. I felt neither hungry nor thirsty, nor in need of anything.

My conversation with the officer who was bound for Mersa Matruh had been sketchy, but a civilian with a briefcase had joined us at a later stop, a neat and poor-looking man, a civil servant, I assumed. I asked him what those village people lived on. There was no visible source between the train and the horizon from which they could have wrung even those five piasters to buy a couple of cabbages. Their stone huts had nothing, no electricity or well, no gardens. Water, from the underground pipeline which follows the coast from the Nile, had to be fetched heaven knows how far. They had goats, it's true, all standing in line, pressing themselves into the little strips of shade along each wall, but what these lived on was equally mysterious.

The man with the briefcase said to me, in English, "Arabs rather live in a hut in the sand than in town." It didn't answer the question, but I was struck by his use of the word "Arabs" for others distinct from himself. Once, in the days before the new Arab nationalism, that was the term Egyptians used for the Bedu (plural of Bedouin) only. I asked him if he meant them. "No," he replied, "Arabs. Just Arabs." But if the platform people, the men in torn galabias, the women in the black uniform of the poor, had once been Bedu, there was nothing visible left from that way of life.

Thus we finally came to the El Alamein station.

The moment I got off, I was surrounded by people looking me over. I had expected a little town with shops, cafés, an old taxi, but the one-room station building was all there was. With nowhere else to go, I went in. A man was sitting behind a desk and sternly asked me, "Name, name?" Men and children followed me in, presumably to see me get arrested. I frowned back at the stationmaster, if that is who he was, and said, "Why? Why do you want to know?" and he came back once more with "Name, name?" I pushed my way out again and went back up to the train, but I had trouble finding my coach. I was afraid the train would pull out and hurried along the embankment, pricking my hands on the cactuses that grew there, till I saw my colonel leaning out of the window. I hadn't realized the train was that long.

"Can you tell me where the battlefield and the monument are?" I asked him, mostly to be seen in conversation with him. I didn't understand his directions, but my followers stopped when they saw us talking. Then he called over a soldier from out of the crowd and directed him to show me the way. I thanked him and shook hands at great length, which is perfectly natural here anyway, where people hold on to your hand while you exchange the "How are you's?" and all that. That did it; my shaking hands with a veteran colonel convinced the crowd that I was all right. They were still interested, but in a different way, and they kept a bit of distance. Once the train had gone, however, the soldier vanished, too, and I started walking up the only road in sight, which led north toward the coast. I had already learned while on the train that, contrary to what I had been told in Alexandria, there wasn't any train back that day.

Presently I came to a military car park, a level spot with barbed wire around it. A lieutenant was driving a truck out onto the road, and he immediately stopped and let me in. Five minutes later we reached the coast road.

It hadn't been much of an adventure after all: I was back on asphalt stretching all the way to Alexandria, with a gas station, a rest house, a pile of old tires, a road block, and various other items of modern civilization. It confirmed my idea of two worlds: that you can drive through countries like Egypt from Western hotel to Western hotel and never realize you're moving in a kind of layer outside it all. Here was the mostly neutral, international tourist world where you could eat and sleep and buy gas like anywhere else, and two miles to the south was the country, where the people might smile at you or arrest you but at least would be interested in your existence.

The lieutenant drove me to the British war monument which borders on the military cemetery. A friend joined him, and they went in with me. Those two were civilians caught up in the draft, as you could tell easily enough from their ill-fitting uniforms, trousers without crease, and the same low, soft shoes they must have worn the day they first showed up to report for induction. I guess I provided some relief in the boredom of their days, but even so they were remarkably friendly.

We looked in the stone receptacles on each side of the gate where the registers with the names of the fallen are meant to be kept, but someone had taken these away. The cemetery was impeccable, though, and several gardeners were working in it.

Steps led up to a flagstoned veranda, and from there we looked out over all those rows of graves and, beyond them, into the desert. Far off, a donkey trotted by with two children on it.

Then if you turned around and faced north, you saw another stretch of sand. Greyish bushes swayed in the wind, and rusty bits and pieces of metal and barbed wire were strewn everywhere. Beyond that lay the blue, blue, empty sea.

I am no monument buff, but I thought it was a tragic setting. It wasn't touching, it was sad; it was finality and futility. One of the officers touched my arm and pointed out some headstones in a corner that were at a different angle. "Moslem soldiers from India," he said, "buried facing Mecca." The other walked down to the flowery hedges and came back with a big light-pink rose. He told me it was called the "Egyptian Rose" and I should take it home for "my lady." There seemed nothing ridiculous about a bedraggled lieutenant picking a rose for a foreigner. It's the kind of thing Southern races can carry off naturally. To me, fresh from all those grim Middle East war years (in the *New York Times,* that is), it felt somewhat strange to stand there with two Egyptian officers while holding a rose.

We walked past the walls in which the thousands of names are chiseled, names of men who died at the age of nineteen or twenty. Then the lieutenant wanted to take me farther up the coast road to the German and Italian cemeteries. I said I didn't want to see those, and they showed they didn't approve of this sentiment. They drove me to the nearby war museum, and there we said good-by.

The war museum was a bit of a mess. It was a low two-room building put there as a kind of counterweight to the monument—a monument, after all, to a battle won by the country that was at the time Egypt's occupier and master. In the first room it said on the wall, "Egypt was then helpless between two Powers," and "It was Nasser only who gave us self-respect." There were cases with arms, and dummies in the uniforms of all the armies—always a very depressing sort of exhibit—and large and hideous portraits of Rommel and Montgomery. The second room was devoted to the October 1973 war, in which, the wall text said, "the Egyptian soldier proved himself." Here the portraits were of President Sadat, and there was a poster of Golda Meir, who wasn't made to look specifically uglier than all the others.

It seemed a pity, perhaps, that this stuff had to be shown in the very place where so many had died; but then you had to remember also that no one had touched the monument and its prideful inscriptions, not even in 1956, when British planes were bombing Port Said. Perhaps it served a purpose, reminding tourists from America and Europe that the third world does not see World War II as a struggle between good and bad guys, for the simple reason that the good guys owned most of the planet at the time and that it took that war to pry them a little loose. And since I was there, the Egyptians have announced that they want to build a Rommel museum at Mersa Matruh.

I walked back toward the rest house, along the empty asphalt with the sun burning on my back. The excitement of my desert journey had evaporated. I felt I had been on a sad and somewhat foolish expedition, to see—to see what? Stones marking spots where bodies had been put in the ground, bodies once belonging to men who had vanished from this earth and who had never known what had happened to humanity after October 1942. There was nothing here really but patriotic pride, walls carrying frozen speeches by British and Egyptian politicians.

Well, anyway, we had beaten the Germans. Nothing relative about that.

The rest house had a trellised terrace, where an Egyptian in galabia and turban was quietly sitting in the shade, doing his Ramadan fast. Inside, two gangstery-looking young men who owned or managed the place were eating spaghetti with a German tourist and a loud young American. A glass case contained El Alamein postcards, all the same, showing a black-and-white photograph of the cemetery gate. I asked for one, and someone had to go find the key to open the case. They asked fifteen piasters per postcard, which was three times too much. There were thousands in there; you couldn't help wondering when they figured to have them all sold.

Later, I took up a position in the shade near an army road block, in hopes of hitchhiking back to Alexandria. In one hour, two rental cars with chauffeurs came by, but they weren't stopped by the military post and they didn't stop for me. Then a major showed up beside me. He was going to stop the express bus from Mersa Matruh, which came through at four, and get aboard, and he told me I could join him. And so I did. I found a kind of seat on the edge of a bench, next to a man in peasant clothes who had a sack beside him which he refused to move for me. The people behind us were ready to pick a fight with him over it, but I asked them to let it be.

The landscape seen from the coast road was a little less deserted than it had been from the train farther south. The sea kept appearing, which gave it some friendliness, and I saw an occasional shepherd or goatherd sitting under a low (two or three feet high) awning for shade. The goats and sheep were nibbling at the bushes, which didn't provide them with more than a blade of green per square yard. Every so often a stone hut appeared, with dogs and goats crowded into its shade, and once a little child ran by with a jar, looking very pleased with itself and happy. Then we passed the first drome-daries I'd ever seen outside a zoo, a small flock by themselves. A dromedary, says the dictionary, is the one-humped or Ara-bian camel; Richard Burton (not the actor, but Sir Richard, who went to Mecca in disguise) writes that a dromedary indicates the poverty of its owner. Only men on camels were robbed in his days; a man on a dromedary wasn't worth bothering with. But the animals don't care about that; they look very haughty, and old-fashioned, too.

A bus passenger on the seat behind me, one of the two who had been ready to fight for my right to more space, bent over and asked, "Well, are you happy now that you've seen El Alamein?" I've since seen his kind of fixed smile and heard his kind of vocal inflection in Egyptians who were trying to start a conversation; at the time I thought he was being ironic. To get that smile off his face, I answered, "Yes. My brother lies buried there."

This was fantasy and I was ashamed once I had said it, but it suited my deflated mood. He didn't ask anything more. I felt and I must have looked as heavy-hearted as if it had been true.

Evening fell. My neighbor produced a large portable radio from his sack and turned it to a reading from the Koran.

Most passengers had closed their eyes by now, and the voice of the Koran reader was the only sound in the bus. In the distance, the first lights of the city shone through the blue dusk.

SEVEN

I stood in the central square of Rosetta, my first real Egyptian town—that is to say, a small town without any Western past—and a great surprise it was. At forty-four miles from Alexandria, it was once more a movement back in time, but not by getting stuck in the middle of an unchanged desert as at the El Alamein station. This was a place where twenty-five thousand people lived their lives.

We become used to a basic disappointment in traveling: that nothing is as remote, as different any more as it once was and as it is still shown to be in ads and movies. Not so Rosetta.

Not so Egypt. From Rosetta on, I expected to find fragments of Edward Lane's Egypt of 1835, and of Flaubert's and Sir Richard Burton's Egypt of the middle 1800's. And I did, almost everywhere. A romantic backwardness—but although bits and pieces of it might have shown a sense of continuity and of tradition, its main ingredient was a terrible poverty that had paralyzed all movement.

Standing in the Rosetta square that hot morning, I found myself in a townscape such as we haven't seen at home in a century or so: no real streets, no wheeled traffic. It was a true town all right, with tall stone houses, four and more stories high, many of them famous for their beautiful façades of red with black brick, and for those bay windows which have finely carved wooden screens instead of glass. They're called *musharabiyas* and they make for a nice, cool draft through a room. Their main purpose, once, was to let the women of the house sit and see without being seen.

But between those houses ran paths rather than streets, fanning out in all directions from the center. Some were roughly paved, but most were dirt roads. The traffic was heavy, and with a few exceptions it was a traffic of pedestrians. (The most important overall exception was the old long-distance buses that connected Rosetta with the Delta and Alexandria. They had to stop at the edge of town.)

When the West rediscovered Egypt in the wake of Napoleon, Rosetta, whose Arabic (that is, real) name is Rashid, was the main port of entry for Egypt. By then Alexandria had become a miserable ruin of beggars, robbers, and fishermen, for Alexandria's waterway to the Nile had fallen into disrepair. Ships docked there because of the safe shelter of its harbor, but travelers then took little boats along the coast to Rosetta, and from there they sailed up the Nile to Bulak, the port of Cairo. Depending on the wind, that could take as long as a week. When Muhammad Ali had the Mahmudiya Canal dug, the balance shifted back, Alexandria revived, and Rosetta at the western mouth of the Nile and Dumyat at its eastern mouth sank back into obscurity.

We have heard of them both, but only through the connotations of their past. Dumyat is our Damietta, where the Crusaders won and lost some murderous battles and threw their prisoners down the ramparts with their heads in wooden caskets (to make them live and suffer longer). Rosetta has its fame from the Rosetta stone, the basalt tablet that a French lieutenant found in 1799 in the local fort. It carried an inscription in three languages—Greek, which was the language of the rulers of its time (the year 200 B.C.), demotic, which was the form of writing of the Egyptian people, and "holy language," or hieroglyphics. With this stone, Jean François Champollion had the key to the deciphering of hieroglyphs, and Europeans and Americans began their long romance with Egyptian antiquity.

I had had a nice conversation on the journey to Rosetta with a young engineer who lived there. But once in town he hastily said good-by and marched off. It was clear he did not want to be seen with me. Not because I was a foreigner; if I'd been a Pakistani or an Algerian it would have been okay. He did not want to be seen with a non-Moslem, an unbeliever, during the holy month.

The very word "unbeliever" must seem a throwback to old adventure stories; but I will get later to the tremendous upswing of orthodox Islam in this country. During my day in Rosetta, the twenty-first day of Ramadan, I did not see any creature except goats and horses eat or drink anything. Well, one small boy was licking off a piece of paper in a grocery shop.

Having been left standing by my engineer, I somewhat hesitantly picked a direction and started walking. The sun was beating down; my path was lined with crowded food stalls, for during the daylight hours of the fast, women and men do the shopping for their nighttime dinners. But nobody so much as munched a grape to quench their thirst. I, in the crossfire of many stares, also went through the day in abstinence.

Here were again the pyramids of fruit, sometimes higher than a man, fresher and less battered than what you saw in the streets of Alexandria; there were bakeries, each with its own coal or wood oven, open-air butcher shops where cuts of meat (all of a sickly pink from the color of the government ink stamps that completely cover them) hung beside calves and sheep waiting their turn; stalls with sacks of beans and pasta, and with dates, yellow or blood-red, freshly picked, dried, or fermented. I counted a dozen different kinds. I passed trestle tables with kitchenware, shoes and sandals, kerchiefs and turbans, galabias next to jeans, and those ghoulish plastic toys which are universal. Wherever you went, you could tell from the smells what was for sale—the slightly sickening smell of bloody chunks of sheep, the decadent mango smell, and the reviving sharpness of herbs and spices. Some small stands had little towers of canned stuff. There were canned Egyptian fruit juices (they are cheap and bad), canned East European pickles and jams (rather expensive and rather good) and very expensive West German juices and compotes. But all the buying I observed was of wares freshly brought in or scooped out of sacks and pots—this was a market that could have been set in about any century all the way back to the Pharaohs. The dusty cans looked as if they were for decoration only.

The town really consisted of a handful of roads, several mosques, a park with government buildings, and beyond that the riverside. I was soon back in my own tracks, and the merchants who had seen me go by before stopped staring. Presently only children took an interest in my appearance. My sensation of remoteness persisted, though. It made no sense emotionally that a taxi and a plane could have had me back within a day in London or even New York. Here was an insulation of place *and* of time which I didn't remember ever having felt that strongly. It was strange but not the least sinister, for it was too bright and lively for that.

I came to a partly covered bazaar I had not yet seen, with articles on view—clothes, tools, and books—that had come from Alexandria. Rosetta is the trading center for the northwest corner of the Delta. People travel from Edku, and fishermen from Lake Edku (fifteen miles away), to buy rope and tackle and to buy or sell salt. You pass the salt flats on the coastal road, glittering oblongs with stakes planted all around them to keep out the blowing sand. People come from the little port of Abukir (thirty miles distant), where I had seen my first Arab warship, a minesweeper, and a sign on the beach saying, "No Photo."

At the corner of the bazaar, and in several porticoes, I could recognize columns taken from Greek or Roman ruins—upside down sometimes or adjusted to the proper length with bricks. Temples and palaces stood once on this ground. The religion then was not of abstinence but of abandon, and public orgasms honored the bull-god Sarapis who had his sanctuary here. I, on the other hand, with not even a chance to drink a coffee or just take a quiet pee, finally decided to make for the river. I had been holding that in reserve: the idea that I now had the Nile, which I hadn't yet seen, in walking distance.

Turning east out of town, I first came to a wide and paved roadway, which wasn't a thoroughfare but a ropery. Two men "walked out" with the rope, while a child turned the crank. He was a small boy and it certainly seemed to me that he was doing the heaviest, if the least complicated work. Alexandria should have conditioned me to seeing children work like mules but it had not; it is not a sight you get used to. (In Cairo I was to be briefed by officials on how all children were now in schools; "Well, maybe not all the peasants' children during harvest," they said.) After that, I came to a boat builders' lane. Men were sitting on the ground with their tools, and several small boats were being built right there; every part but the nails was made of wood. I used to sail, and I could tell theirs was high-quality workmanship; they would have done well for themselves in Holland or at the Long Island Sound. Their boats weren't for sport, of course. Sailing in Egypt is not a sport but still an essential mode of transport. There is usually a breeze on the river and the water is calm; time and labor are cheap. Much will have to change before it will no longer pay to sail rather than put in an engine.

The Rosetta ferries, several in a row, were all sailing boats. I came upon their landing stages when I turned the corner from the boat builders' lane. Here was the shore, the Nile a subdued, almost greyish blue, with in the distance, across the water, cultivated fields with no sign of buildings, and neat rows of palm trees down to the horizon. I followed the river. The shore road was wide, covered with dirt and rubble, and on its left were rows of apartments, but unfinished and abandoned, as if building had stopped years ago. On the embankment, half in and half out of the river, were two wooden ships under construction, looking rather like replicas of the *Santa Maria* as remembered from grade-school pictures; a little smaller, maybe, and with extraordinarily high masts. Two men were hammering away on them. The sound carried through the warm air, for it was very still at the river. Once a ferry had loaded half a dozen passengers and set sail across, there was no one around but those builders on the boats.

The Aswan High Dam has stopped the silt from coming down the Nile and out into the Mediterranean, and when the silt vanished, the schools of sardines that used to come to the mouth of the Nile here vanished, too. The fishermen of Rosetta used to live from fishing those sardines. "The Dam is good and bad," the engineer had said to me, "bad for my town, bad for Rosetta." He had startled me with that remark; I had expected the patriotic pride customary in such projects, especially in front of visiting foreigners. (I didn't know at the time that Kicking the Dam had become national politics in Egypt.)

I sat down on a rock in the shade of a sycamore and watched the river. The Dam has tamed it, and I could just barely see the current. The only traffic on it was that ferry-boat under a lateen sail, cutting obliquely across. A hushed scene.

When I walked back into town, it was the hour for the midday prayer. From the minarets of all the mosques, the voices of the muezzin started to boom through the loud-speakers—there is no God but God, come to prayer, come to salvation.

I had first heard that call twenty-five years earlier, from the minaret in a Moslem town in Yugoslavia which long ago had been in the marchland of the Ottoman Empire. I had never forgotten the spell of that haunting singsong:

Singing Christmas hymns makes me believe in the Christian church; I thought this sound might convert a person to Islam. But that was before electronics came east. Now no muezzin climbs the winding steps of his minaret any more to call out over the town. Instead, he switches on his microphone while, for all I know, he's sitting on his divan—and the amplified call booms out from the loudspeakers at the top of the tower.

The ritual of the call was supposedly created by Muham-mad as a reaction against the mechanical quality of Christian church bells. They're still one strike ahead in Islam, for we now have church bells rung electrically, an awful difference. But the muezzin's call has lost its beauty. (As for synagogues, all they've ever had was a beadle running around and knock-ing on people's doors.)

Perhaps a sober Moslem believer wants nothing but the signal that it's time to pray, so that an electric bell or a siren would do as well. The very reason for having minarets has vanished with the arrival of this amplified sound. I was repeatedly blasted out of bed by it in small towns as, one hour before daybreak, prayer was called. I wouldn't have resented it if I had known a pious man had ascended a tower and was now looking out over the rooftops and calling to us, but I didn't want to be awakened by a loudspeaker, even if its words were, "Prayer is better than sleep."

It so happened that near one of the busiest crossroads of Rosetta a small mosque stood, a true *gama* or meeting place, which is the proper Arabic name for a mosque. It looked like a house amidst other houses: a shop-front mosque. Its muezzin stood in the door, to one side. He was dressed splendidly in a red and black robe with a white turban, but as he had neither minaret nor amplifiers, he chanted the invocation right there in his doorway, following the words from the invisible loudspeakers of some other mosque in a road behind. I thought he had a beautiful voice, but he looked diffident, and the passers-by, hurrying to bigger mosques or to other destinations, paid no attention. His was the only live call to prayer I heard in Egypt; maybe it was the last one in Islam.

EIGHT

The line between the perpetually green fields of Egypt and the wilderness surrounding them is as sharp as a knife. True, there are oases far out in the Libyan desert, and with the new water from the High Dam an effort is being made to move that knife edge between life and death farther out. It has not been a terribly successful effort so far. The line is there; take a step and you have left one world and moved into another.

The landscape within those borders is one of the most worked over in the world. For longer even than in China, men, women, and children have plodded in these fields, seeing nothing but green and mud and the glare of the sky above, fighting nature. Once, in the primeval years of this valley, the work must have been light. The fields that the Nile flooded each year were so fertile that their harvests never lessened. The mysterious red silt left behind by the river was a perpetual virgin soil.

Presently Pharaohs, and then Greek, Roman, Persian, Arab, Turkish, and English conquerors, and finally in our days local statesmen and experts, got into the act and wanted more —the "more" that more work (not by them but by the fellahin) on more land could produce. Thus the peasant nation of Egypt spent its people's lives throughout its history getting

Nile water from low places to high ones. It was bound to the waterwheel by its rulers.

I have crossed the Egyptian Delta in various directions half a dozen times and seen most of the rest of the valley (which is easy) up to where it now ends, at the High Dam. On these travels I have in all seen two tractors (in Upper Egypt), two pumps (in Upper Egypt), and no tractors but maybe six pumps in the Delta (Lower Egypt). If I'm asked why I come up with such haphazard and personal data instead of looking at statistics, the answer is that most Egyptian statistics are worse than unreliable—they're meaningless.

I'm not saying that there are only two tractors in Egypt! I'm saying I've seen only two, and I've seen a hundred waterwheels. I wasn't an observer with any preconceived ideas. It was a total surprise; I had looked at the pictures of all those various contraptions to force water up against gravity, in old books, that is. I hadn't for a moment expected still to see them now. I hadn't read of any recent visitor's mentioning them. But there they were.

Blindfolded cows, donkeys, and dromedaries were going around and around and around in circles, sometimes with a little child carrying a twig behind them, sometimes just left to themselves. They were turning a simple wooden beam on a vertical axle, and two cogs changed this into the movement of the horizontal axle of the wheel. That entire part of the machine as a rule was wooden, too, but the waterwheel itself was iron; a curiously one-step modernization, like the flat-bottomed iron sailing barges one sees on the Nile. The wheel consisted of four or five flattened scoops which spooned the water from the level of the river or a feeder canal into an irrigation canal.

That was the most sophisticated nonmechanized device. I've also stared, right near Cairo, at children sitting on the edge of a little dike, their feet in the water, holding a handle and turning without end a screw-without-end, a water-lifting apparatus designed by Archimedes some 2,200 years ago. Still worse, I saw men in pairs standing in a niche in a dike (wherever the level differences were particularly great), pulling up a bucket of water with a counterweight, emptying the bucket, and dropping it again—on and on, a Stone Age contraption. If you read eighteenth-century descriptions of that procedure, the travelers may tell you that people sing while they do it—a kind of Mississippi rhythmic song—but the men I saw were always silent and grim, as well they might be. The animals, blindfolded, showed no expression. They held their heads high, but only to lessen the strain. They were without exception skinny, as was every farm animal in the Nile valley.

What else did the Delta have on view? The peasant houses, or, better, huts, were more often than not made of nothing but dried mud, and they looked exactly like children's sand castles on the beach when the tide has washed over them once and they are about to crumble: very smooth, very temporary. Roofing was of sacks, palm leaves, corn or cotton stalks, wood, tin; and the firewood, or, better, fire branches, and other supplies were stored on the roof. A better house was built of bricks, which were the same mud, right out of the soil, but baked in an oven. I saw the brick factories in many places, just an oven, a high chimney, and a yard for drying. But more villages had their own home brick industry, little squat kilns. All you needed to have brick rather than mud walls was fuel, and, visibly, many fellahin had not managed to get to any fuel to do just that. It wasn't a matter of primitive and less primitive areas; I saw mud huts next to towns and in fact in towns, and brick houses on their own far from any modernity.

Many Delta houses had a high conical clay tower next to their entrance or, if the house was larger, on the roof. These towers had rows of holes all over them and little sticks bristling out. I had vainly tried to puzzle out by myself what they were for. They were pigeon houses, and once you knew, you saw they were not unlike the pigeon houses French manors used to have in their farm gardens two hundred years ago. The purpose was the same: to collect manure. I was told that the fellahin occasionally sold some birds to buyers from the towns but never ate them themselves. I've been in a tower that harbored ten thousand birds; the stink was staggering. The flocks in the sky, then, were not game birds but part of peasants' households, and pigeon-shooting English sportsmen created one of the great dramas of the British occupation: the village riot with subsequent hangings in Dinshawai in the year 1906.

Every Delta field looked different. Cotton, sugar cane, wheat, okra, and Indian corn were all growing side by side. This was the mixed-tillage business, run from Cairo by a swarm of government people I will write about later; they're making an effort to enlarge the area of each crop and have less of a quilt. There's no winter pause, of course, and planting, sowing, harvesting, et al., go in a nonstop cycle. Some land now produces one crop or another three times a year. In my first month here, cotton was piled up by the thousands of bales in walled yards, for there was a snag in the transport system. Some cotton had been sprinkled on the outside of each bale to show the quality of its contents. The walls protected against thieves, or at least against lazy thieves, and protection against rain was one thing the farmers were spared.

Those Delta roads that were paved and drivable were very pleasant to travel on. They had shade trees, often on both sides, such as eucalyptus, sycamore, and pine. No book I've read mentions pine trees, but they were a common sight. To walk or sit under those trees and watch the green fields beyond them was a color happening.

The green of Egypt makes our green look dirty grey; it

is *luminous,* and with the reflections of the sun, the mirroring water, and (if it is September or October) the red splashes of fruit in the date palms, it is color that almost blinds.

Foremost among the trees were, of course, the palms, and especially those date palms. Strange, tall plants, often scraggly and looking half-bald as if they were losing their fronds the way balding men lose their hair, they fitted so perfectly and embodied so neatly the nature of this land that they seemed to me the precise vegetable-kingdom equivalent of camels and dromedaries, equally perfect and yet unlikely creations, disdainful, poor, uncertain of their future in a smooth new world. (I'm not sure I ever saw a real camel in Egypt. It's mostly dromedaries. They are so heavily loaded that you can't tell if they have one hump or two.) Dates are ripe in the fall, very pink or very red, and they make the palms look even more odd and vulnerable, forming those enormous clusters at the pit of each leaf, around which the peasants put nets to keep them in place, and unavoidably reminding you of testicles.

But above all else the Delta was a landscape of people. Again, it was an old-fashioned landscape, in the sense that everyone was on foot or on donkeys. Assuredly, I use the word "everyone" loosely. Trucks did go by on the roads, just as you found newly built factories and even apartment houses out there. But these were few; the people dominated the scene. They worked in groups, walked in groups, stood talking, sat very erect under white sunshades or old black umbrellas on donkeys that trotted by. The overall effect was of an old painting, here a rather grim Ruysdael, there a soft Watteau. I am not trying to make an artistic image. It took me a moment to realize that I couldn't help thinking of old paintings because of the absence of transport; that it was all footwork and footpaths from one place to another created a totally different frame of time and speed for the people in it, including onlookers like me.

As I have said, it was a landscape full of water, and of men, women, and children moving water. Canals ran everywhere, and the enormous sails the boatmen used stuck out over the trees bordering distant waterways: huge white or red triangles gliding along without a sound or tremor. Children still so blessedly young that no one had been able to think up any work for them were splattering and splashing in the ditches and ponds, cool and content in a hot setting, beside the ducks and the geese. Men and women bathed, too, of course (always in very chaste wrappings), and women did their laundry at the water's edge. The small children were everywhere. They are far too many in the books of the planners and economists, but they added the only really happy note, the happiness of innocence.

By necessity, the sun is an enemy here, its blessings taken for granted and its perpetual cloudless presence a burden. If the Bible had been conceived in England, hell would probably have been a very cold, wet place. When the sun set, it was as if you heard a sigh of relief rise from the land. The work didn't end then, but it changed character. It became more intimate. Instead of in the limitless double glare of fields and sky, it was done within the circles of lamps.

When you drove along a country road in the deepening twilight, you saw the carbide lamps being lit at the roadside stalls where the villagers went for their evening trading. Other stalls just had a flickering candle. Donkeys with two riders appeared in the headlights. Produce was brought to the road and loaded on trucks and carts, all by the light of oil lamps. Butchers went by, carrying whole carcasses on their backs. The village mosque was an island of electric light, its open doors showing turbaned men kneeling on a carpeted floor—very calm and detached from this outside bustle. On the roof of the mosque, a string of little colored lamps, as in our shops at Christmas, flipped on. A town showed a street of real shops with lit windows, but its unpaved side streets ended abruptly in a bluish haze.

Then, as night fell, whole villages glided by without a single light showing. You were startled by a donkey with two small boys on it, in the midst of the darkness and the now empty fields. It was strange to think of the peasants behind those warm walls, in the total familiarity of the breathing of their wives and children in the dark, the stirring of animals, fields of which they knew each ditch, each lump of clay—was there security in that, or did they feel in their bones the strings of disasters, man-made disasters, which have pursued them and their parents and their grandparents and so on backward in time?

Did they make love with passion or in a spasm between worn and dirty bodies? Had the idea of happiness been invented yet for people so poor?

These notes so far have hardly reflected today's or even last year's headlines; but those headlines have little resonance in Alexandria and the Delta. Port Said has been in the front line of what will soon be a thirty-year war/confrontation, but Port Said and the Delta do not touch. There are a desert and a swamp between the two. Port Said is in a different world altogether, although a road now leads from it to Damietta, between the sea and the swamp. But it is a military road; when I was in Egypt it wasn't on any Western map yet, and I think I was among the earliest foreigners allowed to travel it. Cairo is where the politicians and diplomats and foreign correspondents have conducted that war, and while Cairo is in the tip of the Delta, it is a long way emotionally from Alexandria, and light years from mysteriously distant and lonely communities such as Rosetta.

Alexandria had had Israeli overflights and air raids. Most places where the well-to-do lived or worked had brick walls set a few feet in front of the entrance doors, making a kind of screen supposedly protecting against bomb splinters and blasts. Alexandria also had a fair shake of the "No Photo" signs, which meant, of course, "Forbidden to take photos." These were on bridges and the other customary places. The military and the police were suspicious, as you would expect them to be. Once I was picked up by a "secret" policeman in white shirtsleeves. But as usual in such cases, there was little rhyme or reason to an alertness that wouldn't hamper any spy. The wife of the Russian ambassador was stopped by the police from photographing the High Dam at the dedication ceremony, though the plans for that Dam came from Moscow. In Cairo you were told that there were no maps of the city for sale for security reasons, but one day I discovered a bureau of the Survey Service in Giza, and they sold me a sixteen-square-foot plan of the city for about fifty cents. As for the general public, they stared whenever I pulled out one of the old or new maps I went around with on buses and trains, but they stared anyway. No one busybodied or interfered.

Thus, although I had meant to get away from the headlines, it came easier than I had expected. In the end, in the government or newspaper offices or at the receptions in Cairo, it had to be me who brought up the subject of Israel and Mideast politics, as everyone else was determined to ignore it.

This is not to imply that the Arab-Israel issue was cooked up by politicians or is not genuine. But then, and as of now, the word among the establishment here was that it was bad for business, bad for the new relationships with the West, and so the motto was, "Cool it." As for "the people": that brief and rare moment in their history, when they identified with the state and even with the government and made the enemies of the state their enemies, has passed for now.

The Egypt of these pages, though, was not floating in timelessness. Much of it may have looked and tasted like the eighteenth century, but the fact that it was actually the last quarter of the twentieth century was as well known to the man at the waterwheel as to the man at the wheel of a new car. There was no going back to King Farouk or Lord Cromer or Muhammad Ali. The Turkish system of social justice, with the judge and the executioner making the rounds together and people's heads chopped off right then and there in their doorways, was no longer practicable—no matter how much some statesmen might regret it. The water-wheels hadn't changed but the people had, and the Egypt of 1986 will be very different from my Egypt of 1976. These were Cairo thoughts, but I am moving them up to my Alexandria days lest it be assumed I was going around there imagining myself Flaubert.

My last evenings in Alexandria I tried to lose myself, to become one of the crowd. I knew it was a slightly ridiculous illusion. But I am still proud of the fact that I used to walk through Montmartre at night without being accosted by a single tout, that is to say, without sticking out as a stranger. Alexandria isn't Paris; still, it's on the sea, which gives its character a certain accessibility. I got close enough to taste being part of it—the excitement of being someone else, utterly removed from the fears and from the securities of our world.

Those were days toward the end of Ramadan. The shops were open after nightfall and everyone was out on the street, not buying, but walking and walking. Neatly well-off couples, neatly poor couples, and outright poor ones lugging their small children along or carrying them, fast asleep. Teenage boys raced and screamed and yelled and pushed one another. Young girls went by in groups, meeting everyone's eyes with a mixture of defiance and pleasure in their own youth. (Not so long ago you wouldn't have seen "nice" girls alone on the street here. The town youth of Egypt is in matters of sex and chastity where we were in the thirties: hanky-panky is daring, going "all the way" absolutely out.) Many couples consisted of men or boys who, as in Greece, walked hand in hand or arm in arm in complete naturalness. There was much bodily grace, and boys moved and gestured in ways that in the United States would be thought effeminate. I don't think this has anything to do with homosexuality unless in the argument *ad absurdum* that all male friendships, et cetera. I do think this aspect of Islamic society explains the romantic notions about the Arab world held by so many Englishmen—Englishmen who *were* gay, and who now imagined they had landed in a dream world where their public-school days could be taken up again, but without masters, freezing dormitories, and smelly toilets.

In a cluster of people, I stood in front of a radio and TV shop and watched a movie in which soldiers in beards and swords chased long-haired virgins; we stepped aside when a man appeared, carrying an entire skinned sheep which he delivered to the shop. I sat on a café terrace—that is, on a kitchen chair on the sidewalk—with a cup of Turkish coffee. A man pushing a cart piled high with figs stopped in front of us and passed out one fig, which went from hand to hand. Nobody bought. The waiter, a boy in a white robe tied with a piece of string, brought coffees, each with its glass of water, or teas with mint, and water pipes. He kept the pipes going by puffing on them on the way to the client. If you didn't look at him, you could just sit there without ordering anything, which is what several of us were doing.

Men would recognize one another and exchange greetings and news while holding on to one another's hands, but it was not a French (or any Latin) café scene, where people sit for the pleasure of sitting and watching and being watched. The passers-by and the occupants of the chairs did not make a point of observing. Once, I now think, these places had been coffeehouses in the Oriental tradition, where men went to talk quietly, away from the women, to enjoy the cool of the evening, and to listen to passing storytellers and street musicians. Most of those reasons and conditions had dropped by the wayside, and if there had still been a storyteller around, he would soon have been run over. New manners, such as going out with your wife or girl, or having cocktails, hadn't taken their place. We were sitting there in a bit of a social limbo.

There was animation in the air, even excitement, but of a tired and nervous kind. It touched me, too, although I didn't know its origins or even if anyone else knew. I climbed up the staircase to a little restaurant on a second floor, with its windows over the street. A man and a fat woman were eating without talking; the other tables were empty. I asked for rice and lamb and was immensely pleased that they seemed to understand what I was asking for. When I came back down, there were fewer people in the streets and many more cars, honking away as always.

I decided there were no pickups on the streets of Alexandria, at least not visible ones.

I came to a large, white, rather new and ugly mosque, took off my shoes at the edge of the mat in front of the door, and, carrying them sole to sole, entered.

I stood in a very large hall, behind a few kneeling men. The corners were dark, but a chandelier made a circle of light in the middle of the carpets. People kept looking at me over their shoulders. Finally I knelt, too. I wasn't trying to make them think me a Moslem. It was because I wanted them to stop looking at me; and even more it was because it was so still in there. Not the quiet of our churches, where you may feel you are on the sidelines of life; the quiet of some inner chamber of decision.

TEN

I went to Cairo on the last de luxe train left in Egypt; or perhaps, given the way things are going, I should look to the future and call it the first one. It was the Alexandria-Cairo Rapide (trains listed as "Expresses" made all the stops), leaving at 7:50 in the morning and arriving, on time, at 10:25 in Cairo's central station, covering the 129 miles at an average of 50 miles an hour. It was air-conditioned, and waiters brought breakfasts of eggs and coffee to your seat, and not on plastic or in paper, either.

There were no foreigners in my car, but the passengers all looked rich and angry and all kept to their newspapers. (The rich in the third world, and as far north as Greece and Italy, look angry in public.) After stepping over the chickens and sleeping peasants on the station platform in the early morning and getting aboard, I found the train damn cold, and the electricity spent on achieving that seemed a wicked waste. But there I was, for a few dollars, and the icy train—blinds down, frowning faces over headlines—rushed through the Delta to the capital like an alien body without sympathy for or even awareness of its environment.

The first view I had of Cairo was of a movie house, way at the edge of town on a corner in a crummy suburb. They were advertising, in English and Arabic, *Death, Dynamite, and Dollars* with James Stewart when he looked about twenty, pointing a gun of course, and made very ugly by the poster artist. After that, nothing but slums followed, of the kind Alexandria had prepared me for. But looking down on them from the embankment, I saw them as oddly countryish—the flat roofs piled high with firewood, the straw, the debris of decades, and goats, chickens, and children, and women hanging laundry—like (poor) villages sitting on top of (poor) city streets.

No book gives you advance notice of what the crowds of Cairo are like. The railway station and the square in front of it were something beyond my experience. The newsreels of President Nasser's funeral obviously did not show the daily reality, but, then again, they did give an inkling of what Cairo can do. I managed to locate and struggle through to the telephone office in the station, as I was to phone the *New York Times* correspondent, who was a friend from my school days. He had said he'd find me a hotel. Of the three telephone booths in that office, only one was working and the line in front of it was long, but I assuredly do not mean to say you've got to come to Cairo to experience that. When my turn came, the number was busy; and when it wasn't, I botched the intricate way in which you had to coax two piasters into a slot. Though they were patient behind me, in the end I gave up.

I got a taxi (beginner's luck), but as I only had the postal box number of my friend's office, we had a problem. Egyptians are patient and even amused about that kind of thing, though, and my driver pulled up at the first corner and consulted various other drivers and bystanders. It was hot, dusty, a total traffic jam with everyone blasting their horns, and the square and the dry fountain and the statue of Ramses II all seemed very different from the photographs in books on Cairo. (The statue looked new, and it was the cleanest thing around; I assumed it was a modern copy, and a bad one. Only back in New York did I read that it had been found in Memphis and was three thousand years old. Someone must have decided to sandblast it.)

At that point I thought that here was a town so bewildering that I would never be able to master it. It wasn't a wilderness—nothing intrinsically frightening in a wilderness —it was a huge city, with everything from the alphabet on up totally alien; it was indeed like being on another planet.

After a while, things did fall into place, though. I did master it, up to a point and as far as possible in a brief period. By that I mean that I learned its rules, its tricks, and its tabus, enabling me to get around, to cope, and indeed to survive. I didn't find many foreigners who had gone beyond what I got to know and understand, but then very few wanted to bother. And everything is in flux: the best book in English on Cairo that I know is by James Aldridge, an Australian writer; it is wise and finely detailed but, as it was written in 1966 or 1967, the present it describes is already like that of another city.

My cab did make it to the office building where the *New York Times* is housed. And by the end of that day I was installed in a sublet half-apartment of a friend of a friend, having learned, first, that hotels cost three times as much as the official prices given in the latest government brochures but, secondly, and eliminating any worry about prices, that there were no hotel rooms to be had. I've always declared that reserving rooms spoils the spontaneity of traveling and that there is always one more room, but the hotels of Cairo beat me.

Cairo came out of World War II with about a million and a half inhabitants. By 1955, it ranked twenty-first in the world, with three million. Proper counting has long since stopped, but supposedly well over eight million people now live in the area and make it the third or fourth most populous city in the world, after Shanghai and Tokyo and perhaps Mexico City. In 1975 its governor said that a hundred thousand country people moved to Cairo each year, and other estimates doubled that number. The arrivals settled in funeral vaults, on roofs, in huts, behind screens in rooms of others— setups that would have appalled the poorest nomad in a tent of a previous century. If Cairo's birthrate is only half that of the entire country (forty-four per thousand), five hundred babies a day are born here. Deduct a hundred deaths, and another hundred and forty thousand new citizens are added per year. Some districts are said to have four hundred thousand inhabitants per square mile, which is three times more than the worst areas of Calcutta.

More visible and tangible than these figures is the hard fact that nothing has been done to the municipal services since the city was a quarter this size. Housing, public transport and utilities, telephones—they're all disasters. Pavements buckle or have vanished. As for hospitals, a Cairene said to me, "If you want to die, why not do it at home?" Like cockroaches in garbage, the only things flourishing in all this are cars, two hundred thousand of them now. (More than eighty percent of Egypt's cars are in Cairo.) And as those two hundred thousand precisely represent the people with power, the driving classes being the ruling classes, for them money has been found—to build the Nile Corniche, which is a shoreline highway, and the new bridges and overpasses and traffic circles to dash around on. Gasoline, at less than forty cents a gallon for high-test, is shamefully cheap for a broke country.

I knew most of these bare-bone facts in the abstract, but I did not know how life in a place like that felt. I did know that whatever fate, neglect, or corruption had created these conditions, they were not the result of governmental lack of interest: Cairo *is* Egypt to the politicians and to the establishment, and its very name in Arabic, Misr, stands for the capital and the country both.

There has been a town at this spot since the days of the pyramids. The original one was founded on the island of Roda. It still stood in Greek times and was called Babylon. When the Romans had taken Egypt, that Babylon was the headquarters of their army. The words in the first letter of Peter the Apostle—"The church that is at Babylon salutes you and so does Marcus my son"—may mean that Peter wrote from there. Saint Mark was the first bishop of Egypt. In our year 641, the year 19 of the Islamic calendar, the Arabs came and ended Egypt's Christian era, except for its Copts, who stuck to it through all the following centuries of blood and tears. The Arab conqueror was the Caliph Omar, and his new town was called El Fustat. From then on, different dynasties followed one another in unending wars and assassinations. The name "Cairo" comes from the Arabic "El Kahira," which means "the victor" and is derived from their name for the planet Mars. Mars had been in just the right place, the astrologers said, when a caliph from West North Africa moved in and erected his new capital some miles north of El Fustat; and thus the new city was named El Kahira.

El Fustat is now called Old Cairo, and of El Kahira, roughly the area around the El Azhar mosque, wall fragments and town gates survive. As Roda, long an island of wheat fields, has been built over and become part of town, all the different Cairos through forty-odd centuries are now within the confines of this enormous city.

Early in the sixteenth century, the rule by Arabs, in a vague sense of the term, came to an end. A new power appeared: Turks. They took Cairo in 1517, and it stayed in the Ottoman Empire until World War I, when Turkey came in on the side of Germany and England made Egypt its "protectorate." This was a formality, as England was already running the place. Turkey's betting on the losing side in 1914 was a very close call, hinging on nothing more than a German warship that got through the blockade to Constantinople. But think of its long-lasting effects! With the collapse of the Ottoman Empire in 1918, Palestine, Syria, Lebanon, and Jordan were cut up between England and France, and our Mideast drama started in earnest.

The Turks had had things more or less their way in Egypt for nearly three hundred years, and being Moslems had not stopped them from bleeding Egypt white in a way not seen before. Peasants or Cairenes who rebelled, or seemed to be about to rebel, were flayed and burned to death with candles stuck in holes in their bodies; the population of the country dropped from eight million to two million. Turkish power was exercised through the local Mameluke princes, who thought of themselves and were thought of by their unhappy subjects as supreme warlords rather than sadistic bullies. This continued until Napoleon showed up in July 1798.

His men, in wool and felt hats and uniforms sticking to their bodies, carrying forty-pound packs through clouds of mosquitoes and all with diarrhea from a diet of watermelons, knocked the Mamelukes hollow in one afternoon at the Battle of the Pyramids. Napoleon entered Cairo and put up in a palace in Ezbekiya, which was to remain the fashionable center of town for the next hundred and fifty years and where later Shepheard's Hotel was built. Napoleon had a flair for starting things though he didn't always finish them, and presently he went back to Paris and left the mess (Cairo was rebelling once more) to General Kléber. *His* name lives on in the Avenue Kléber, but he was stabbed to death in the Ezbekiya Gardens by a Cairene student in the year 1800.

Though this was but the year 8 of the Revolutionary Calendar, a new era of humanity, the French had the assassin impaled It took him three days to die.

The French left. Muhammad Ali and his inglorious offspring appeared, increasingly under Western control—until the day in January 1952 when the poor of Cairo, rebelling one more time, set the city on fire. This led to the officers' coup, to Farouk's departure on July 26 of that year, and to the presidency of Gamal Abdel Nasser, meant to bring in a New Deal.

This was the city where I went to sleep in a room in the district of Zamalek, at the northern edge of Gezira island, looking out over the river. Or, anyway, tried to sleep, with the mosquitoes buzzing around me, and the uninterrupted car horns from 26th July Street blending into one high chorus as of gigantic katydids that continued into the early hours of the morning.

ELEVEN

The first printing press with Arabic letters brought into the darkness of Egypt came with Napoleon, and when his troops had to get out, they took it with them. The next printing job in Cairo was the *Egyptian Gazette,* founded in 1828, the first Arabic newspaper. It didn't become a daily until the 1870's and was always only a government sheet. But in 1876 two Lebanese brothers arrived and started a real newspaper, *El Ahram* (The Pyramids). *El Ahram* became the best Arabic newspaper. It probably still is the best-known one and its former editor, Mohamed Heikal, the best-known Arab journalist, though it now prints the same dreary government boiler plate as all other Cairo papers.

El Ahram was one of my Cairo destinations. Even if journalists don't print what they think, they might still say it; I am a great believer in traveling with letters of introduction, and I carried a slew of them for *El Ahram* people. These originated from the paper's American and UN correspondent in New York, whom I had known for years and who had conjured up a picture for me of a devoted but informal bunch of people talking politics through the night in smoky composing rooms.

El Ahram's reality was different, and it was more interesting as a phenomenon than as a source of information. It turned out still to be a power in the state, but the direction of that power was downward only, power over and not from the people. The editors in their huge, wood-paneled, air-conditioned offices looked and sounded like cabinet ministers. They were all men; the only woman on the Power Floor (the twelfth) was an extremely efficient lady whose official title at that time was "Secretary to Mohamed Heikal" (who had already been sent on leave by President Sadat and was shortly to be fired). Once I found her in conference with a group of impressive gentlemen, each behind a copy of a report in German on the mineral wealth of the Atlantic Ocean. I've no idea what her real function there was or is.

The fact that editors sat in air-conditioned offices may not seem worth remarking on, but it was. Other high-ups in Cairo had air conditioning, but you knew it with a vengeance: a creaking machine in their window would direct a blast of cold air into a very hot room. The *El Ahram* men had invisible apparatus purringly providing them with a different climate from the rest of the city. You knew you had entered a different world when you came into the building, a gleaming glass high rise facing filthy El Galaa Street with its bulging streetcars; *El Ahram* doormen smiled rather than scowled at foreign intruders; *El Ahram* elevators were all in working order, and no one had to stand in line to get on.

"What has happened to Egyptian socialism?" I asked one of these extremely comfy men. His name was Ahmed Baha el Din, and his office was even higher-ceilinged and woodier than most. As for my question, while President Nasser was certainly considered a socialist in the West, especially by his enemies, it seemed clear to me that his successor Sadat had gone back to capitalism.

Mr. Din, like all Egyptians now, assumed that a Western visitor hoped to hear that devil had been exorcised, and he reassured me accordingly. "We cannot abolish the public sector," he said. "It was paid for by government investment and foreign aid; it couldn't be handled by private business. Also, its workers are a powerful pressure group. But we can and will *trim* it. Land," he told me, "will be returned to expropriated owners, but within the land reform law" (which sets limits on holdings). "Beyond that, there'll be compensation in money."

Mr. Din was a pleasant and soft-spoken man, and in those few sentences he summed up a situation others would envelop for me in clouds of words. When we got to talk about the social legislation of Nasser, he shrugged. "We do not have the resources to implement those laws," he said. I thought, "Well, better an honest conservative than a half-baked liberal," although the remark he followed this up with was rather chilling in its Victorian finesse. "Perhaps it is better for children to work than not to work," he said.

My next editor, Professor Butros Ghali, was a different type. His colleagues called him an international man, and when I met him he was, as usual, just about to dash off to a congress or conference—in Canada, this time. Ghali had but one subject, overpopulation. He told me that Egypt either needed a Chinese-type revolution or had to break out of the Delta and the valley, across political borders, through federation, integration, or what have you, and people the Sudan, Arabia, and wherever else there was space. "Call it imperialism, if you like," he said. (I'd sooner call it exporting poverty.) He literally refused to talk of or consider any other problem; this was the key, and the only one. Would he be willing to go himself? Well, he would like to organize the operation.

Then there was an editor I'll just call Mr. M. He was very self-satisfied. As he seemed doubtful of my credentials, I said I could show him one or two of my books. "I certainly can't show you mine," he replied, "for there are fifty-four of them." He had written books about philosophy, existentialism, languages, linguistics—"virtually everything." He used to be absorbed in work and study at Cairo University and had ignored politics and the war with Israel. He had never known Nasser. "No one could get to see him except Heikal," he said. "Nasser was a *deus ex machina.*" By that he meant that Nasser had been a superdictator. Mr. M was full of such malapropisms, about which there was nothing funny, for he used his semi-education to push his readers around. "Whom do you write for?" I asked, and his ambivalent answer was, "We've fifty percent illiteracy."

Actually, the figure from the best sources, such as UNESCO, is seventy percent for men, eighty percent for women, because building schools (as Nasser certainly did) isn't enough to break a pattern in which poor peasants need their children's work on the land and better-off landowners consider education for peasant children a threat to their labor supply. But the political illiteracy in which the government keeps the nation, or tries to keep it, is nearer a hundred percent. The few opposition people who cared to speak up told me so; the books written by political exiles documented it. But to see they were right, all one had to do was read the papers for a couple of days. Those air-conditioned newspapermen weren't harmless stooges or, even less, newspapermen champing at the bit of censorship. Many of them were what the Latin Americans call *vendidos,* sold ones, bought with cars and comforts in a very poor and uncomfortable country. Their job was to convince the readers that what had been so nice and profitable for them would be nice and profitable for everyone. That was the job, anyway, for those whose names still carried some weight. Others were just sent out to graze—which in their case meant to get on planes, carry tape recorders, and attend conferences.

El Ahram has about half a million readers; the other big daily, *El Akhbar* (Information), has six hundred thousand and over a million on Saturday, when it carries a magazine insert. The difference between the two, the editors told me, is only technical. *El Akhbar* brings its message home in a more popular, more low-brow form. *Akher Saa* (Last Hour) is another magazine produced by *El Akhbar,* more jazzy, and it has a hundred and thirty-five thousand readers. These are vast numbers, for in Egypt they mean that virtually everyone who can read buys one of these papers. All of them are cheap; and heavily subsidized. But I could tell precisely from *El Akhbar's* shabbiness how much further removed it was from the center of government, i.e., from the fleshpots. *El Akhbar* also had a nice Power Floor, though (the ninth), with rugs and fresh paint, and was different from *El Ahram* in that you could see the city, at least through the windows in the corridors. From that height, Cairo had still another face: the craggy, dirt-covered roofs and crumbling walls gave it the look of a World War II bombed-out German town seen from a plane. Judging from their paper, the editors rarely looked out.

Cairo again has an *Egyptian Gazette,* which is now the name for the English-language paper. Its editor is an Egyptian with a West Indian mother, a man who speaks beautiful American English and is the only journalist I met there who sounded like a journalist. His paper, with a circulation of seven thousand, is the one self-supporting newspaper in the country.

As for the well-known independent left-wing weekly, *Rosa el Yussuf* (named after the woman who founded it fifty years ago), the last two of those adjectives really belong in quotes. Besides political directives, the government also sends it its paper, in careful rations. When I visited the offices, I thought both the pop-art, with-it wall decorations, and the excitement everyone felt because Sadat had said they could set up a free "rostrum" on Friday evenings, equally depressing. Rosa, by the way, was the mother of the present chairman of *El Ahram.*

Earlier in this century, Cairo had become a newspaper-oriented society in the Latin tradition. In 1938, the country had two hundred newspapers and magazines. Buying the papers, or if necessary sharing a copy with friends, was an important ritual, and men read and discussed the news together over their coffees. Admittedly, it stopped there, for politics were made by the British high commissioner (later ambassador) and a few power brokers, but a habit of interest in politics was formed without which the officers and Nasser could not have succeeded. After 1952, the press—public debate—bloomed for the first time in Egyptian history, but Nasser curtailed it again, though, at least until 1960, not as drastically as we were made to believe in the West.

I am not a liberal, and I think an argument can be made in favor of a populist administration's curtailing its rich enemies' attacks in the media while it's trying to survive in this wicked world. Allende was one of those who tried to survive without doing that. But that's not what is happening in Cairo. The papers don't present dull, unbalanced, progovernment information and data; they present Potemkin villages in words, endless enumerations of speeches and plans from various officials who are always, in utter respectful humility, given all their titles and first names and middle names (even if these occur ten times in a piece), and shown shaking hands, patting children's heads, and smiling, smiling, smiling. I don't think it's even effective, for to the Cairenes these papers are an insult; and as for the fellahin, they assuredly have no time and no money to read them, assuming they can read.

But there is indeed also information in them: low-level complaints and answers, religion, a few sifted foreign items, neighborhood news, and, of course, entertainment. This provides the raw material for what one Egyptian writer called "the new silence." "We don't discuss political decisions," he told me. "We talk about the telephones' not working." An issue of *Akher Saa* had a gossipy conversation with the

President, His Excellency Anwar el-Sadat, talks with foreign students in Cairo about how they celebrated Ramadan, a lot of fashion material (including a full-page photograph of newlyweds), a large article on fishing as a family outing (they'd have enjoyed that one in Rosetta) with pictures of ladies and children catching fish, a play review, ads (few), and, as the only vaguely "real" subject, a piece on how pilgrims to Mecca now use this holy duty to come back to Egypt with loads of smuggled goods. This last item is a well-worn one, clearly an acceptable and easily popular piece for general indignation. *Rosa el Yussuf* had a cartoon that same week showing a hadji, a pilgrim, about to board his plane to Mecca and a friend saying, "Don't forget the cigarettes, Pilgrim." It's a funny item on the list of changing mores in this world: fifty years ago the pilgrimage (one of the five Duties of the Moslem), by boat and camel, through a thirsty and hostile desert, was as great a sacrifice as a medieval pilgrimage to Jerusalem. But it is not particularly relevant to the decisions made and being made, crucial to the lives of the people of Cairo and Egypt.

Mrs. Korkmaz was the widow of an importer of chemicals who had made a fortune in the twenties. Originally from Lebanon, he had been not just very rich but also one of the socially prominent men of Cairo. When I was given a letter of introduction to her, I was assured she still knew "everybody." The man who wrote the letter for me, a London amateur art-collector, was one of those Englishmen full of Middle East nostalgia. It took me a while to realize he hadn't been to Egypt in a decade or more, for he sounded as if he hopped over every weekend. But once, in the old days, when he had wanted to buy or rent a piece of church property, a phone call by Mrs. Korkmaz had got the patriarch or archimandrite in action within minutes ("on the stick" would be a more precise, if too disrespectful, term). Mrs. Korkmaz was now in her sixties and lived with one or two of her middle-aged, divorced daughters in the old family house, in a district of Cairo that is still called by its original name, Garden City.

My Dutch pre-1940 education was old-fashioned and continental enough to teach me how to present myself to such people as the Korkmazes; or at least I've always credited myself with that. Many countries now have survivors from an *ancien régime* in their midst, and you have to see them on their terms and not to hear yourself talk. My first visit consisted of properly dropping off my letter of introduction one day around noon, and declining to stay beyond a few minutes. Mrs. Korkmaz turned out to be a woman with a pleasant smile, nice looking, still in her dressing gown but very neat; her daughter Bea, who put in an appearance to have a look at me, was rather disgruntled and not fully awake yet. We decided to have dinner one evening that week in the Gezira Sporting Club.

The Gezira Sporting Club still occupies a vast acreage on what is now a built-over part of town, Gezira, an island in the Nile. (*Gezira* is simply the Arabic word for island.) Gezira sits midstream, facing the center of town, which is on the east bank of the river; but the west bank is now virtually "downtown" too at that point, and the many bridges are in a perpetual jam at rush hours. The club has lawns, swimming pools, and tennis courts, and it was once the most exclusive place in Cairo. As it happened, the night of our dinner was better for praying than for dining European-style: it was *Leli el Kadr,* the Night of Providence, when all the angels descend on earth to bestow their blessings. It is the night the heavens open and all prayers are heard, and salt water turns into fresh water. (The faithful used to sit over a bowl of sea water, tasting it through the night to catch that moment.) Thus it is also the night that even sporting clubs, in their privacy, even after sunset, do not serve alcohol in Cairo right now.

As Mrs. Korkmaz, a lady friend of hers, and I arrived at the club in her car—twenty years old, but a Cadillac—we found Bea standing near the gate to the garden restaurant in what was definitely a sulk. Although the temperature was still near ninety, Bea announced she was cold and had just realized there would be nothing to drink. We sat down anyway at one of the tables on the lawn.

It was the first time since my arrival in Cairo that I found myself out of earshot of car horns; with the stars shining overhead and an almost cool breeze, I thought the place was very nice. Still, it was clear enough that the exclusivity days of the Gezira were over. The lawn, once without doubt as carpety as the British roll them, had become ragged with bare spots. It wasn't crowded, but the guests were middle-class Egyptians in open shirts, and many young people were in jeans. Dogs and cats in abundance were slinking around.

Mrs. Korkmaz ordered the chicken dinner for everyone, and the conversation turned naturally to the fate and state of the club. Mrs. Korkmaz apologized for it. "It used to be so nice," she said, "when only English officers came, and just a very few Egyptians were allowed in." I protested politely that I was quite happy as we were. "We'll have a dinner at home when all this is over," Mrs. Korkmaz answered ("all this" being Ramadan). "Right now that's impossible. Formerly the servants wouldn't have dared talk about Ramadan all the time."

A waiter brought lemonades, and then chicken with squash and salads. "Cromer wrote the only good book on Egypt," Mrs. Korkmaz told me. That was the Lord Cromer who had run Egypt as British high commissioner at the turn of the century. "And you must also read, what is it, Jarvish Pasha, *Oriental Sidelights.*" She mimed a person making violent gestures and quoted from Jarvish Pasha (a 1920's British police chief), " 'An Egyptian takes his exercise by making a ten-minute telephone call.' " "But I'll invite some writers for you," she promised me. I mentioned the name of a novelist I knew, and Bea looked up from a morose stare and said, "But he's a Comm—he is very leftist." I said, well, no, he was a mild liberal (which was the truth).

Then the conversation, having done its duty by my profession, turned to their mutual friends and mutual enemies. I was told a story about a restaurant started by a Copt, a Moslem, a Jew, and a Catholic. "I was sure the Jew would stay last, but he was the first to quit," Mrs. Korkmaz said. As she and her daughter speculated on who would end up as sole owner of the place, the lady friend told me there was now one Jew left in the rowing club, one in the golf club, and one in the shooting club. "Not the same one," Mrs. Korkmaz interjected, and that made even Bea laugh. A lady was mentioned who suffered from cancer. "I wonder who'll get to buy her furniture," Bea said.

During these bits of talk and gossip, Mrs. Korkmaz had conducted a running battle with the waiters and the cook, who stood behind a buffet table not far from us. They didn't say much to her scoldings and reacted by staring into the middle distance. Daughter Bea, in the meantime, was distracting herself by throwing all the chicken bones and remnants, from her plate and those of the rest of us, onto the lawn. This resulted in all the loose dogs assembling around our table, amidst much growling, yapping, and barking. Two very unappealing curs, after fighting over a chicken bone, started copulating. No one reacted, and finally it was I who chased the lot away. Bea was half-smiling over that, and I was sure she was doing this chicken-bone act to show her contempt for her surroundings, proving to one and all that the genteel days of the Gezira Sporting Club were over and that it now had only the name in common with its predecessor of the British days.

Mrs. Korkmaz (to me, in an undertone): "I get eight percent on my Swiss investments, via Luxemburg. . . . I lost this year on the New York Stock Exchange." (Egypt has currency control, and these activities were illegal.) She asked me what was happening of late to the rate of the Swiss franc vis-à-vis the dollar, and I said I'd look it up in the *Trib* and call her the next day. "Local real estate gives a good return," Mrs. Korkmaz said, more to herself than to me, "but you can never tell what will happen."

The next time we met was at her house. Ramadan was over,

and drinks and very elaborate and delicious hors d'oeuvres were brought in by her two servants. We were sitting on a second-floor balcony, looking out over the street. The house was large, decrepit on the outside but full of fine furniture and art objects. It was half-hidden behind a huge advertising billboard and the site of an excavation, started and then halted, for the subway project Cairo has been toying with. The house had been sequestered in Nasser's time and now it was going to be returned to the Korkmazes, although the affair had not been settled yet. It stood near a very busy crossroads, and there was a touch of melancholy and maybe even pathos to that supper on the balcony: it was cold, the noise of the traffic was deafening, and the exhaust fumes easily reached us. But everyone ignored all that, as if determined to hold on or return to a way of doing things that had been so easy and pleasurable once.

One of the guests was a Lebanese lady, formerly of Cairo, who had come back to escape from the civil war in Beirut. She told me she received sixty-five percent compensation for her share in her husband's sequestered Egyptian firm, and it had always come promptly, in monthly dollar checks to Beirut. Her husband, being an Egyptian, hadn't received anything for his share, but now he would, too. His brother would get his land back, and none too soon. Wasn't there a good side to the land reform? I asked. She looked at me with something like pity. "Nasser gave the peasants an empty box," she said. "The old owners used to give them machines, seed, everything. An empty box."

We talked about "new" and "old" society and the way people brought up their children. "They're aping us," Mrs. Korkmaz said. The American University had been given back to the Americans; it was rather expensive, but there everyone knew everyone. All sorts of people went to Cairo University. I showed surprise that the teaching at the American University was totally in English. "There exists no Arabic to teach medicine," I was told. "When I was a girl, we were forbidden to speak Arabic in school," Mrs. Korkmaz added. "Kaddafi," she then said, "pays five pounds a month to every girl who wears the white turban" (the Women's Lib badge in Cairo). "Isn't that true?" she asked the company, but no one confirmed it.

A European diplomat, a young counselor of embassy, and his wife were shown in; she was a very pretty black woman from Zambia. There were introductions and some small talk, and then Mrs. Korkmaz took them aside. It turned out that they had come to sign the lease on an apartment of hers. No writers or other such people showed up for the party. The Korkmazes had nothing to offer just then that would bring them to the circle on that dusty balcony, over the crossroads gas stations.

When the diplomatic couple had left, a buzz of comments started such as you might have heard in Queens in the 1940's or, for all I know, now. Mrs. Korkmaz explained that she had accepted the couple only because the man was quite important and they hadn't questioned the rent. There were jokes about whether the color of the lady would come off on her husband. I was informed, and not as a joke, that the Congolese chargé d'affaires, on his wedding night in the Cairo Hilton, had eaten his wife. "There was a 'No Disturb' sign on the door and so they didn't dare come in when they heard her scream. They thought, well, you know, maybe it was ecstasy. He fled the next day, back to the Congo." As these ladies were rather dark (what Lord Cromer icily would have called "touched by the tar brush"), it all seemed rather sad. How unlikable the human race can be!

Korkmaz was not the real name of this family; I have changed it, along with other minor details. My picture of their conversations may seem caricatural, but I have toned it down, if anything. I realize that what seemed unpleasant in it to me may be perfectly all right with the Korkmazes, but they received me and I want to protect their privacy anyway. Nor do I have any intention of ridiculing them. There were many families like them in Cairo and many, assuredly, all over the world; and even their being at war, in a sense, with their government and people is not that unusual any more in our part of the world either.

They didn't receive me quite as cordially and interestedly as I would have expected, but this was not connected with my likableness or lack of it. In the small circle of an *ancien régime* society, a letter of introduction from the right person establishes one, for at least as long as one remains a visitor from abroad and not a competitor. People like the Korkmazes, stranded among their fellow citizens like *émigrés* in all but geography, always welcome outside messengers from the world of dollars, francs, and stock exchanges, whence cometh their deliverance. I do not mean they want or need handouts. A rich man who has become poor is still richer than a poor man doing all right. But they do like to have contacts for their many journeys, who can change money, have a piece of jewelry taken out for them, or what have you—or simply serve as one more insurance against a future calamity.

I thought I understood why the Korkmazes were just a bit different in this from, for instance, dispossessed Argentinians I knew in Buenos Aires. I thought the point was that they were coming back.

It hadn't completely happened yet, but it was in the air. They smelled the turning tide. And thus they were about to become hard again, "exclusive." Soon there might be no more cause for inviting and receiving writers. Not even writers from the hard-currency city of New York.

What, then, is happening in Egypt?

"They breathe again"—that's how a history-minded old inhabitant of Cairo described it to me. "They're walking their mistresses again, they're driving their Mercedeses . . . and you must admit, they are more amusing than the new bourgeoisie who have no culture."

"They" in his statement were the disinherited former ruling classes, the great landowners, the international industrialists. He talked about Egypt in pure French Revolution terms: we were in Cairo now as in Paris under the Directoire, when the red Jacobin revolution had been sidetracked and a bourgeois republic had taken over which would lead straight to Napoleon.

"There are power conflicts, surely," he said, "and Sadat is involved in them. But the Nasser bourgeoisie has most of the power and will keep it. They're flirting with the old upper classes, though, and marrying into them, as the Sadat family, for instance, already did. And that is like Napoleon and the old aristocrats."

As he was so amused by his own images, I answered sourly, "But the people suffer," also a sentence from the French Revolution. "Oh, less—well, maybe as much as ever," he said, "but not more."

One thing wrong with the parallel is that Egypt never had any Jacobins in power to have a go at a totally new society. The King and the *aristos* were toppled, but the people never took over. The national revolution never became a social one, though some in the West hoped and most feared that it had. There are many versions of what happened here, but on this, there's agreement in Cairo.

Agreement among whom? When I quote anonymous speakers, these are never government people (which includes newspaper men and women), who as a matter of principle confine themselves to vaguenesses; my informants are professional people mostly, politically minded, with an occasional foreign diplomat or long-term immigrant.

Take a step back into the British days. Contrary to cherished beliefs, the lack of independence did not buy general progress. After 1914, the overall health of the people deteriorated and the British statistics show they had fewer calories to eat. In 1938, Egypt had the highest death rate in the world. Egyptian manufactures would have competed with English imports, and they remained a bugaboo to London, which thus forced the levying of duties on *local* products. The British fought the plans for a state university, and for most of their years in Egypt there was ninety-five percent illiteracy, with less than one percent of the national budget devoted to education.

Presently the threat from Mussolini and Hitler had gone, and King Farouk had lost his credibility, if any, in the whorehouses of Cairo. The army lost its credibility in the 1948 Palestine war. After a year of guerrilla battles by native population and constabulary against British troops in the Canal Zone, the European section of Cairo burned on January 26, 1952, Black Saturday. In July came the coup of Nasser and his fellow officers.

In August of that year, the "Free Officers" responded to a strike in the Misr textile factory in the Delta by hanging two of the strike leaders. They put themselves on record then and there that law and order came first to them, too—not British law, but not law per se either; their law.

In 1956 the British troops got out, after the "temporary intervention" that had taken them seventy-four years. That was in June; a month later, Dulles had his tantrum over the financing of the High Dam, and a week after that, Nasser nationalized the Canal. In October, Israel invaded the Sinai and was joined by Britain and France. The United States, Russia, and the General Assembly of the UN all found themselves pulling at the same end of the rope for a change and forced an armistice and new evacuation. The Suez war, far from overthrowing Nasser, became his hour of glory.

Mahmoud Hussein, an Egyptian Marxist exile, wrote about this: "The regime gave the people a renewed national dignity, and that satisfied one of their aspirations. But it did this in a bourgeois framework . . . the support remained passive, and what began as a mass movement, a genuine popular revolt, ended up an alienated, powerless, mob."

The point is, of course, that Nasser *wanted* that support to remain passive. He could have had a mass uprising supporting him then, and probably at almost any point in his presidency. Mahmoud Hussein and other Egyptian radical writers (they're mostly in Paris) will tell you he did not want it precisely because the aid and cooperation of the new middle classes, the Nasser bourgeoisie-to-be, was lent to him on condition he'd keep "the people" in check. I don't doubt that is true, but, to Nasser's credit, another reason may be added: mass uprisings are particularly ineffective except in guerrilla actions. To have stirred up the fellahin to march against British or Israeli cannon would have meant killing them off.

Nasser felt that the national struggle was the good and pure one, and that any social-equality plans were a very painful added ingredient. They were needed to make Egypt a modern country with modern conditions of work and life, and they were painful because they disrupted the unity of the people (a unity, however, that existed in political speeches only). He and his fellow officers started out as exponents of free enterprise. One of them, Kamal el Din Hussein, since years out of power, became my neighbor in Cairo, and we spent a hot evening sitting in front of his huge seven-speed electric fan while he described to me his grief when Nasser turned away from that ideal and eventually made him, Hussein, feel obliged to resign.

After the coup, the officers actually canceled a law from the year 1947 which had required fifty-one percent Egyptian control in all companies. And the first Agrarian Reform Law of 1952 was precisely meant·to get Egypt out of feudalism into modern free enterprise (they wouldn't have used the word "capitalism"), to break the enormous power of the 280 great families, including the left-behinds of the royal court; and it did that. It gave a new fillip to the rural middle class and the most enterprising local manufacturers. And—indeed—justice was served.

After 1956, the government veered, not really toward socialism (by now one of the most misused words over the globe), but toward statism. The new bourgeoisie had shown they knew the facts of life, and their new money had therefore not gone into the planned new industries at all, but instead into solid downtown real estate, where you can count the rooms and the baths and the johns before you begin; or it went, even more solidly, to a bank in Zurich or New York.

I hate to keep using the word "bourgeoisie," which isn't English and which tastes of pamphlets and lectures, but there's no proper synonym, maybe because the United States doesn't have a real bourgeoisie. It is not property owners, for a German high-school teacher who is as poor as a church mouse is certainly a bourgeois, and it is not exactly the middle classes, for a woman running a candy stand is middle class but no bourgeoise.

Anyway, the Egyptian bourgeoisie had been doing what such people always do in countries where the politicians talk too much for comfort about nation and sacrifice and unity rather than prosperity, and Nasser had to get the money for his investments elsewhere, that is to say, from the state and from abroad, which meant the USSR, as there were no other takers. In 1952, two-thirds of the investments had come from private sources; in 1960, two-thirds were undertaken by the state. The Egyptian economy was getting nationalized, and a legion of new state institutions appeared.

Nasser got away with that because the people, passive as they were kept, went on supporting him, the first ruler of their Egypt who showed them some basic good will, who didn't "eat their blood"—and thus it was clear to one and all that he and he alone kept the masses off the streets. There was a lot of political organizing but it was vertical, trade by trade, fat farmer together with thin farmers as against factory owner together with his workers; all had to be Egyptians for the greater good of the country. Obviously, Nasser was helped in this by the permanent confrontation with Israel (which was a terrible economic burden, though) and by the mood that had been created to make the Egyptians (who had rarely called themselves Arabs) feel one part of The Arab Nation.

But by about 1960, Nasser had become very serious about his social reforms. Only Allah knows what his motives really were, how heavily a sense of new justice for the people weighed with him, how heavily his ambition to be the leader of a modern nation. As the reforms had to be put through without "the people" and without sacrifices (except by the people), the results fell a long way behind intentions; there was a depressing limpness about them all. Still, schools were built, village social and rural-health units were organized.

Higher education blossomed, as Nasser got the most ultra-conservative religiosos off its back.

The middle classes were at the front of the line taking advantage of these things. Principle doesn't seem to enter then. It doesn't buy gratitude. On another level: Bea, the Korkmaz daughter, did sculptures. She was quite satisfied to have her pieces circulate and sell through exhibits in Europe, organized and paid for by the red regime of those years she hated so. The middle classes filled the new places in the new colleges, and presently the government got to guaranteeing a civil-service job to each and every graduate—so as not to have a growing intellectual proletariat on its hands.

It was a ramshackle structure, the new populism—a structure it was, though. If it didn't stop very many from profiteering, at least it provided those who did with bad consciences, or maybe just with sleepless nights from fear.

Egypt had always been a poor country; no, a country with many poor and a few insufferably arrogant rich. In between sat an immoderately numerous bureaucracy.

Now the country was slightly less poor and its rich were less rich and less arrogant. But the bureaucracy was becoming elephantine.

FOURTEEN

The new state civil servants shared with the existing bourgeoisie the determination not to do any suffering. (Galal Amin, an economist at Heliopolis University of Cairo, wrote that there was a definite government promise: no development plans at the expense of the present generation.) Apart from some old-time officers who at least showed up at nine o'clock and kept their desk tops dusted, no one had discipline, let alone fervor. And only fervor could have made up for the incompetence unavoidable among so much new personnel.

Nor did the new civil servants show any of that crusty professional exclusivity you'd find even in a junior postal clerk in a French village. They knew their jobs hung by a thread, dependent on the political fortunes of one man. Below them gaped the open mouths of the hungry peasants, above them stared the jealous or contemptuous old-old and old-new bourgeoisie. They thrashed around for more footholds, in a fearful hurry to consolidate their new powers and turn them into something tangible, something you could stash away, job or no job. "A network developed of personal relationships, collusion, and complicity, between the different state organizations and the private sector; the circulation of capital and commodities began to escape from control by the central administration . . . the control of liquid capital, spare parts, raw materials, fuel, finished products, all became impossible as those responsible learned to use both the means of production and the products for their own benefit. The black market spread everywhere, even to consumer co-ops. In the countryside, with its backward transportation system, black-market monopolies sprang up. The state tried new controls, but they were administrative, within the same setup, and enabled the controllers to strike deals with the controlled. There was no popular control to stop either of them." This description is by Mahmoud Hussein. He may be exaggerating, but not much. In today's Egypt, corruption is an omnipresent fact of life, and you are constantly told—though it's difficult to see how it could have been—that it was worse under Nasser.

Nasser is dead. "Socialization" is all over. His successor, his vice-president Anwar el-Sadat, originally supposed to be a bit of a joke and good for six months in office, has dug in beyond anyone's expectation. You see him everywhere—on posters, that is—saluting smartly and with an Avis-type "at your service" smile. He had the army cross the Canal in the October 1973 war, which helped, but he is still no hero and no father figure. In other words, the various bourgeoisies (plural) that have come out of these turbulent years with their flags still flying and their cars still running don't have to take any nonsense from him. He, unlike Nasser, cannot act the people's tribune with them. Thus there is no need any more to be patriotic or Arab or interested in anything but business. Or, if you want to be charitable to them (which I don't), you could also say they can now concentrate on a quiet, good life for themselves and their families.

To use the word "socialism" is still okay here, just as it is in Mexico, which went through something like this in the 1940's and where archconservatives love to call themselves "revolutionary." But apart from such word games, the people are no longer wooed. Now you hear that "the right to work" cannot be called absolute, that "we cannot indefinitely afford to subsidize food," and that "our labor cost has to remain competitive." Restrictions are lifted on investment and on once sequestered or nationalized properties; the clock is turned back, and no one knows yet to what year or epoch. Unfortunately, the state apparatus does not seem to do any visible shrinking; leaving the economy to the private entrepreneur doesn't seem to have made one control by the bureaucracy redundant. In the Central Government Building, the Mugamma, in Cairo's Liberation Square, the people still run up and down the endless stone corridors and staircases, in search of a permit to stand in line for another permit, while the civil servant needed in the link is having his coffee break; it still looks there like a scene out of Lang's film, *Metropolis*. But the foreigner, that selfsame white-bleeder and dry-squeezer of Egypt, now has tantalizing prospectuses printed for him in red, blue, and other gay colors, explaining Foreign Investment Law Number 43, inviting him back into the new Free and Investment Zones for Arab and Foreign Capital, and promising him, "We'll never be naughty again."

And that, of course, also implies a definite good-by to the Russians, whose weapons, we are informed, never functioned properly anyway. There is the matter of some very large debts indeed still to be paid, but no official is willing to discuss or even put a figure to these. America is cordially invited to take the place of honor instead. America will get the Israelis out of the Sinai. And it will bring (or lend) prosperity, so much of it that enough drips through to keep the poor quiet, who in Islam as in Christendom are always with us.

Or to sum it all up much more briefly yet, in the remarkable words a government agronomist spoke to me (he made thirty Egyptian pounds a month and moonlighted as a chauffeur): "We hate poor people like the Russians. We love rich people like the Americans. They'll give us things."

FIFTEEN

O ne evening at a party for the British ambassador who was about to retire from his Cairo post, I found myself on a balcony with a fellow guest who called himself "an oil man" (our latest power elite; there are many in Cairo, and the Cairenes are always making bitter jokes about them). If the guest had been an American, he'd probably have asked me in turn what I did for a living, but he was an Italian. Clutching my arm, he suddenly cried, *"Oh, les nuits du Caire!"* ("Oh, nights of Cairo!"). As we were but standing on the balcony of a third-floor apartment, looking out over a street full of parked cars and the Omar Khayyam Hotel in the process of being torn down, he startled me somewhat. You don't expect oil men to have such poetic fervors, too.

Still, there were stars above us, and the nights of Cairo used to be the favorite Egypt topic, taking first place before treasures and mummies in royal tombs. Quite a number of books of turn-of-the-century travel memoirs had those very nights in their titles. When you got to read the books, you found that the mystery of the Cairo nights consisted mostly of Victorian sin—the ease with which you could buy the use of women's and boys' bodies. It's the other way around now: very hard to achieve in Cairo, very easy on Lexington Avenue, but this has not led to any rhapsodizing on the nights of

Lexington Avenue. What I mean is, I don't think there *is* any mystery to Cairo, or to the Orient, day or night, beyond the universal mystery of human love and death. There are dark and narrow streets and alleyways, pathetic occupations, unbelievable conditions, sights and smells of the Middle Ages; and, undeniably, a certain magical, bitter charm.

At least I thought so, but only toward the end of my time there, and it was of course as subjective a feeling as the words are to describe it. Most of my days Egypt just all seemed chaos, chaos and poverty, mitigated by human contacts.

It sorted itself out slowly, because I lost much of my time dutifully working down the list of introductions I had brought and going through appointments. These were mainly with official personages who were, in turn, supposed to introduce me to others more exalted than they were; a fragile chain in a city where the officials are as afraid of sticking out their necks as Russians and as lazy and absent as Washingtonians, and where the telephone system is of no place and no time. Eventually I had the satisfaction of dropping this whole business of interviews; and I found recompense for the waiting and the no-shows when I was telephoned from the government press center about an appointment with a minister and I could answer, "Well, no, thanks, I think I'll let it pass."

The press center made a fine bridge to the official world of Cairo: it was the embodiment of the clash between plans and reality. Located on the second floor of the big communications building known as "Television," it consisted of mostly empty rooms, with rows of broken-down and ribbonless typewriters, two telephone booths without the phones, and a teletype clicking away on a reel of paper which always got stuck and shedded torn fragments of world news onto the floor without anyone's bothering to fix it. Outside, all along the rooms, a veranda with many chairs stretched, giving a view of the Nile Corniche, the river, and beyond. You could see how once in the past someone had planned this, visualizing journalists from all over the world gathering here in professional discussions; but not a soul was ever on that veranda.

But I spent a lot of time in the never-never land where forever the nation's future was planned and announced, or if not forever, at least till lunchtime. If I had had a chauffeured car and had been shuttled between a hotel room, the press center, and the government bureaus, I could have carried this on for months without ever really knowing where I was. (At that farewell party given for him, I had asked the British ambassador how things had been different in 1944 and 1945, when he had also been posted in Cairo. "Well, we had no Scotch in those days," he answered. "But the Egyptian wines were better then." I don't mean he wouldn't have had more to say on the subject; still, that was his answer.)

Luckily, though it didn't always feel that way, my days didn't originate in any hotel room. My Cairo apartment belonged to a Cairene who had rented it to a photographer who had sublet it to the present tenant, my landlord and host. He was a young man who wrote about the economy for foreign publications; he told me he'd be an actor next and then he'd direct movies. I'm sure he will, for he had the show-business talent of being ruthless in a jolly, friendly way. Built in a colonial past, the apartment was huge, and its cavernous rooms were much the worse for wear. The tap water was black—not just when you opened the tap but all the time—and the remnants of enormous meals were always rotting away in the kitchen. Those meals were cooked for my host by men in white jackets whom he hired in a vision of gentility as antiquated as the kitchen; there was a kink in his labor relations, and it was a different man almost every week. Several early mornings I was wandering down the side street on a round of the many washing and ironing shops there, trying to locate where the next-to-latest cook had left the laundry, to find myself a shirt and a towel. A nightclub waiter who lived on the corner, and who even at those early hours was in a good mood, helped me with the language problems this entailed, and with such hangups as finding a cylinder of Butagaz for the shower without having to return an empty. Cairo, one of the early cities to have gas and then electric street lighting (1898), has at this time no piped cooking gas. The waiter was really interested in buying dollars at the black-market rate, he said; but my host thought he was a police *agent provocateur*.

That little side street also had a string of groceries, where I'd occasionally buy food for a cold supper by myself: bread with Spam or corned beef or packaged cheese. The shops, catering to a middle-class and upper-middle-class area, had those items in abundance, as also mineral water, Scotch, Nescafé, ballpoints, radios, cameras, tape recorders, cosmetics, and everything else, all hard-currency stuff from France, Germany, Holland, Switzerland, and the U.S., for which Egypt at least in theory had no funds available, and for none of which she had a hard need. The canned food was of mysterious brands and (sometimes) taste, and maybe it was part of one of those Western aid deals we use to unload our less desirable products onto the third world. As proper in a desert-bound country, water was the most expensive part of my meals. A French or even a local bottle of water cost between seventy and eighty-five piasters, which is at any rate of exchange well over a dollar, and twice as much as the rest of the supper added up to.

I tacked pieces of gauze in my window to keep out the mosquitoes, which in Cairo show up in irregular attacks through the year. Malaria is endemic. But the one thing impossible to keep out, and my greatest bane, was the everlasting din. Cairo is to Rome as Rome is to Sleepy Hollow.

One night a hoarse cry was emitted every few seconds or so from a window in the adjacent building, across the courtyard from mine. It echoed in the concrete stairwell and sounded like a donkey braying. Toward dawn I thought I discovered a human quality to it, as if someone were being kept prisoner or being tortured. I got up and went to ask the doormen about it, but they professed not to know. It ended around noon, and I concluded later it had been a professional mourner, a keening woman such as Saudi and other families from Arabia still employ. It was a terrifying kind of sound, expressing horror rather than grief, but at least it seemed a legitimate noise to be kept awake by.

Those "doormen" are really watchmen; they don't come in, but are employed to sit outside front doors day and night, just as in Spain fifty years ago. Wages, of course, are a pittance. Next to my building, excavation was in progress for a new house: a dozen men and women were going up and down a hill of dirt all day long, emptying baskets of earth. It was a method unchanged from Pharaonic times; just as you could, outside the Egyptian Museum, see men making bricks in the same way as on the hieroglyphs inside.

This is then pointed out to tourists as a sign of historic continuity. It is only a sign of such lopsided poverty that it's cheaper for an entrepreneur to hire a crowd of paupers than to get one machine or a few men with decent tools.

SIXTEEN

The buses of Alexandria were vile, those of Cairo much worse. Supposedly there were three thousand on the road; the papers were repeatedly announcing orders placed in various countries for new ones, but I was told that this had been going on for a long time without visible results. The fare was low enough, two piasters (about four cents), and unless you boarded them at or near a terminal, you wouldn't get a seat, you wouldn't get standing room—you'd be hanging on outside beyond the reach of any fare collector anyway, and beyond help from anyone but God. Because half the passengers hung on outside, from starboard, so to speak, the buses listed like sinking ships, one side up, one side almost touching the pavement.

The next step up the transport ladder, and a big step it was, was the jitney taxis, which picked up and dropped people going in vaguely the same direction. Almost all taxis in Cairo ran that way. They didn't have fixed routes but they tried to keep all seats occupied, unless some sheik or American wanted the whole thing to himself. The jitney was still cheap —to a foreigner. You paid more or less what the meter ran up during your tenure, and that wasn't more than thirty cents for a ride all through town, three or four miles.

The snag was that these taxis, gilded luxury compared

to the public transport system, were tough to catch. Many a Cairene would inform me they were impossible to catch at most hours, but as a New Yorker I knew better. It is a matter of training and determination. You have to find a street pointing toward your destination and walk there; no use to stand somewhere else. On that street you have to post yourself at a spot where some obstruction of man or nature will force cabbies to slow down. Then, at the precise moment, you shout your destination at any cab that has room. It worked.

On my first morning free from efforts at interviews, my first place to visit was the Ezbekiya Gardens. They're not one of Cairo's sights, but they're its equivalent of Alexandria's Place des Consuls, a setting for recent history it is nice to poke around in, to try and fit the old photographs onto the present. When Napoleon set up headquarters in Ezbekiya, most of it was still a lake during the four months the river was in flood: a thirty-acre lake with boats and boatmen to handle the traffic. In the course of the nineteenth century, the lake was drained and the gardens laid out by a French designer, and an admission price of five milliemes (at that time, two and a half U.S. cents) was set to keep out the natives. It remained the very heart of the establishment until the day of arson and rebellion in 1952 when its Shepheard's Hotel, focal point of British rule, was burned to the ground.

A line drawn along the eastern side of the gardens and running south divided Cairo into a native and a European part; but from that day on, things changed, and Egyptians began invading their own streets. The division holds in a different way now, very poor east of the line, less poor and prosperous to the west of it. With the European exodus after 1952 and especially after the 1956 Suez war, the Europeanized cafés and restaurants and shops and hairdressers disappeared; the poor who until then had crossed the line to serve or beg from the foreigners now came for their own purposes. The city became shabbier but more genuine.

Another section, though, became the domain of the rich, and especially the rich foreigners (few Englishmen these days, but Americans, Germans, Arabs); they moved from Ezbekiya to the shore of the Nile. Here sits the new Shepheard's Hotel, which, however, has nothing but its name in common with the old one. It is an international chunk of stone, barred from the town around it by a racetrack of fumes and car horns, the Corniche, where one inadvertent step will bring sudden death. Its concierge cheats when you buy stamps from him.

Admittedly, those colonial pigs of the old Shepheard's handled things better for themselves. On the old photographs you see them sitting very nicely in rattan chairs on the large terrace, right over the shady street, with a policeman at the foot of the steps and a servant huddled next to him on a stool. With a magnifying glass I discovered a scales on the terrace near the garden door, surely to check whether one hadn't lunched too heavily.

As for Ezbekiya, it is pronounced "Ezbekeeya," with a heavy stress on the third syllable, which I found out trying to get there, for no other pronunciation was recognized. The gardens were, amazingly, still in good shape. No admission price any more, nice rattan chairs—who knows, maybe saved from Shepheard's—and a buffet selling coffees and lemonades. Old men and women were sitting in the shade, members of that well-nigh vanished class of poor but educated Westernized Egyptians, retired employees of Western firms perhaps, still receiving some tiny pension from London or Paris. There were many children playing, and vendors of balloons and candy, and workmen saying their prayers on matting they had brought. At the garden gate sat a street photographer with tripod camera, black cloth, and buckets in which to develop the pictures on the spot. He took my photograph and let me sit on his chair while he developed it. He spoke Italian; he told me he had worked many years in Italy during the Mussolini time, on construction sites.

When he handed over the photo, I saw that its background was formed by a house across the street called Hotel Roy. It was a little place of quite unbelievable filthiness, facing the corner where the Shepheard's lords and ladies, officers and gentlemen, had been sipping their sherries. In the space once occupied by the main bulding of the hotel stood a gas station, and behind it, a newly built insurance company office.

That was all Ezbekiya produced for me. I walked through the gardens to the southeast corner, where the Muski begins, also a famous name in the past of Cairo and once its finest shopping street. It was built a hundred and fifty years ago and named after the Muski bridge over the Nile-Red Sea canal, which used to go by right here. That bridge, in turn, had been put up by and named after a man called Iz el Din Musk, and he was a cousin of none other than Salah el Din, Saladin the Great, the chivalrous opponent of Richard the Lion-Hearted.

The Muski played a big role in one of the most popular Egyptian novels of the 1940's, *Midak Alley* by Naguib Mahfouz, and from that book I got my idea as to how it would look. Midak Alley was a slum street in the Khan el Khalili market area nearby, and to the people of that alley the Muski was the unreachable land of gold. The beautiful but wicked girl of the book was seduced by a rascal in a posh Muski apartment, and it was the Muski, not the man, that had done the seducing. Thus its narrowness and its darkness came as a surprise to me.

The Muski was the first Cairo street to have stores with plate-glass windows instead of the traditional open kind.

Both types were still there, and its sidewalks were lined with stalls. While more modern stores had concentrated a mile farther west, in the Kasr el Nil area, the Muski was now just an honest local shopping street, organized with rows of shops that concentrated on selling the same things. A jeweler said to me, "If you want silver, you have to walk two blocks up. We sell gold articles only." It wasn't any wicked girl's dream any more, nor was there anything "Oriental" about it: no one accosted me, no merchant ordered coffees for his clients, and when I went into a store to buy a dress for my daughter, there was no bargaining and as little commotion as you'd have at Bloomingdale's, though the service here was better. Bookshops had large collections of paperback manuals, very expensive Western textbooks, and much comic-strip stuff. There was always one shelf with dusty old British novels abandoned long ago by their once owners. In old-fashioned merchandise emporiums at the end of little turns off the main street, knowledgeable-looking men unrolled huge bolts of material for their customers. Open-air stands were loaded with lamps, glassware, and tinware.

The goldsmiths sold earrings, chains, crosses, calligraphed Koran covers, and hangers with "Nile keys" (♀ is really a stylized sandal strap, and the hieroglyphic symbol for "life"). They said their gold was all eighteen-carat, though it seemed light and the workmanship was not very fine. On the sidewalks, women in black *meliyas* (dressing gowns without sashes) were trying to sell squares of mirror glass and matches. But most of the shops were down-to-earth hardware stores, dress stores, shoe stores, shops for kitchen articles, and much of their stuff was locally made and priced below our level if you converted at the free/black-market rate. Some was quite cheap in our terms, but in terms of wages earned in Egypt, it was all expensive.

The crowd of shoppers was very thick, though. Without

the hassle and noise of car traffic, it was a pleasant crush, and people looked more good-natured here. Personal contact —between perfect strangers, that is—could play its role in mitigating the harshness of life. It is a role it plays everywhere among the poor, and in Egypt very much so; contact and touch are crucial. Where a New Yorker shrinks away, if possible, from the touch of strangers in a crowd or from sharing a cup or a seat, here people liked it. Donkey carts were the only vehicles, and the drivers used some of the old cries—"*Shimalak ya sit*," "*Yaminik ya bint*," which meant, "Watch your left, lady," "Watch your right, daughter"— traditional warnings elsewhere replaced by claxon blasts.

I sat down outside a little café and had tea with mint. The two waiters took turns smoking the unfinished waterpipe left behind by a client. A man with ballpoints was besieged by buyers for reasons a mystery to me, as I had seen the same pens all over town. In front of us, a cart pulled up, loaded with bags of nuts and beans which the two little children who had been riding on it started carrying in. The driver—and you could see he lifted those bags with a bit of an effort— put two bags at a time on each child's back, which they then, bent double, shuffled away with.

THE BURDENS

The streets of Cairo in general are crowded with cars, but they are also crowded with carts pushed by men or pulled by donkeys, with dromedaries loaded up high, and with boys bicycling, each with one hand on the handlebar and one hand holding an enormous basket of bread on his head. The loads are heavy and the methods the same as long ago, but the city has lost its patience. I watched a cart loaded with cement pylons at a traffic light. Two men were pulling and pushing, and when the lights changed, they could not get it going again. The sweat was running down their faces. Finally the cart started moving, inch by inch. But the cars behind it hooted and hooted, and passing cab drivers cursed as if the cement cart had been a sports car with someone dozing behind the wheel.

THE ACCIDENTS

I think the discussion of automobile mores is a bore, but the driving habits in Cairo are so crazy that I do have to mention them (I know I have already gone on and on about the horn honking). The driving is very fast and very bad. At one time I rented an old car and started driving around myself, and it did not worry me too much, but I had been an army driver for a year. I'd like to know what psychology would make of it. Childishness, frustration? Most cab drivers are so reckless that you do not have to be the old lady from Dubuque to be scared. I was told that on each journey out of town I'd pass five or more fresh car wrecks, and that was precisely true. Cops have no mechanical means to chase drivers, and they write down the license numbers. When you come to renew your license, once a year, you're made to pay for the offenses, alleged or real, that have been written down.

I had never before witnessed someone actually being knocked down by a car. In Cairo, I saw two girls being knocked over by a motorcycle; the one who could get up afterward took the other by her legs and dragged her to the sidewalk. If she hadn't, the other girl would have been run over half a dozen times, for no one stopped. They were little girls. I saw a red sports car knock down a boy, who started to scream and was carried off the road by a passer-by. Two soldiers were sitting in a jeep, talking, and I shouted at them to chase the red car, but they paid no attention and drove off in the opposite direction. This business of not stopping after an accident is particularly vile here, since the people knocked down will, as a rule, have no money for proper medical attention. But Egyptians assured me that it was too dangerous to stop; you might get beaten up or, in the countryside, killed.

When men, like Egyptians in red sports cars or like our General Westmoreland, announce that life in the Orient is cheap, they mean it is cheap to them. The "ruling classes" hold the lives of others very cheap. But the poor and the fellahin take immense care of and show great love for their children and even, as a rule, their animals. All you have to do is observe the tenderness with which little children, at the end of long and hard days, have their hair brushed by their mothers; the immense grief over disease and death; the patience of a man bathing a horse or a cow in a canal.

THE CHILDREN

Some Cairo children look smug and happy bumping along on top of the crates and bales of a donkey cart, happy with the ride and still in innocence of the chasm between them and the children in the backs of the cars that hoot at them and then dash past. Some children look heartbreakingly miserable and you can tell they are sick, with hollow cheeks and swollen bellies, not bothering to chase the flies covering them, but going through their day's work all the same. You also see amazingly beautiful faces, Pharaonic princesses reborn in the city slums.

I sat behind a flat-bottomed truck one morning, on the railway and car bridge from Bulak across the Nile. We were all creeping along at about three miles an hour. Beside the truck a man was walking, holding a tiny girl by the hand. He lifted her up and put her on the truck, then trotted on beside her. She laughed out loud with sheer delight.

A little boy was hanging on to the back of a bus, and when he saw me look at him, he started stepping on the pavement with one foot, with an enormous grin, making believe he was pushing the bus on that way. A barefoot boy was dragging a cart along, placed between its two handlebars like a donkey. He was looking at his feet only, and singing to himself.

Older children jeered and made faces—but only around the places where foreigners and tourists came: in front of the Hilton, where there was always a crowd of pimps and touts, and upcountry in a place like Luxor.

THE SIGNS

The European exodus, the wars and disillusionments, Arab nationalism, and our own crises and tantrums haven't spoiled the Egyptians' idea that the West is glamorous. Cairo is still, or again, full of inappropriate names from over here: shops and restaurants are called Lolita and Miami, My Fair Lady, Champs Elysées, and The Godfather. Two dismal hotels are called the Claridge and the South Victoria & St. James, and the man who scooped up and served me a plate of beans and sinews had called his place The Automatic.

In a country like Egypt everyone may hang out signs, not just shops and hotels. "Dr. Victor Bromberg—Médecin —Chirurgien—Dentiste" in large letters: what fate brought this man to practice medicine, surgery, and dentistry behind a tiny window of matted glass on the second story of a decrepit Cairo office building? On a wooden slat over a door: "Gynaecologist from the University of Paris." Was this once a young man full of hope and expectations, promenading in Montmartre? I sat in one of those waiting rooms up an unlit staircase, for I had caught a kind of desert bronchitis. It was a dark little room with dusty cabinets, as of an abortionist in an old European movie; the doctor was an old man who spoke a mixture of Arabic and a German that no one in Heide(l)berg ever heard. (His sign said, "Formerly of the hospitals of Frankfurt and Heildelberg.") He wrote me a prescription for a long list of drugs and antibiotics. Cairenes like to swallow lots of medicines for everything. He also told me to get a daily injection of vitamins at the pharmacy; these are given for ten cents a turn. But I decided to skip that part of the treatment once I had had a look at the shop.

SEVENTEEN

It had been pleasantly abstentious not to be in a hurry to see the Pyramids. I was keeping it in reserve. There was also the fear of being disappointed: they've shown us so many pictures of them. (Egypt has dozens of pyramids, but the Pyramids with a capital *P* are the three at Giza.)

One morning I got up at dawn, around six, walked across the Nile bridge, and on the Giza side found a taxi just setting out on its day's work. The road to the Pyramids used to run through the fields, and when these were flooded by the Nile there was a point where the silhouette of the Great Pyramid was reflected in the water. Now the whole way, some seven miles, lies within the confines of the city and looks like any U.S. highway running out of a big town: a mixture of high rises and slumminess, with, toward the end, lots of nightclubs. That stretch used to be sin road, and rumors have often circulated in Cairo that some orthodox Moslem group or other was on its way to burn it down. Lastly, Kaddafi's unification-with-Libya lobby were supposed to have this on their program. Nowadays the sin consists of nothing, though, but ladies doing bowdlerized belly dances in an overabundance of gauzes and bangles.

I got off at the Mena House Hotel, from which the road climbs up to the plateau of the Pyramids. Nobody was about yet but the very first of the guides, vendors, and others who do their hustling here. Avoiding everyone's eyes, I reached the plateau unaccosted. (I've never been to a famous sight anywhere where you weren't better off alone—unless you were lucky enough to have a scholar as your companion, someone busy studying the place, or digging it out, or restoring it.)

I walked through the sand until I had the Great Pyramid, the Pyramid of Cheops, between myself and the town.

The sun was well up in the sky now.

I looked up along that triangular wall that pulled my eyes toward the light. I turned the northeastern corner of the Pyramid (the diagonals of all three run precisely northeast-southwest and northwest-southeast) and as soon as I had passed it, the hum of the town was absorbed by the enormous body of stone. I was in absolute silence and I stopped being half-afraid to watch. I turned the next corner and was surrounded now by sand and stone, out of sight of the environment; the sun, though it was early, was white, a truly pure white, and the sand and the stone surfaces were shining and shimmering under it. Complete stillness. Mathematically, an outer edge had been created here, a platform onto a void.

I had read up on facts and history, but I had not prepared myself for any particular emotions. I was surely not trying to come up with any literary reflections fitting the occasion. But I was, immediately and in that instant, overwhelmed by a feeling of understanding, and it was an understanding that did not get any more complete from all the hours of wandering I did thereafter. On the contrary, I felt I had to hold on to it as hard as I could, not to let it slip away as the day wore on.

I was plodding through the sand and looking up at the sun and at the two Pyramids visible to me, the Middle Pyramid of King Khephren and the Great Pyramid, which the Egyptians once called Ekhet Khufu, meaning "the horizon of King Cheops," or perhaps "Cheops is infinite."

My sudden understanding was of nothing less than what this had been *for*. It was outside the theories and truths of Egyptology, but I was in no doubt about it. The Pyramid of Cheops was not built to be bigger and more impressive than the only preceding ones, those of Sakkara, which are the oldest stone constructions on earth. Sakkara had made Cheops possible, but with Cheops, mankind had taken off; no matter how many learned men have counted its stones for us and weighed its weight, there wasn't a feeling of building, or work, or effort. Cheops was an asterial monument, and it gave the people in that dawn year of humanity, 2700 B.C., an experience of ecstasy, of fear, and of immortality. I wasn't surprised that this hadn't been seen clearly before, because it is, also, an experience of our time. Ridiculous as it may be, I have to use our slang to be precise about it. I am not in the least talking about "eternal beauty" or about the immortality of mummies —five thousand years or five years are equally nothing in terms of immortality. Nor am I thinking of art. I am trying to say that this setting was one to get high on. It expressed immortality, and fear, as pure and unreasoned experience.

I had to try my damnedest to keep my hold on the first flash of this idea. There were so many distractions, so many deteriorations. Forty-five hundred years ago Cheops was completely covered with white limestone, *glazed*. Only a few pieces of this remain. It was a white star, and its dazzle must have been unimaginable; it must have shone into the universe. For even now, when most of it is rough surface, the sunlight and the reflections, the blue and the white, are so intense that the totality is an experience of outer space.

That is what I meant with the words, "it is an experience of our time." Perhaps there was nothing like it between then—

when it was done with stone and in the one possible setting in the world, the desert, which belonged to space as much as to this world—and now, when it may be done with light and color created by electricity, surreal music, drugs, imaginary cameras in imaginary spaceships.

After feeling that, I thought there were only two ways to be on that plateau. Either this, some kind of (maybe hysterical) sense of a man-made outer universe; or, on the other hand, the measuring and digging and deciphering of the professors, which reaches other valid truths about the place. Everything in between, the usual bit of looking plus a bit of data, seemed useless and sacrilegious.

I climbed onto the higher part of the plateau. "It is everywhere," I wrote down at the time, and I cannot recall precisely what that was supposed to mean.

Far below me a policeman or soldier appeared and waved and shouted at me to come down, as I was entering the closed area of the Old Kingdom tombs. But I shouted back, *"El Umum el Mathahda!"* which was Arabic (I hoped) for "United Nations!" and angrily waved an (expired) UN press card, and he did not persist. There was a welter of abandoned diggings here, and what I took to be empty tombs—deep and dark chasms between slabs of stone—and many caves and deep tunnels. Birds (I think they are called sand merlins) swooped down very low, and huge dragonflies drifted and buzzed past my head.

I saw a tombstone covered with hieroglyphs sticking out of the sand, and another one with a contour outline of a woman's nude body. I held my hand against those stones to be in contact with the oldest human artifacts I had ever seen. In the gullies it was already very hot.

I had thought I was all alone here, but then I saw two men in bedraggled galabias at the end of a gully stare my way. They looked as if they were considering robbing me—it was surely a fine spot for hiding a body. But their presence fitted. When the first foreigners came and rediscovered this, the pauperized Bedu were lurking around, begging or stealing or robbing if they could. A man came out of a stone hut and crouched in a hole in the sand to relieve himself. A girl with a pot on her head appeared and started the descent down the slope of stones and light-yellow dust. People lived here, as they live everywhere in Cairo where there's some kind of shelter and a chance to be left alone. Later, when I left the plateau, I saw there was a tap at the exit, where all the ghost dwellers of the area came with jugs on their heads to get their water.

I rounded the second pyramid and came in sight of the third, the smallest one. Now I really was by myself: rolls of rusty barbed wire kept people from coming up here. Because I could not see the visitors' road, I got a precise feeling of where I was, at the beginning of the great Libyan desert. My desert boots, bought on Connecticut's Route 7, had finally found their destination.

I was going east now, almost straight into the sun.

The sun. I am aware of the facts of astronomy, and I know that the sun isn't any closer to Cairo than to Manhattan. But it was such a presence; as if everywhere else in the world it was always behind a thick veil. This is how Egypt came to its sun god Ra.

I had almost walked a circle now and had not found the Sphinx, but if I asked someone directions I might not be able to get rid of him afterward. Thus I marched on. And then suddenly the Sphinx peered up from out of the hills that hide him, in a very different way from the impression photographs give. I was glad I had resisted asking; it was a nice discovery.

He had a sweet head, or at least that's what it was now; perhaps it had been awe-inspiring once, as he sat guarding what was then the only entranceway to the plateau. I didn't want to turn my back on him for some superstitious reason and walked slowly backward through the sand till he had gone under again behind the crest of the sand dune.

I sat down and watched.

It was mid-morning now, and buses were pulling up below in large numbers. The visitors didn't climb up to anywhere near me, but local children did, shouting the international cry, "Hey, mister!" The valley of the Sphinx, I now saw, looked out upon some kind of concrete slabs, behind which metal chairs were set in straight rows. They glittered in the light, and at first I thought they were the graves in a military cemetery. Behind the chairs sat an open-air theater, with a motel-type glass building behind that, and then a parking lot with buses and taxis.

I hastened away from the edge of the plateau, so as not to lose all of my first marvelous moment. A boy came running after me, calling "Mister, mister, wait!" I kept shaking my head and he kept following, until I couldn't think of anything but pulling out that blue and white UN card again. I waved it in his face and screamed, "*Bolis!* Leave me alone!" *Bolis* means police, and he looked at me with fright and turned around. I went down toward the road.

Streams of people were everywhere, and a scramble of men selling hieroglyph tiles and tickets for all the separate enclosures, men with camels and donkeys, and men with Bedouin headgear for the tourists to put on when they climbed onto a camel. These camels and donkeys were of course sheer idiocy, as there were no more places left that can only be visited by animal, and only at this spot were they still for hire, for tourists to be photographed on. On the road, a man was sweeping their dung together, and a very old fellow in rags carried it off in a basket for manure or fuel. The sweeper went carefully around all the newspapers, beer cans, and sardine tins strewn everywhere. Two guides were having a violent argument with a policeman and each other about the price charged to a tourist for being photographed on a camel. The tourist, in a checkered shirt and Arab headband, sat rather miserably on the camel and kept saying, "You'd better let me down," while the camel growled, as camels do, and pulled at his halter. And everywhere wires ran, connected to loudspeakers and spotlights that sat on the stones and in the sand, with red, white, and blue lightbulbs, for the *son et lumière* (sound and light) shows they stage, where people in impossible crowds under impossible colored lights are made to listen to a multilingual spiel about Pharaohs and mummies.

I had been saved by arriving at dawn, and I thought I was also lucky to be there as a kind of reporter who could at least make something out of this present mess; how bitter it would have been just to have to undergo it as a tourist. And I felt I'd have been happy to come here in the July heat in a uniform of Napoleon's infantry, just to have seen it as virginally as those soldiers did—for the first time almost since Herodotus.

But there is no need for this criminal mess. It is the government (which used to administer the monuments of antiquity under the Department of Tourism) that is alone to blame. In one week all the new stuff, the wires and lamps and speakers, the stands and the glass motel and the chairs, could be thrown out, the whole area walled, one entrance road for pedestrians restored along the line of the original roadway past the Sphinx, with an entrance booth if money was indispensable, and that would be it. I know this will not happen. On the contrary, in January 1976 a developer signed a contract for a "Pyramid City" to be built, with golf courses and the whole bit. That kind of real-estate proposition is the one kind of plan that usually quickly becomes reality.

Luckily it was at least a Moslem holiday. An Arab village lay at the foot of the steep eastern slope, with stone houses that fused into the hillside, chickens and cows, and boys carrying whistles and firecrackers running down the dirt street. From this village families now appeared, climbing up the zigzag footpath along the hillside, carrying picnic baskets and water bottles, all in new clothes, little boys and girls both in long trousers of bright red, green, or yellow. They looked festive; they looked very much better to me than the harassed tourists, although I realized that my attitude was maybe just anti-anti-prejudice. At least they stayed outside the racket mills the tourists were nilly-willy ground into.

It was worse than the rackets at the Acropolis or in Pompeii (which are bad enough), because these, the Egyptian monuments, were not *à la mesure de l'homme,* made to man's measure.

I hurried down the road then all the way to the Mena House, where I sat down in the garden. It is a very nice and modern hotel, and American to the point where they make you sit uncomfortably here rather than comfortably there, with little signs saying in English, "Section Closed."

Cheops and Khephren, above the line of palm trees, were now background only. No one looked at them as the guests sipped their coffees and juices or splashed their feet at the edge of the pool. Here the Pyramids were properly obliterated and finally done with.

I sat there and was sorry I had yelled at that boy. Under other circumstances, if you reshuffled the deck, my little daughter would be running up the sand hills and asking for a handout. I was ashamed about it. Police, indeed.

I thought about the sun god Ra and tried to imagine living under his sign. He was not a merciful god.

One of Allah's epithets is "The Merciful One," but killing is part of Islam, and Muhammad had a woman poet slain in her bed, with her children at her breast, because she had written mocking verse about him. Christ's god was merciful, but those who ever really lived under that law are so few and far between that it made no difference.

Ra was not a loving god, as was clear in the light of the plateau. He must have been neither merciful nor unmerciful; his journey through the sky and back through the underground river of the night was but an unhuman, a-human, never-ending circle. But the dead King entombed within his pyramid became part of the cycle, and so did the onlooker in that dazzle of light outside it—

EIGHTEEN

A Cairo literary critic invited me on a visit to his country
place in the Fayum. He wrote a general column in a paper,
and he was a man with political interests. Under Nasser, he
had had his time of troubles, like many writers. I shall call him
Dr. Philip; he came from a Coptic family.

To say that he had invited me is stretching the point. We
had some talks, once a hectic one in his newspaper office, once,
much nicer, during an evening in the bar of the Meridien
Hotel. (The Meridien, on the northern point of the island of
Roda, was built by West Germans who went broke, was then
taken over by the French, and is now the Air France hotel.
It is the nicest of the "de luxe" places in town.) The bar was
empty that evening; machines made it cold. We were both
tired and talked very quietly. Perhaps lulled by that intimacy,
he told me I had to see the Egyptian fellahin not just as a
passing traveler but from close up, and he said, "We will go
to my country place one Friday." I later realized this was the
equivalent of a New Yorker's "We really must have lunch
one day," but the opportunity was too good for me to be
politely self-effacing about it, and I pursued the matter until
I finally did find myself on my way one Friday morning.

I had had to rent my own taxi for the purpose, for at the
last moment Dr. Philip let me know that he already had two

guests and that the cab that always took him on Fridays had room for only three passengers. Thick-skinned, I said I'd come with a bigger taxi, and he gave in. The two other guests were Arabists, one a Lebanese professor, the other an American one. Dr. Philip sent his own taxi ahead with the food supplies, a tape recorder, and battery-powered lanterns, and he and the others joined me in my cab. Everyone was friendly, pleased to be on an outing. Soon we were on the desert road which, skirting the Pyramids, runs in a straight line, south-southwest, to the Fayum.

The Fayum is a phenomenon. It is often called "the first oasis" as it is outside the Nile valley, but it is not an oasis proper kept alive by wells. Life is brought to the Fayum by "Joseph's Canal," a branch of the Nile that flows out into the area, which is partly below sea level. Some of the Fayum is lake, Lake Karun, a famous place for duck shooting, where a very nineteenth-century *pavillon de chasse* still has a plaque stating that Winston Churchill met there with Kings Farouk and Ibn Saud. In antiquity, it was all marshes and water. Dikes and canals built through the years drained it and made it the most fertile province of Egypt, one large garden. In the days of the Ptolemies (the successors to Alexander the Great), it was very much part of the Greek world, famous for its olives and bearing the melodious name, the Arsinoë Nome. Its capital had been holy to the crocodile-headed god Suchos, and the Greeks took over his worship, named the town Crocodilopolis, and had a cemetery for mummified holy crocodiles.

These marshlands were crawling with crocodiles at that time, and the worship was anchored (also) in fear. In a book of ancient hieroglyph verse, I read a poem about a peasant mourning for his wife, who had perished when they crossed the lake; he was grieving "for his unborn children who already had to look the crocodile god in the face." Words that have haunted me. There are now no crocodiles left in Egypt.

As our taxi raced through a landscape of nothing but sand, dunes, stones, and the asphalt ribbon of our road, the professors and Dr. Philip got involved in a heated political discussion, in English, about the unification projects of Egypt's recent past. The plan for the Union with the Sudan, Dr. Philip said, had as its only purpose to suppress and hang the Communist leaders there, the same purpose as the Syrian Union had served in Syria. "The bourgeoisie will go to any length, even submerging national identity, to save themselves," he told us. "Union with Libya? A theocracy would have been installed here." In Egypt, the rightists were now in charge. "Well, let them try," was the consensus.

I said something about the land reform laws being maintained.

"The land reform handed the countryside to the kulaks," Dr. Philip said. "At least they're not absentee owners like the pashas, but in some ways it's worse. . . . They're against industrialization, they've never asked for education in the villages—in the Socialist Union, that is—where they're the representatives from the land; they're against birth control. They don't want it. Ninety percent of the religious establishment is against birth control. We've a great religious revival now, but it's financed by the oil states. Two million children work on the land. If they went to school instead, wages would shoot up. We've seventy-five percent illiteracy, but fifteen thousand Egyptian teachers work in other Arab countries."

"That's where all that loose money comes from," the Lebanese professor said. "We're exporting the experts we need ourselves, and importing the black-market dollars they send."

"Yes, indeed," Dr. Philip answered. "Everyone I know has a new car this year. Where does the money come from? Saudi, Kuwait—and corruption. Formerly only the junta stole. Not Nasser. Now everyone steals. My neighbor in the Fayum planted fruit trees just to fool the inspector into believing he had fruit gardens. These get three times more water allocated than ordinary crops. He does not grow fruit. But he has all that water. Too much water. It is the kulaks' fault that so much water now drains and soddens the earth. It's not the High Dam, it's their greed. Greed and ignorance.

"The middle classes have nothing to contribute, neither the kulaks nor the city. And we have a minister of culture who writes glossy novels and says that culture should be entertaining."

"I wish they made you minister of culture," the American professor said, and Dr. Philip gave him a vague little smile.

We came to Kom Aushin, where a few struggling trees marked the border of Fayum province. They were the last remnant of the "Trees in the Desert" plan of General Muhammad Neguib, the leader of the Free Officers for a brief time after 1952. When he lost power, his tree plan withered away, too.

We drove through semiarid terrain now, with some bushes and gorse. Then, quite abruptly and linearly, just as when one enters the Delta or the valley, there was an explosive greenness, green so bright it was well-nigh blue: the Fayum proper began. Fields amidst palm trees and walled gardens reached to the horizon; at our right we saw the lake, greenish-blue, with high, barren hills beyond it, and at the shore fishermen huddled around wooden boats. We passed through a little town, Sanhur, and then we left the paved road and bumped down a dirt road following an irrigation canal.

A high-backed stone bridge, sitting in thick sand, crossed the canal, and Dr. Philip told the taxi driver we had to go over it and follow the canal on the other side. The driver refused; he said this might break an axle, which seemed reasonable enough to me. A bitter, shouted argument began; Dr. Philip and the professors got out and started walking. I produced my wallet, but Dr. Philip came back and said to me,

"I forbid you to pay him here. He'll get his money at the house. He's doing this because he's holding out for more money." I obeyed my host and followed, and the driver, looking intimidated and crestfallen, came up in the rear. It was about half a mile's walk, down a narrow road, before we came to the place: a five-acre fruit farm. The land, like all fruit gardens, had a high stone wall against thieves; its metal gate was opened for us by a girl after considerable banging and calling. I was then allowed to pay the driver the agreed sum (five Egyptian pounds, about eight to ten dollars, for the journey of eighty miles each way) but was expressly told not to give a tip.

Another servant appeared, an older man, and rattan chairs were brought out for us and put in the shade of a bower about thirty feet from the house. One of the professors thought he had left his overnight bag in the cab, and the words "theft" and "police" were spoken, but then he found it. We sat down, and various drinks were brought out along with plates of fruit from the farm (oranges and mangoes and figs). The driver of the other cab, Dr. Philip's, who was already there, was sent to the nearest large town, El Madina, for ice. His cab was a very old high-wheeled Renault, which had no trouble negotiating the road; my taxi had been a more recent American make. The conversation stayed on cab drivers and their dastardies, how they had now taken to refusing certain trips and how you had to don an Arab oil-sheik robe in Cairo if you wanted one to stop for you—the same kind of remarks you can hear from Santa Barbara to Hong Kong. The American professor began to tell lengthily how he had taken a cab to The Sea Horse Restaurant (in Cairo) and asked the driver to wait there while he had dinner, and how the man had said he'd want five pounds, and what *he* had told *him*. . . .

At our right hand we had the brick wall, and facing us the one-story main house with a stone terrace around it. At our left the farm gardens began: rows and rows of trees, and galleries of trellises with grapes, narrow irrigation canals following the paths, and white stone columns supporting the trellises. It was a classical garden. I had never seen a place like it except in Roman mosaics and Pompeii wall paintings. Tunnels of green, and in the open space between us and the house, poinciana trees in a cloud of red flowers and jacarandas with blossoms of a lovely fresh blue. Birds fluttering from tree to tree looked like glorified woodpeckers, woodpeckers with peacock plumage; they're called *hud-hud*s. Later, when the irrigation hour came and water started running through the ditches, ibises descended everywhere—literally hundreds, snow-white.

I complimented Dr. Philip on the beauty of his place. A servant reported to him on the state of some masonry that had to be repaired. But then the talk returned, via rebellious cab drivers once more and unreliable handymen, to, of all things, the fate of the Movement in America. Both professors agreed on, and spoke about, the nonsense of all this neighborhood and minority work of their students. "Minorities have nothing to offer us but food recipes," the American professor said. "Culture can come about only from the melting pot." That was an expression I hadn't heard in a long time. I thought, I'm going to say something to-the-point to them, about abstract liberalisms versus relations with cab drivers and students, but I didn't. I told myself that I had not come to the Fayum to chat about the Movement.

The local village began right beyond the north wall of the property, and I wanted to see it before it got too late. "You must excuse me," I said. "I'm going for a walk, to have a look at the village."

Dr. Philip shook his head. "That's not a good idea."

I sort of shrug-smiled and got up. "I've lived here for over ten years," he told me, "and I've never been in it. They've sent delegates to me, but I never go there."

"I'll be all right," I said.

He was visibly annoyed. He answered (in French; why, I don't know), "You will be going then at your own risk and peril. I won't come to your rescue if you are in trouble."

"I'm not afraid of the people," I said nobly.

NINETEEN

Lest it be thought I'm acting the adventurer, let me say right away that nothing happened to me and that there was of course no earthly reason why something would have happened. But Dr. Philip's attitude helps define the local political spectrum. Here was a man who thought of himself as somewhat leftist, whom we might call a liberal, and whom Ms. Bea Korkmaz called a Commie. In the Fayum, toward his neighbor fellahin, he was a *seigneur,* which is not French for country squire but something worse.

What a walk it was, though. Turning left outside the gate, I followed the path until I came to a crossroads. To my left, the path led into the village; to my right, another little bridge crossed the canal. At the intersection stood a stone column and here was the tap, the village source of non-infected water (more on that subject later in these notes). A lot of women and children were filling jars and buckets, and they did all stop and stare at me. I decided to go on a bit first and on the way back venture down the village road.

I crossed the bridge and continued past the canal. The air was dry and still, the road very dusty. The sun, about an hour above the horizon, was hot. To my right lay fields of sugar cane and what I think was young wheat. Perhaps the Lit.D.'s remarks made me feel more alien in that landscape than I would and should have; I thought it was very much like southern India, tropical, old, remote, outside my ken. I tried to see myself as the few men in the fields, looking up, would see me, or the men or women passing me in the road on a donkey or herding some cows or goats with a tree branch. Each time I greeted them by bowing slightly and bringing my hands together in Mahatma Gandhi style. They answered the greeting and stood still after I had passed, to have another look; I could see that out of the corner of my eye. I was wearing jeans and an old blue army shirt, but the gap between these and the odds and ends of cloth they wore, the gap between the races that have made themselves at home on this earth and take for granted meals, medicine, law, and the reasonableness of fate, and all the others . . . Until about thirty years ago, white people walked here, as everywhere, taking their lordship of mankind as a matter of course. Now we're withdrawing, and in places our presence is as remarkable again as if we were crew members of Captain Cook. It's not an economic withdrawal; we need the raw materials, and if force is feasible to get them on the cheap, well, why not. A trickle of the general violence we visited onto the world for the previous five hundred years now occasionally reaches back to the innocent in the mother countries; this is terrorism, and it has taken us completely by surprise. I am not using a walk along an Egyptian country lane to hold forth; I was aware of this then, I am a political man, and the fellahin were on my side of the political fence. About that there was nothing remote or exotic. I realized the people didn't think any the better of me because of it, nor would they if they had known, but that I couldn't help. Later, in Cairo, the correspondent of *Time* Magazine would tell me rather ironically that my countryside expeditions reminded him of his youth in Louisiana, "when we thought the darkies were all happy and laughing with us, while they were unhappy and laughing at us." He said I was fooling myself if I thought I understood anything about the fellahin. But I wasn't laughing or watching them like an outside observer, friendly or not friendly. "My defense," I said to the man from *Time*, "is in one word: politics. Politically, there's nothing hard to understand about the fellahin."

The road became empty of people, but ducks and geese were running across it and swimming in the canal, circumventing an enormously swollen dead donkey floating in the middle. Ibises stood motionless in the reeds. Then at my left an arm of the lake became visible in the distance, and I continued till I reached its shore. The water was blue here, not green; behind it, almost pure red, stood what are called (though they are in the heart of Egypt) the Libyan Mountains. A light wind blew from the lake and dried my forehead.

When I took the turn toward the village, all the children within sight came running and stood around me, and we were all smiling and greeting one another over and over again. I was clearly a distraction, not seen before, and when I hesitated, they took the lead and walked ahead of me toward the houses, squares of baked mud with roofing of straw or corn stalks and mud. In front of the door openings were porches of sticks and palm leaves, which made shade and gave the mud-walled room behind them a bit of protection. Cows so skinny they looked like walking spareribs stood munching on piles of corn and cane stalks, and unprepossessing dogs slunk away at our approach. A few men were about, some sitting quietly in the shade of a wall, others staring at me—angrily, I thought. Women and girls were doing chores. For instance, one was pushing a hanging goatskin bag to and fro, which is their method for making butter (the skin is filled with milk). They did a lot of giggling, and I wondered if I was trespassing against a tradition of decorum.

But the children wanted me to see something, and we all

marched on to a piece of wall. A boy was sitting there, a broom in one hand and an old yellowish woman's veil over his head. When I saw him, everyone stopped and watched for my reaction, and when I looked properly surprised, they were satisfied and all began to laugh. I laughed, too, and the boy with the broom jumped to the ground and improvised a little dance.

That evening I'd hear that the villagers had a running complaint against Dr. Philip's beehives because people had been stung, and he had promised to move them. The boy must have been a kind of watchman against the bees. But he was also considered, perhaps for dramaturgical reasons as he had donned a woman's veil, the main attraction of the place.

I walked back, trying to look without staring at this Stone Age or, better, Mud Age settlement. The dwellings were very close together, sharing walls, with a kind of village square off center. Not a single twentieth-century amenity was visible, but there was certainly a feeling of close security and shelter about it. The women who were now busy laying cooking fires on the porches and filling pots seemed busy in a pleasant and homey way. No outsider could state they weren't happy—if it weren't for the fact that they, the fellahin of the country, provided the surplus that paid for the towns. That's not politics but simply arithmetic, and I will explain it later.

It was the hour now for people to return from the field. This was the first time I saw it from close up, and I have come to think of it as the sweetest moment in Egypt's day. Everyone was hurrying so and everyone was so pleased to get home. Small children led donkeys and geese; slightly bigger ones came riding in on oxen and buffaloes. Men rode dromedaries, and women usually walked, with baskets or jars on their heads and babies pulled by the hand or tucked up in their dresses. All the children and the animals that had the chance, ran. Cooking fires were already burning, and every creature was making for the safety of food and closeness.

When I had passed the houses, I got up on Dr. Philip's wall. I figured it was a kind of no man's land, and my presence would not be resented. The passers-by stared, of course; the children waved, the women smiled or looked away, and the men mostly answered my solemn nods. Then the road got quiet, and all you heard was the water rushing down the ditch along it. In some houses lamps were lit, throwing a yellow glow over the straw on the porch.

When I came back to our garden chairs, the professors and our host were having Scotches while the boxes of food from Cairo were being reheated and put on the table. I sat down and awaited some reaction or question from my host, but all he said was, "Let me give you a drink."

"They're very poor," I said. "Well, you'd better not write that," he answered.

TWENTY

The dinner in the garden was nice, but the conversation was a bit dreary. The late, reddish light shone through the rows of trees, and when it had gone, all the ibises in the garden flew off in one great rush. We were waited on in a manner a Manhattan housewife with a servant problem would dream of, but that kind of thing doesn't fit any more and it makes me uncomfortable. Dr. Philip told us about a literary conference in Scotland where "shameless but vain" efforts had been made to get him to sit together with the Israeli delegate for a photograph. This led to the subject of writers, and hence to Lawrence Durrell. That was when Dr. Philip told us that, although Durrell was a friend of his, it had to be said that the *Alexandria Quartet* novels had no meaning in Egypt and that no one here had heard of them. The Lebanese professor had been praising Durrell and objected, "I was thinking of the intellectuals here." "They haven't heard of them either," Philip assured him. I remembered Durrell somewhere calling the Egyptians "verminous apes in nightgowns," and quoted this. "He is contemptuous and patronizing," I said "Well, maybe he's right," Philip answered.

These two men had known each other during World War II in Cairo, and I thought that although Philip called Durrell a friend, he actually resented him but had a vague nostalgia for the drama of those days of his youth. I also thought I had made myself not very popular with Dr. Philip, but while I wondered what to do about that, he said, "I've arranged a surprise for you."

He got up and welcomed some people entering the garden. They were professional singers, an older man and woman and their daughter or niece, who was carrying a baby. Our host had sent for them from the little town nearby, Sanhur. Our chairs were carried farther back into the garden and set to face the west side of the house. The singers sat down on the tiled terrace there, but after some to's and fro's, three straight chairs were brought out for them. A carbide lamp was hanging from a post, and another was now put on the ground near them. Dr. Philip and one of the professors started setting up a microphone and a tape recorder. "Note the dignity of the people," Dr. Philip said. "They don't want to sit on the ground in front of strangers."

The three singers began their recital, an epic song dating from the twelfth or thirteenth century, a drama, I was told, of love and war. They accompanied themselves on a drum stretched over an earthenware pot, which is called a "taraboukeh," and a tambourine without bells. I do not know anything about this form of art but I thought it sounded beautiful—the words almost spoken, against a perpetual rhythm with the mysterious inversion of Mediterranean and Arab music. The three were completely absorbed in their song, and when they had to do a passage again because the dogs in the garden barked, they shifted effortlessly back to a previous point and its mood and tone.

Then all around us in the dark, dogs started to bark, and we heard people shout in the road. The singers fell silent, and the sound of a shot was heard. "No, let's keep a low profile," the American professor whispered to me as I got up, but then, as he saw how frightened the singer with the baby looked, he jumped up, too, and led her into the house. Dr. Philip got up and vanished into the dark. He came back after a while with two men carrying a six-foot snake, the discovery of which had caused the commotion. No robbers, no riot, as everyone had assumed.

The singers took their places, but Dr. Philip remained standing to one side with a youngish man who had come in. He was in a galabia, an extremely elegant and neatly pressed one. I was called over and told that this man, a kind of headman or comayor of Sanhur, would take me on a tour of his town, since I wanted to witness country life. And I obediently followed after him, as behind us the song was taken up again.

The mayor had a recent-year Peugeot waiting out in the road, and he drove us very fast over the dark paths and bridges into town. Along the unlit streets, people were sitting in their doorways in the cool evening air. But once we got into the center, there was a blaze of electric street lights. Sanhur had received High Dam electricity in 1972, and this had been a big event. The poor section of town was still on oil lamps and communal taps in the street, but the richer part had electricity and piped water in all the houses. We got out of the car and started a walk through town, attracting enormous attention. We soon were accompanied by a throng of people, and I had a chance to find out how presidents or royalty feel on such occasions. When we sat down outside a café in the street, everyone came up to shake hands and say something. The mayor made jokes and they all laughed, and he greeted the passers-by; a few were ignored or ignored him.

I am sure our reception was partially due to my being a one-man freak show, and also to my showing up just at that moment in their history when the motto was, "No more militancy, friendship with the West." Still, the excitement and all those smiles and handshakes and teas and colas were an overwhelming display of hospitality. The high-school teacher came forward and was told to say something in French to me, and when I didn't understand it there was loud jeering and cheering. The vet sat down beside me and told me bilharziasis, the parasitical disease, had been wiped out in the Fayum by a German project of chemical treatment of the Joseph's Canal water. He also said that all sufferers of the disease had been cured. The mayor's son approached to say something in English.

Through all of this, there was a very precise order of rank: some people sat down next to the mayor and me, others at a distance, and others still remained standing, while the lowest ring of citizens squatted on the ground. When we moved on, there was a similar order for shaking hands, and when I included a servant of the mayor there was a second's silence and the certain feeling that this was considered a faux pas.

We took a tour of the mayor's house and that of a farmer named Ali. (The people working the land in Egypt live in town or village agglomorations; isolated farms in American style are quite rare.) The mayor and Ali had the same sort of furniture I had seen in the Cairo apartment of the ex-Free Officer Kamal el Din Hussein, a kind of Oriental Biedermeier with much gold, pink, and white. It is in every window of the more expensive furniture shops, in the country towns, that is. In Cairo, it's in the side streets. Their houses were large, prosperous, uncosy, with bright naked lights everywhere; the family—women, children, servants—sat around in one room and looked somewhat embarrassed by my appearance.

We also entered a less rich place, a big medieval house with a warren of rooms, very messy in a nice way, where several families lived. There was a huge stairwell in that house, and as we came down the stone steps, I saw a swarm of children sitting below us, all sifting flour in big sieves. I thought we had came to a bakery with nighttime child labor, but they told me these were the children of the house, sifting flour for cookies. They had the sweetest faces, all tilted up at us as we came down. Women appeared from the kitchen, where they were frying fish from the lake, little spratlike creatures. They insisted I take half a dozen along in a piece of newspaper, and I had to fill my pockets with small orange-colored lemons to go with the fish.

The farmer Ali had said he would take me back, and as we stood in the road waiting for him, we went through long good-by's and thank-you's in the same feudal pecking order, while a servant of the mayor's held the parcel with the fish; I wasn't allowed to carry it. A garage door was opened, Ali came out in a very large American car, and off we were, tearing through the dark outskirts whose people ducked and pressed themselves against the walls as they were caught in the beams of the headlights and all that speed and noise flying by.

Back at Dr. Philip's, the singers were gone. I realized he had sent me on the tour to counteract my village walk somewhat, but I was properly grateful that he had bothered: bringing a foreigner in on a connection with a town official was a nice thing to do and a potential embarrassment for him. Again he didn't ask anything. Ali sat down with us and we ate the fried fish. We had tea, and Ali ordered himself a coffee. (Visitors in Egypt order the servants of a house around with as much authority as the master or mistress does.) The conversation was in Arabic, and with the little I understood and the rare bits of translation the American professor whispered to me, I gathered it was about fertilizer and corruption.

With the Nile no longer depositing its yearly layer of

virgin silt, artificial fertilizer has become a crucial ingredient in Egyptian agriculture, and it is rationed and eagerly black-marketed. Ali said he was not getting his proper share but had to buy what he needed in the black market, and he wanted Dr. Philip's influence in Cairo to help him. Even with fertilizer at the black-market price he was doing well enough; a new Chevrolet in Sanhur was like a private jet in Dutchess County. "There's a kulak for you," I murmured to the professor, but he wasn't amused. He said the treatment of Ali was a disgrace.

Dr. Philip was clearly not happy with my sitting there and trying to follow what was going on, so after a while I wandered away into the dark, along a row of fruit trees. The water had stopped running, but the wet ditch made a gleaming trail in the moonlight. Bats fluttered around everywhere. I had been told in Egypt, "We have more stars than anywhere else in the world," and that night it seemed true. I had also been assured that on some Egyptian nights you could read by starlight, but I didn't experience that. The farm dogs kept following and growling at me, for I had thrown sticks at them when they were barking during the song recital, and I tried to dodge them. You hear a lot of rabies stories in Cairo.

When I came back and went into the house, I found Dr. Philip's cab driver sitting beside a little oil lamp and drinking Egyptian brandy. He told me that on these weekends he always had to sleep in his car, but he didn't mind. He poured me a glass, and it was delicious. "Pure Grape Brandy, Distillerie Zottos & Co., Alexandrie," it said on the label. I brought a bottle home later, for about a dollar, and everyone thought it was French cognac.

After a while I went to the kitchen and, groping in the dark, found a jar of water, which I used to wash my hands. Then I said good night to the cabbie and lay down in my bedroom. It had little windows both to the outside and to the other rooms, and in these windows, pictures of ancient gods had been made of colored glass: the cat-headed, the ibis-headed, and the ram-headed gods. The servants were puttering around everywhere, each with his oil lamp, and the moving glimpses of colored light through my windows played over the bed; their voices mixed with those of the farmer and Dr. Philip still in discussion outside, and the cab driver, slightly drunk, talking to himself in the next room—a muted *son et lumière* of country life. Dogs were barking haphazardly at the moon, and from beyond the garden wall came a sea of soft sound, the shuffling, breathing, and scratching of animals in all sizes from cattle down to, who knows, scorpions. I rolled myself as well as I could in the bedspread and closed my eyes to the lights in the animal-headed gods.

TWENTY-ONE

Within my lifetime the Suez Canal has gone through a list of myths. As a schoolboy I was taught that the Canal was an essential link in the modern world and that its closure would be a global disaster. A French historian, Gabriel Hanotaux, wrote that "the immense human chronology" could be divided into just two periods, one before and one after the opening of the Canal. It was also understood that no one outside the West could run it.

But then we discovered, first, that Egyptian managers and pilots could learn overnight to handle the job, and, second, that once the Canal was closed, everybody was ready to forget its existence in a very brief time—everybody, that is, but the ships' crews stuck in the middle.

The Canal was reopened in the summer of 1975, after it had been cleared of the debris of war, mostly by the U.S. Navy. Now Egypt is in the uphill struggle of making the shipping companies, with their new supertankers, Canal-conscious all over again. When the Canal opened in 1869, the toll rate per net loaded ton was 13 gold francs or about $2.60, and in 1928, the last really "normal" year in its history, that rate had been pared down to 6.90 gold francs or $1.35. In that year, the Canal Company took in 225 million gold francs —45 million dollars, some 30 million of which went as straight profit to the shareholders.

The rate per loaded ton is now figured in SDR (Special Drawing Rights, a mix of hard currencies) and, in 1976, is almost precisely a dollar per ton of actual cargo.

The gross income for 1966 was 180 million dollars, and the first full year of operation after reopening it was hoped to take in 120 millions. Egypt stated it had received some 75 million Egyptian pounds for the last six months of 1975 alone, or 187.5 million dollars at the commercial exchange rate. (This seems a very high figure: it's known that the original response from the shipping lines was disappointing.) For the year 1976, an income of 210 million Egyptian pounds is budgeted.

The Canal is 38 feet deep; it is meant to go to 48, then to 67 feet, and its surface width is to double. At Port Said, a separate channel is to make for one-way traffic at the mouth. Every visitor is given these figure, and the plans for the bigger canal hang above all Port Said desks. It took me a while to realize that they were but plans, and that the studies needed on canal profile, currents, and all, had not even begun on January 1, 1976. The plans must hinge on how ships take to the reopened route, and so does the enormously ambitious Canal Zone development scheme, which foreign (mostly English) engineers have drawn up in a dilapidated house in the embassy section of Gezira, and which has been paid for by the UN. The final report is in thirteen fat volumes.

The Canal is stuck in Egypt's history like a bone in a man's throat. No other human construction has had such a staggering influence on the fate of a nation. Panama is the comparison that comes to mind, but it is a weak one. The Canal killed thousands of laborers and their families (who were left to starve to death in the villages); it made foreigners rich and bankrupted Egypt; it put the British army in the country, caused the 1956 war, and made Nasser a hero and ruler for life. In local terms, the balance so far has been on the side of almost undiluted misery. Novels set in Port Said used to dwell on that town's many and wicked ways of taking the Westerner's money, from gambling and whoring to selling hashish and trick-diving for coins, but at least all of these offered thrills of *some* sort in return—and what penny-ante robbery it was compared to the Compagnie Universelle du Canal Maritime de Suez, which has scooped up its millions during eighty-five years without so much as leaving a smile or a tickle behind!

The Port Said Control Bureau is now run by a Mr. Sassi and has been since 1962, right through the years of war and evacuation. He is a big, jovial man, and he made a point of immediately telling me he was a different, no-nonsense kind of person who believed in getting the job done, who'd get me whatever I needed, and no red tape. His joviality was one-sided, for his servants trembled and saluted at his appearance, and while he was on the phone, he used to bellow for an ash tray and make his assistant come running from another room to move the thing from a corner of his desk to within his reach. But I thought that he, and the men running the Canal shipping agencies, were indeed a different breed from Cairo officials.

There is a need for commitment and no-nonsense in the running of a ship, be it the oldest tramp freighter, for without, no ship will survive for long. Port Said ashore seemed to have a lot of that same spirit, with people doing their jobs instead of dodging, and files appearing on desks with great speed and orderliness. Every day a convoy of some fifteen ships traversed the Canal from north to south or from south to north, and that was a reality you could not muck around with as you could with memos.

The Canal shipping agencies, each of which had the responsibility for a number of ships in a convoy, worked once more in the old buildings, patched up after years of bombardments. The furniture was improvised, the mood that of squatters. It was all for the best; it was workaday and friendly and the contrast with the ministries couldn't have been bigger.

Several of these shipping men told me they were Christians. It wasn't surprising that they were, for many had been on the job since before nationalization, and in the old days England and France always employed Copts rather than Moslems in their administrations. I was surprised, however, that they made a point of telling me, even the watchman and the messenger. Their reasons must have been complex. Once, they had been chosen over their fellow Moslem Egyptians by the foreign bosses, but then they were discriminated against and kept in lower posts in the company, with Europeans over them. Now they were often in charge as the best men available, but, not being Moslems, they were still and again somewhat on the outside of things. Copts are not quite second-class citizens in present day Egypt; the term would be too strong. But there is an awareness around them that they are different, comparable to the ways the Russians or the French have with their Jewish colleagues.

Mr. Sassi did not "get me whatever I needed." I had had the sudden idea of asking for clearance and permission to get on a ship in the northern convoy and travel through the Canal to Suez. I began by sitting some three hours in the Government Security Office, not a Canal institution but pure Cairo. Here, every few minutes, one official or other would appear and ask me the same questions, take down my passport number one more time, and have one more look at that expired United Nations Correspondent card of mine.

From the intelligence men I ran back to Sassi; Port Said had no taxis, only horsedrawn carriages, and these were thinly sown. The same officer of the watch who had okayed my entry into the Canal building before was still or again having a rest. Again he had to be waked up, had to put his shoes back on, and had to tell the guard, smiling painfully at me, to go ahead and let me in. But Sassi had gone now, and his assistant Mahmud (the ash-tray carrier) would not take the responsibility of allowing me through one of the gates onto the dock. He sent me to the Harbor Police this time, for a pass to leave through Gate 10.

The Harbor Police captain, to whom I penetrated by a mixture of smiles and Victorian nastiness, had a whole slew of questions ready whose points I could not fathom. Then he told me to sit down and wait while some invisible higher-up pondered my fate. I declined his offer to smoke (a difficult thing to do in Egypt) and sat and sighed as a stream of citizens came and went, all saluting him, all holding papers and cards and folders, all in need of stamps, permits, seals, all bowing and scraping to the captain as if he were their savior, which is what he could choose to be or not to be. An unshaven and very sad old man, holding a card with all his ten fingerprints on it, refused to leave the office after the captain had refused whatever it was he needed; he stood in one corner and then in another and even cried behind his hand. I don't know what he wanted; the captain himself seemed to have trouble understanding him. The captain ignored him for a while, then suddenly jumped up and shouted a string of curses at him. The old man shuffled away and posted himself in the corridor outside, from where he kept eying the captain like a beaten dog.

In due time, a scrap of paper was filled out somewhere and sealed with stamps somewhere else, allowing me to pass through Gate 10. I paid for the stamps, waived my right to a piaster in change which would have had to be fetched from still some other place, and hastened back to the shipping agency. This time I caught a carriage, halfway back to town. At the agency, an American tanker, the *Pioneer Crusader*, had been designated for me, and a message had been sent to the ship. Agencies frequently do this kind of thing, and ships comply although they don't have to. My ship was in "Three Black," one of the berths of Port Said harbor which are identified each by a color and number. I just caught the agent before he left for home, and he signed the papers while I sat in a chair and tried to catch my breath.

The convoy was to sail south at three in the morning, and, my pocket full of documents, I went to my hotel to get my things together, with the smug feeling of having scored a victory over red tape and officialdom. I changed shirts, for I had run myself into a sweat, and enjoyed the surprise of a journalist in the hotel that I had pulled it off, and in one day. Back at the dock area, and through Gate 10 (no one looked at that pass), I found a note awaiting me from the American tanker. Its captain had rejected his agency's request and let it be known he didn't want anybody aboard his ship.

TWENTY-TWO

Port Said had been a real *Scoop* situation. I'm referring to the book by Evelyn Waugh. I recognize Waugh's unpleasantness and his racism, but he was very funny; and life repeatedly imitates the messes his nonheroes got into. When they studied my UN press card and asked if I had been sent by the United Nations, when I was driven through Port Said in a carriage vainly trying to find my hotel (the long Arabic name of which I could never remember), I felt exactly like William Boot of *Scoop*. Port Said's two fashionable seaside avenues have been mostly destroyed; the only functioning hotels now are rather sad little affairs in midtown, as is the restaurant where Canal officials and foreigners eat if they have the chance. I could never remember its name either, although now, looking it up, I see it's simple enough—Gianola. But in the search for my hotel, my salvation always came when, going around and around, we finally passed Gianola, where someone would be able to set me and the coachman on the right course. The essence of *Scoop* situations is, of course, a breakdown in communications.

Westerners, from way back, have left it to the others to understand them. Lord Edward Cecil, a British diplomat in Cairo in the early 1900's, wrote a book called *The Leisure of an Egyptian Official* which had a great success in its day. Its humor was based on the bad English of various Egyptians and the way they got tenses and gender mixed up and called someone's brother his sister. If you think of what even the few Westerners who try, do to Arabic (admittedly a complex language with a terrifying morphology), Cecil isn't very funny, but most Anglo-Saxons still become Lord Cecils as they get south of the Rio Grande or east of Calais.

Maybe the captain of the *Pioneer Crusader* thought I was in a conspiracy to grab the wheel and strand him; anyway, I was glad it was he and not an Egyptian official who tripped me up in the end. He gave me a salutary perspective to look back from on all those irritating Egyptians. Few nastinesses or corruptions anywhere that can't be matched with similar or equally frustrating habits somewhere else.

The reason Port Said turned my thoughts to Evelyn Waugh in the first place was its old-fashionedness. It was, again, an old-fashioned place, full of "natives" and things the way they used to be in the old days. This doubtful distinction had been achieved for it when the government declared it a Free Zone and gave the green light to all the traditional delights of free enterprise in general. Port Said had been rewon by and for the West. Signs in English along the main roads said, "Welcome," and, "7,000 Years of Civilization Are at Your Service." The truths of both texts were immediately borne out as a young man came up to me on the terrace of the hotel and offered the services of a guaranteed virgin for only thirty Egyptian pounds.

MONEY

No better place to discuss money than Port Said, where there was no black market in dollars or, if you will, where everything now was black market. Port Said's new freedoms included the freedom to wheel and deal in all currencies.

The Egyptian pound (£E), equal to a hundred piasters, is

formally and commercially pegged at about $2.50 or £1.40. As no visitor to the country would long fail to see that's an artificially high rate, a visitor's rate of exchange has been decreed which allows the changing of currencies within the country at £E 57 for $100 or £E 1 for $1.75. This is still below the black-market rate in Cairo, which is as high as £E 70 for $100 cash (checks are worth less). And the Port Said money changers, who don't have to look over their shoulders as they do it, give £E 72 for a $100 bill, which is also close to what you'd get in New York or Geneva. Be it noted, however, that rates of exchange do not per se reflect "true value." Supply and demand enter into it, supply depending on tourism, speculators, and other tricks, demand depending on all the Egyptians who want to travel or buy tape recorders, for which there is officially no currency available. At the free Port Said rate, a piaster is 1.4¢, and Egypt is a cheap country, *for foreigners*. (To its own people it offers the lowest standard of living in the Arab world.) The fact that there is no genuine rate of exchange also means there is no genuine rate of financial comparisons, and when *The Economist* writes that Cairo has a budget of a hundred million dollars, no one can say what that means.

THE PORT SAID APPROACHES

I have mentioned the new road I traveled from Damietta to Port Said. It follows the shore, the Mediterranean on one side and the salt swamps of Lake Menzaleh on the other. When I drew it in on my map of Egypt, it looked as if it were enclosing a considerable chunk of new territory for the country. But actually, this strip of asphalt through flat emptiness would have been a total waste of funds and machines so badly needed elsewhere—if it weren't for the military angle, which was clearly the only one. The hinterland of Port Said is water and morass in all directions for thirty miles or more, and without this road it would be tricky to get supplies to the town or even to defend the coastline against a landing. It must have been an expensive undertaking, and I was told that after each winter the road surface needed major repairing. In the meantime, it made for a spectacular approach: it was like driving through the sea. The water and the sand blew everywhere, and there wasn't a tree or a stone in sight. In the old days, a little steamer used to cross the lake from Damietta to Port Said on three days of the week. The crossing took nine hours and was often canceled because the water was too low. That was farther to the south, though. Near the road, the lake was only inches deep, just a sheen of water over vast cakes of salt. Now you could race from Damietta to Port Said in not much more than half an hour.

Closer to Port Said appeared army tents, tanks, and bunkers buried in the sand with stovepipe ventilators sticking out. The heat on the ribbon road, with the sea and the wind blowing about, was great; the temperature in those bunkers must have been beyond hope.

Then the only human figure in this landscape emerged: a man rushed up from nowhere, stood in the wet wind on the side of the road, his rags flapping all around him, and waved a fish-for-sale at me.

Near the town, bomb damage had been suffered; a bridge was out, and the road detoured over a World War II Bailey bridge. I saw missiles sticking out behind the dunes, but a bit later they turned out to be the thin masts and sails of fishing boats. Then the sand strip to the side of the road widened and the beach villas of Port Said came into view. They were all empty shells of houses now. On the roofs of the most solid ones, soldiers were posted, staring along Bren-gun barrels over the metallic sea.

TWENTY-THREE

As I couldn't get to Suez on the MS *Pioneer Crusader,*
I went through the desert. It was a ride not so different from
the Port Said approach, but with, instead of water, sand on
both sides of the road. Here, too, the only activity was military. But there was more of it: convoys of trucks, soldiers
sitting or standing around in the timeless boredom of army
life, a real missile site on top of a dune, and, once, a tank
going around in circles, with a plume of sand behind it making it look as if it were on fire. At a reservoir, men were filling
plastic jerrycans with water and listlessly ranging them on the
back of a truck. For a while, bushes sprouted from the sand
gullies, but then all signs of life ended and there was nothing—only sand and stones.

The first sight of Suez was of the new satellite towns they're
building, prefabricated blocks of houses going up in a half-
circle around the old center, financed by Saudi Arabia and
called King Khalid City. Then, all of a sudden, I entered the
Suez that was.

Eighty-five percent of the houses of Suez were destroyed
or heavily damaged during the artillery and airplane bombardments by the Israeli army. At least, that is the figure given
out, and it looks accurate enough. A strange sight, those mostly
ruined streets, with improvised dwellings, bulletin boards with

personal messages, burned-out tanks, people sweeping and cleaning and going about their business, sidewalk stands with fruit and bread and meat. All this in the hot sunlight, and with the clean smell of sun on stone dust and rubble, a smell like no other, unforgettable once you know it. I closed my eyes and was back in Europe in the summer of 1945 as I (sergeant in the British army) drove through the towns of Germany. How oddly the wheels of history had to turn to copy that image after thirty years in an African desert town, shot up in an Arab-Jewish war!

Later, a Canal employee I got to know, a native of the town, insisted on taking me on a tour of the fighting that had been. But after I had followed him along the Sharia El Gesh (Army Street, so named in 1952), where the fiercest battle had taken place, and had stood a while in silence in front of an Israeli tank on which children were sitting and playing, I managed to convince him I was not interested in military heroics, and he took me on a visit to his mosque, El Charib.

El Charib is in the middle of the Salamania district, named after Selim I, the "Grim Sultan" who built it in the beginning of the sixteenth century. This was the oldest part of town and it was mostly destroyed; the mosque has been restored, and it sat shiny white and ugly amidst the remnants of almost colorless stone ruins. Perhaps the passage of time will give it a new beauty, and some wise man may one day remove the fluorescent circles now lighting its interior and once more hang up a chandelier.

Suez was the most war-minded place I visited in all of Egypt, which was not surprising, as it had seen everything: bombardments, evacuation, the wars of attrition, street fighting. The mood was full of nuances, though; what I could gauge of it was not particularly belligerent, but detached in a way. (That Canal man, on another walk, along the bay, pointed to an island and told me, "That is where the Jewish cemetery was." And he added, half-aloud, "We lived peacefully then. But they always kept to themselves.") Suez also had bits of the mood of colonial days, but indeed only bits and pieces, very different from its sister city at the other end of the Canal, Port Said. The Belair Hotel, once French, was still standing, for instance, and the same old waiter who had once served the French administrators went around carrying glasses of water (a finger in each glass), pouring wine, and bringing out plates of sha'ur, a Red Sea fish. The tablecloths were stained, faded old smells drifted under the ceiling. Suez had nothing of that Happy Days Are Here Again atmosphere of Port Said; no moneychangers, touts, or whores were in evidence. The new housing of King Khalid City was the big topic, and the generosity of the oil Arabs who were rebuilding the town. The Canal employee had a friend who had recently been allocated an apartment there, and at my request we went to look at it. It was in the section called Jidda—each section was named after an Arab town.

Jidda was all finished and inhabited, although its grounds were still mostly churned-up sand; trees were to be planted later. The apartment had two bedrooms, a foyer, a little bathroom with a sink and a shower that drained in the floor; no hot water. The kitchen had the universal Butagaz. All rooms had balconies, though, even the kitchen, and the building material everywhere was thick stone, which isolates and protects against the heat. It was not well built, and much cracking and chipping could already be seen. The drawing room had four red chairs, a couch, and two paintings. It was all very neat and poor, and, as the couple who lived there stood in the doorway to watch my reaction and wait for my admiration, it was a scene of unbearable pathos, or perhaps bathos and sentimentality.

But I've visited so many of these places. The rent is always only a few pounds, or rubles, or yen, or pesetas; they are built in the aftermath of war, and the new tenants are terribly lucky and know it, for behind them a dozen or a hundred other people are waiting and hoping for a place like theirs. These apartments have been built on the cheap and in a great hurry, and you can already see how much will go wrong with them eventually—the woman of the house has hung a little colored print over a crack or a hole. A spoiled Westerner sees all the things that aren't there and feels ashamed as they open a cupboard for him or show him that the tap works. It is all so new and hopeful to them—how pathetic the human condition seems at such moments, and how sad the contrast between what people need to be happy and what their statesmen and politicians dish out.

I stood on the roof of the Suez harbor building at the end of the causeway one afternoon and looked out over the roofless houses and the Gulf of Suez (the very tip of the Red Sea and with water of an even bluer blue, if such is conceivable, than off Port Said). An American free-lance journalist and a harbor official took turns looking through the telescope, for it was supposedly the day on which for the first time a cargo of Israeli destination would come through.

I got my turn and swept the telescope across the empty bay, over to where the Sinai peninsula was shimmering under the sun, and along the line of buoys to the lighter blue stretch of water which was the Canal. Then I turned it up and to the right, west that is, and focused on those dark-brown mountains called Gebel Ataka. Even in that light the ridge looked dark. Those never-inhabited slopes seemed outside our world, part of prehistory, and part to be of posthistory.

I drove back to Cairo along the desert road in the late afternoon. In the morning light, the emptiness of this landscape had not been painful. Now, in the vaguer light of a setting sun, the landscape seemed filled with a feeling of intolerable abandonment. It was so far—far from everywhere. It was a none-ness that had taken form.

The desert, this kind of desert, is not in the least a "howling wilderness," as the English language has it. There is nothing howling, there is nothing wild. There is nothing.

Sir Richard Burton quoted the Bedu on it: *"la siwa hu,"* where there is nothing but he, "he" being God.

It was the earth not without human beings, but as it will be after the last human beings have vanished; and it was very sad.

Islam is a *word* religion, and Egypt is part of a civilization of common language. In our fourteenth century, the Bible was virtually on the Index, but in the present, Islam's fourteenth century, the Koran is all. It is quoted in every conceivable situation way beyond what the most Scripture-minded Calvinist ever aspired to. Reading the Koran is the essence of grade-school education; learning it by heart used to be what education was about. In Cairo's religious television programs, a Koran text or just a few words remain on the screen for minutes at a time. In a religion without preachers or ministers in our sense, there are no godly words but the words in the Koran, and—though this is considered superstition—any such words on a piece of paper are still widely invested with special power. The word "Koran" itself is an ever-repeated decorative motif, and calligraphy of its text takes the place of all our holy and saintly paintings and decorations.

For this is a civilization basically without "image making," though with exceptions in the past (such as the Persian miniatures) and ever more exceptions in the present. But it is still orthodox to believe that whoever makes an image of a living thing will, on Judgment Day, be commanded to give it life and, failing to do so, will be cast into hell or purgatory. In such a society, language gains force the way sounds and smells gain force to a blind man. The Koran is never to be put under another book, the Koran is not to be shown to an unbeliever, and it is against the law of Islam for a Moslem to translate any of it into another language. For not just the meaning of its words, but the words themselves—the Arabic language— count. No Western example will give a proper parallel: the King James Bible may have had great influence on English, but Arabic literally begins with the Koran. There was nothing before, and little after; no pagan classics, no worldly litera- ture. Arabic is the key and shibboleth to the entire Islamic world, the Koran's Arabic.

It seems to me, without hazarding into theology, that this word religion is monotheism at its purest or, if you will, at its extreme. Muhammad was fighting the pagan fetishism of the tribes of the Hedjaz.

Within Islam, the purest of the pure, the Wahabi sect, are now most powerful. They originated in Islam's Arab desert, they destroyed the tomb of Muhammad himself to serve no- tice that nothing outside the Message was to be a subject of veneration; and when a leader of theirs a century later be- came a king, his kingdom was the first Wahabite nation. The king was Ibn Saud, the year was 1926, and the kingdom is now called Saudi Arabia. In this world fanatical believers are usu- ally poor, for "live and let live" is the motto for business, but if you produce three hundred thousand metric tons of crude oil a year, you don't have to worry about that.

There is an Islamic revival in Egypt, and many will tell you it is financed by the oil Arabs. Dr. Philip assured me that was so. A Coptic film producer, a young woman, told me that she had never lived through a Ramadan "as hysterical" as the one in the autumn of 1975, and that behind it was the hand of King Khalid, Ibn Saud's great-grandson. But aren't human affairs more complex? King Khalid's money is rebuilding Suez, and beyond that, the oil money subsidies are all that's between

Egypt and bankruptcy. Undoubtedly such money buys influence in many ways: religious influence, antisocialist and anti-Communist influence. But it isn't as if indifferent people could be bribed into religious enthusiasms.

There was an emotional vacuum after Nasser's death, and the turn toward Islam seems natural enough, even or perhaps precisely because political Arabism was pared down. Of course it would help that the orthodox but formerly poor and backward cousins in the desert suddenly appeared to have the rich West at their beck and call. Nasser had suppressed the Moslem Brotherhood who, in many ways, were Egypt's Wahabis; and for some time after 1970 there were instances of religious terror. Coptic churches were burned down, and at their trials the arsonists claimed that under still-valid Moslem law, those churches had been illegal. They were technically in the right, and the government announced that the law would be revised (it hasn't been yet). That kind of thing does not happen any more, but the Copts, the Monophysite Christians of Egypt, while strictly left in peace, do not play the role their number would entitle them to. These people, whose very name comes from Aigyptos, Egypt, still live under a cloud, and you cannot get a decent estimate of their number: I got figures ranging from three to no less than seven million.

The Islamic revival is in the air, it is even an aggressive one, but not an arsonist's brand of aggressiveness. Islam in Egypt is no longer emotionally on the defensive. It now shows the same somewhat contemptuous tolerance toward others that in the first half of this century the Christians here showed toward the Moslems. When I ordered a beer on a terrace in a Delta town, the café owner snorted, kept me waiting half an hour, and charged twice as much as he should have. Little did he know that I hadn't asked for beer to defy Islam but because his fresh lemonade, which I'd much rather have had, came from a carafe black with flies.

Islam is in the highest degree concerned with the Kingdom of This World, which it wants to regulate and prescribe for in detail, as medieval Christianity tried and as orthodox Judaism still does. It could hardly be expected to flourish on a planet where the West seemed to do and know everything better; but that belief in the West has now been very badly dented. All rules and commandments of Islam, from moral precepts to the number of months a divorcee must wait to remarry or the way to draw up an IOU, are part of one law, the law of Islam, the Sharia. And Sharia also means nothing more than "street," for the original meaning of the word was, "a path leading to water," and thus, in a forever thirsty society, "the right way."

My support in bridging the language chasm was an Arabic dictionary and grammar published by Hirschfeld in London, in a 1969 edition. It turned out to be a very flimsy bridge. It was supposedly the latest thing available, but its conversational pointers turned on such sentences as, "This is not the horse they showed me yesterday," something I rarely had occasion to say. I created great bewilderment when I announced myself, in answer to a policeman's question, as being from *Bilad elfalamank,* which is the phrase my dictionary gave for Holland, my birthplace. I was later told that it meant, "the land of the diamond cutters," and it must have been used for Holland in days very long gone.

Another pitfall is the transcription of the Arabic alphabet. I have spelled names, such as Mohamed Heikal, the way their owners did. His, the most popular of all first names, used to be spelled Mahomet in the West, and you also see Mohammed, and Muhammad, which is now the official way according to the internationally accepted system for transcribing Arabic into English. The system shows immediately what the original Arabic letters were (if you are a scholar), and to be complete, it also demands various accents and dots and dashes. Pronunciation is something else again, for Arabic is pronounced differently as you travel through North Africa and into Arabia and Syria. For instance, one of the big things is the two *K*'s (kafs) the language has; one is transcribed *K*, the other, a throaty one, is now spelled *Q*. My "Kasr el Nil" should really be "Qasr el Nil," but on the streets of Cairo they don't say either; they swallow that first letter and say, " 'Asr el Nil." "El Kahira" should be "al-Qahirah"; "Sakkara" is "Saqqarah," and the "Koran" is the "Qur'an," while our familiar "sheik" becomes "shaykh." The Libyan colonel is most properly spelled "Qadhhafi," and a "Moslem" is better as a "Muslim."

But these notes are not concerned with scientific linguistics, and I thought "Qur'an," and all that goes with it to be consistent, could be confusing and pedantic; I've tried to stick to the most familiar spellings everywhere.

As for reading anything at all, I never graduated to that. I firmly felt it was going against (our) nature to write and read from right to left, until someone pointed out to me that the West had accepted the Arab traffic directions in its addition and subtraction, which we do from right to left like them. We learned in school that our numerals come from the Arabs (and a vast improvement they were over the Roman letter symbols), and it came as a bit of a shock to find that the Arabs don't have our figures. Theirs are all different, with, for instance, a zero that means five, and a little black square for our zero.

Arabic still has the vocative which we, sadly, have abandoned to unread poets. "O . . . !" is *"ya!"* and it is used all the time. Once I found myself on a café terrace in Luxor with a lot of foreigners and felt immensely smug about not calling "waiter" or "garsong" or "hello," but *"Ya re'is!"* as is the tradition.

TWENTY - FIVE

The university of all Islam has always been in Cairo: El Azhar—mosque since the year 971, place where the first Fatimid caliph came to pray, and where his son founded what was to be the center of learning, center of orthodoxy, and then also center of reaction and obscurantism for almost a thousand years. The name still has a ring, to any Moslem and to anyone who has ever read about the Arab world. Students came here from as far east as Java, as far west as Morocco, and lived in tiny rooms in the mosque or in streets nearby, for a course of study that lasted fifteen years. Fifteen years of exegesis of the Koran and all the commentaries and documents written about and around it, of studying Islamic law and Arabic grammar, logic, and syntax. It was purely medieval (in our sense of the word) but pre-Aristotelian, a vast amount of knowledge; the school was free, and bread and pocket money were distributed to the students who—outwardly— lived lives of staggering squalor and asceticism; and this situation went on right into our days, when only the 1952 officers' revolt changed and ended it.

I had read Taha Husayn's memoirs, *An Egyptian Childhood* and *The Stream of Days*. Husayn, born in 1889, was a writer and scholar who went blind in childhood, and he describes how he learned the Koran by heart in his village school and was then chosen to go to El Azhar. *The Stream of Days* tells about that life of sitting day after day in the circle around a "sheik" (which is a professor or also any distinguished or venerable man), and learning the enigmatic rules of a scholasticism that played with the words used to describe itself and gave them a meaning beyond their meaning; thus an ancient scholar had, for instance, written a comment on the Koran while using only half the letters in the alphabet, and a deeper meaning would be found in that.

Taha Husayn was eventually expelled for rebelling against El Azhar dogma, and his books helped make the later changes. "We are Mediterraneans," he proclaimed at one point in his life, though he was to return to writing about Muhammad and the caliphs.

In the 1930's, royal decrees were issued to turn El Azhar into a more modern school, but nothing really changed, and only after 1952 was a university built adjacent to it, around a Western-style campus, to teach medicine, agriculture, sciences, and also, still, Islamic studies. In 1961, it came under presidential control. The rector is a powerful man, though— more so, once more, than in Nasser's days—and when efforts are made to change the divorce laws, or to promote birth control, El Azhar (which means "the blossom") is always on the other side of the fence.

I had addressed myself to the rector for a visit, for I didn't want to be turned back at the door or wander around conspicuously like a tourist; but his answer was so long in coming that I set off on my own. For all its fame, the mosque isn't easy to find, sitting at the far eastern end of town, near a remnant of the old El Kahira city wall, on the edge of a rabbit warren of little alleyways and packed market streets. In fact, I came upon one of its unadorned doors so anticlimactically that I went into two different shops asking what the name of that mosque was, which created a certain amount of annoyed surprise.

I left my shoes at the door and stood in a vast courtyard. There was a feeling of letdown; the blind student had evoked a more ancient and mysterious world than this reality. It was a vast columnaded space, and it looked forgotten on that weekday afternoon, not just used but used up. A few men were sleeping here and there, as in all mosques—these are easily the quietest, coolest, cleanest places in town for that purpose. The sleepers were by no means real tramps, down-and-outers; I never saw those inside a mosque. Men with not enough rags on them to cover their nakedness, with swollen legs and sores, do not venture into mosques for shelter; you find them behind the trees, in little parks, against walls of houses at night, or in the shelter of the gates in the old city wall.

The inner court, with carpets and mats, had some men sitting around and talking. One sheik, surrounded by ten students, was sitting against a column: there are a few classes left in the old style, open to everyone and attended mostly by villagers who want to return to their home ground with some of that faded glory. Blind boys often still go to these. The sheik was reciting Koran verses; in that large, empty space his voice carried oddly. At the other end of the court, a young man was sitting in front of a bench which he used as a desk to write on. A cat walked by.

I made the rounds of the series of open courtyards, past what were once the Door of the Turks, the Door of the Natives of India, the Door of the Natives of Mecca, the Door of Bagdad—all now shut on empty dormitories or on littered little staircases ending at other shuttered doors. A large court, with pillars and chandeliers, was used as a storeroom for mats and pillows, and I saw two men go in to pick the makings for their beds. They looked at me until I walked away. I came into a washroom with rows of taps in the middle and, along the walls, latrines of rather indescribable dirtiness. I had a plan drawn by "Herz Pasha," one of the Europeans who around 1890 set out to catalogue Egypt's Islamic architecture and save it from the looting antiquaries. The plan indicated a library, but I could not even locate its door, no doubt locked for good. I traced my steps back, to get to my shoes. Three children were now sitting in the large open yard between the columns, and one of them was copying a lesson into a notebook. That would not have pleased Taha Husayn, who hated all learning by rote; but their presence helped cheer up the visible decay.

I left El Azhar in a different direction from the one I had come in, and found myself on a square. Facing me was another mosque, El Hasanein, that is, "The two Hasans," dedicated to the brothers Hasan and Husein, but mostly to the latter. This Husein was a son of Ali, son-in-law of the prophet, and he died in battle in the year 680, fighting his father's enemies. He is one of the great martyrs of Islam; this mosque, where his head is buried, is the most popular in Cairo, or in Egypt. Non-believers used not to be allowed in here, but as I entered from a side street, where some women were standing and talking in the doorway, no one bothered with me. Everything was fresh and new; the chandeliers were burning, the carpets were thick and bright. There were many men sitting and talking, and many were praying.

These two are not tourist mosques, which are places where the steady stream of sightseers trooping through is taken for granted and ignored, the way Rome churchgoers in the Saint Peter's basilica ignore the tourists. At Saint Peter's, they rent out jackets and scarves for the sport-shirted foreigners; in Cairo there's a man at the door with felt slippers to put on over your shoes. It may be more hygienic than going around in socks, but I stuck to the latter system. It gave me a different feel of the place, a different relationship with the rough stone floors, the rugs and the mats, and with the people, who looked at me differently because of it. Maybe it was all imagination. But I would feel insulted if I were a Cairene and saw foreigners go through in that kind of hygienic getup. Nor do I want to pay tips in what is meant to be a house of God.

My 1929 Baedeker warned that "the visitor should carefully abstain from any manifestation of amusement or contempt." In our enlightened days, Westerners wouldn't dream of manifesting either. They're anthropologically tolerant, or they just worry about their camera's light meter. But surely the point of mosques—the minaret of Aksunkur rising like an arrow out of a dark, disheveled street—just as of the churches of Rome in that slummy city, is that religion has fitted them into the day, that they are part of life and treated by their users and neighbors with total familiarity. That is after all what they were built for, as bridges from here to heaven. If you want to understand anything about their success or lack of success as mosques or churches, you have to look at them like that and try to partake in that familiarity. Otherwise, what is the point? They are not monuments, they are functional buildings.

The conducted-tour mosques are, first and foremost, the one Muhammad Ali built in the Citadel, then the Blue Mosque and the Mosque of Sultan Hasan. Hasan got two stars from Baedeker, which was his highest praise (for anything in the world). It is inspired architecture because it is so stupendously big and yet ungigantic: the walls of its open court are more than a hundred feet high, and when you have entered, you are cut off from the city, and in a world of light; tamed, cool light very unlike the hot sun outside on the dust of Cairo. Once this mosque was lit by hundreds of glass lamps, pale green with flowers, blown in Aleppo and Damascus, but most of these were stolen long ago by "collectors," and the few that weren't are in museums. All that is left in the mosque is a forest of long and rusty chains dangling down empty-handed.

The Blue Mosque is really called Aksunkur and has a lovely minaret, but what puts it on the tour circuit is the decoration of blue tiles which some Turkish bigwig put in. This gives it an easy name and is the kind of handle guides like.

As for Muhammad Ali, he had his mosque (and mausoleum) built by a Greek architect and Greek workmen imported from Constantinople, who copied the design of the Nuri Osmaniye Mosque there. The contempt for Egypt implied in that gesture makes it a fitting monument and tomb to Ali's life and actions. Architects have for a hundred years agreed now that its minarets are too slender, its style debased Turkish, and the whole thing "Byzantine." In the more drastic terms of today, it is pure Disneyland.

I had been aware from my books of its lowbrow standing in Islamic architecture and had decided not to go see it. But once you are on the hill that holds the old fortress, Cairo's Citadel, you're right in front of it. The fortress's forecourt is the parking lot for all the tour buses. As I was standing there, a lady appeared holding a stick with a sign saying "Caravan." She looked mysterious, but it was all explained when a tour bus pulled up labeled "Caravan Tours" and its passengers obediently lined up behind her. A row of children had planted themselves at the door of the mosque, and they all insisted on shaking hands with each tourist. They weren't after tips; it was just a game they had thought up. The Caravaners, mostly elderly Americans, happily shook all those little hands, everyone smiled, and it was the nicest thing about Ali's mosque that day.

There used to be a famous view from the western wall of the mosque all over town, as far as the Pyramids and up north to the Nile, but Cairo has enough modern smog to have put an end to that. I could still make out some few of the pipe ventilators on the houses; these are another Cairo speciality, metal pipes used to trap the cool wind from the north and lead it into those oven-hot rooms. A new generation of Cairenes has settled on top of the first layer, and amidst the welter of shacks and huts that have been put up on the flat house roofs, those pipes have mostly got lost in the shuffle.

The buses in the courtyard were all waiting for their tours, and so were the taxis. I tried to hitch a ride in a taxi marked "Press" but was rejected. Thus I had to walk the steep road down the hill again. Both sides of the road were all built up now, but they were still separate from the city, a little hill town. Here was another of those places where no one looked up at the stream of cars and buses going by all day, but where a person on foot, a stranger, would be eyed with great interest. The life of that town was on the sidewalks and was more countryish than five hundred feet away and below, in Cairo. It would be a nice thing for the Caravan folks if their bus would break down and they'd have to walk through it, too.

At the bottom of the hill I found some sidewalk chairs, and I collapsed on one and drank a glass of coffee from the café there. We were almost in front of the Er Rifai Mosque, and later, as I walked past its door, a gatekeeper beckoned me to come and look.

He unlocked a wooden door and there, in a narrow dark room, furnished with a rug and the kind of glass showcase people once used to put their holiday souvenirs in, were the grave and tombstone of ex-King Farouk, come back from exile.

TWENTY-SIX

I cannot write about minarets and desert car rides and villages at sunset, I cannot write about Egypt, without talking about agriculture. Writers from Nerval to Edward Lane have done it, but it isn't right. It's the peasants who keep things going, and things are kept going through them but without them. Here is a rural proletariat straight out of Mao's book. Anwar Abdel-Malek, another Parisian exile, has written, "Egypt should have had a Long March," but Lucie Duff-Gordon, a very gentle and unpolitical lady, already pointed out in her *Letters from Egypt* a hundred years ago that this country, eight hundred miles long and one to fifteen miles wide on each river bank, can be kept down with one gunboat and one regiment. There's nowhere to march to. Only Cairo could stir up trouble, and Cairo is pampered (in a way) as Paris used to be pampered: Cairo gets the cheapest bread in the world through government subsidy.

I'm sticking to what I wrote before about those government interviews and statistics: just thinking back to the frustration of them makes my heart sink. But I had to start somewhere. You can't use impressions to count acres. I got to know, privately, two men who were serious, very helpful, and uninterested in "public relations": Mustafa Kamel Murad, who headed the "Cotton General Organization" (official but rather independent), and Dr. Kamel Hindi, who was the technician, under the minister, who decided how much land was to be used for which crop. And within certain margins of error, and using somewhat dated data, I collected figures from them that tallied with one another.

Murad was a swarthy, heavy man, very calm; he was hard of hearing and put me "at his good side." His office was old, with plastic covers over the best chairs, signed photographs of Nasser and Sadat behind him, and a Koran in a red velvet box. He was late, for which he apologized, from a visit with the German ambassador. While waiting for him, I had noticed on his desk the booklet *Facts About Germany,* left open when he must have rushed off. As for Hindi, he had an office in a dirty beehive of a building, but in Dokki, which is an airy, green section in the outskirts of the city, and he had the luxury of open windows with a nice breeze blowing through. He was a gentle, quite elderly man.

Items:

The fellahin are *obliged* to grow cotton as in the days of Muhammad Ali, who started that. They don't want to, for it is a hazardous crop and pays less than other crops for much more labor. They are forced to with staggered fines, starting at £50 per acre. "They don't care too much about the fines," said Murad, "they're so poor—we'll take his cow, et cetera, et cetera. . . ."

The government sets the price at which the cotton is bought from the peasant. In 1975, it was about fifty cents a pound (I'm setting the Egyptian pound here at two dollars, to make sure I am not unfairly underrating it). I derived this price from the £23 to £30 (depending on quality) the peasants receive for a kantar, or 99 pounds, of cotton. That's what the government paid; but the world price was about twice as much.

In rice, the fellahin have to sell two-thirds of what they

grow at a fixed price, with forced delivery. In 1975 they got £60, about $120, per ton of refined rice. The export price received by Cairo was $400 per ton.

With wheat it is a similar story.

Only if you grow fruits and vegetables are you left alone; and these are "rich man's crops," says Murad.

"They're paying for a lot of all this," I said, pointing through Murad's window. "Yes, indeed, they get us one-third of the national product," he answered. "We couldn't plan, if we couldn't force them. If we couldn't, the minister of agriculture would quit the next day." I didn't venture to suggest that it could be made attractive to them to do what they were told to do. Murad sounded so comfortable with what he said, so lacking in doubts, that I felt he'd have thought me very odd.

But "one-third of the national product"? That includes such vague products as "transportation" and "public services." Actually, "the fellahin earn sixty-six percent of our hard currency" (Dr. Hindi) "and if you include raw materials going into industrial export products—most of our industry is based on agri raw materials—you find he earns eighty percent of our hard currency."

The fellahin carry Egypt, or whatever part of Egypt is carried by Egyptians and not by help from abroad. They build the offices, pay for the cars, the conferences, and the tape recorders.

Egypt now has six million acres under cultivation. That means a crop area of twelve million acres, for all land is counted as averaging two harvests a year. The old Nile rhythm, around which an entire mystique was woven of ceremonies and festivals, is of course gone. There's no low Nile any more followed by a high reddish-brown flood as from a goddess river. It is all steady through the year now; and the High Dam has, apart from increasing crops, added about a million new acres. But almost nine-tenths of these have already been eaten up again by urban sprawl, industry, and the military (Dr. Hindi).

Dr. Hindi was also willing to talk about the "new areas": Tahrir (Liberation) Province at the western edge of the Delta, intended to add some 150,000 acres, and the New Valley, which is to run parallel to the Nile through the oases, fed by underground irrigation and spill water from the High Dam reservoir, Lake Nasser. These projects are still in the shadows, and I never got permission to visit either. Dr. Hindi said the development would take time, and the sandy soil of the New Valley and southern Tahrir could not reach the proper level of fertility with nitrates alone. They would need silt for that, such as didn't get through the High Dam at present. "Northern Tahrir will be all right," he said. I asked him why they didn't want visitors. He shrugged and answered, "It's probably a military area."

Who owns those six million acres and their priceless water? "Well . . . there are four and a half million working peasant families, with some twenty-two million people in all. Two million own their land, and two and a half million families are laborers or pay rent." That was Murad. He couldn't split that last figure. Hindi said, "Well . . . one point seven million families hold land through ownership or tenancy." And he added, tortuously, "Not less than ninety percent of them own less than five acres." (I know there's no possible tally here, but it's the best they would come up with.)

And the land reform?

"The land reform was meant to break up the large feudal holdings and, perhaps more important, to force a shift of capital from the countryside, where it did nothing but boost land rents, to industry" (Hindi). It didn't quite work out like that, of course; it went into real estate and Swiss francs. The land-reform law, as it stands now, allows a man fifty acres, a family one hundred acres. "Yes, it is circumvented," Hindi said. But the basic snag was that it hadn't freed enough land to end landlessness.

Had it raised the standard of living for the poorest?

"Only fifteen percent of our land was involved," Dr. Hindi answered. "It is hard to judge the result. But land rent was fixed at seven times the land tax, and that was important. Some suffering was lessened."

He was an honest man. I asked him, "Isn't the enormous gap in price unjust, the gap between buying and selling?" "Yes—in a way. The government is boosting its buying prices, at five percent a year." (Prices go up at least five times as fast: for 1975, inflation was supposed to be thirty percent.) "And," he added, "we do try to increase yield. We've got seven hundred agricultural research workers, we've raised the yield of cotton from four to six kantars of lint per acre, and corn has almost doubled, to eleven and a half ardebs." (An ardeb is about two hundred quarts.) "We've got to get the results to the fields, though. And supervise, and follow up. That's hard."

What interested Dr. Hindi more than my social worries was the reorganization of land use. The land reform has allowed the government to reshuffle pieces of land. After- ward, they started doing the same outside the land-reform areas. The idea was to make large single-crop fields. Since a peasant couldn't and wouldn't grow just one crop, because there'd be peaks of labor demands beyond his powers, he was given patches of land in different crop areas, through exchange with others. Thus, instead of seeing a patchwork of cotton, wheat, corn, and barley, you have large fields of cotton and of corn, and the patchwork is an invisible one of ownership. "It gives much more efficiency," Dr. Hindi said, "and the farmer will be able to use tractors." That would have been my cue to say, "Well . . . tractors . . ."

Land had been fragmented from way back, through the Islamic laws of inheritance which divide it among all heirs, through mixed tenures of working and renting out, and through all the other fates that have befallen such an ancient valley through the centuries. I asked if the system of giving a man patches here and there in different crops didn't force him into endless wandering around. Hindi said, no, every village was traditionally sitting in the center of all village land, and thus it made no real difference.

There was a cooperative structure in operation behind all this, but nothing Dr. Kissinger would have had to worry about on his visits: no socialism, just administrative units. Every beneficiary of land-reform land was to become a member of a co-op, and everyone else was invited to. It is not really enforced now, but joining entitles one to fertilizer at the official rate (hmm hmm), and it helps get credit. If the co-op as such gets a loan, the interest is four percent, and a member can get a private loan at six percent. Before 1952, the owner of the land had to be the guarantor, and thus the tenant was at the mercy of his good will. After that year, the crop became the collateral, and the tenant could get a loan without an okay from his real master. After 1957, supervised credit was given, whereby a local rural inspector watched over the use the loan was put to and there was no interest to be paid. Co-ops were also important then as donors of land for new schools or social centers.

I asked when the interest-free loans had been abolished, suspecting Sadat, but Dr. Hindi said it had already happened in the sixties. Murad told me agricultural loans without interest were still available now, but my money in this is on Dr. Hindi.

So there you are, or there they are. Thirty-seven million Egyptians, or thirty-eight or forty million, sixty percent of them in rural areas. More than half of those, no matter whom you listen to, don't own their land, and maybe a quarter are just laborers. There is now a minimum adult wage of forty piasters a day—say eighty cents. Children's wages are not regulated even in theory, but of course they are all supposed to be in school anyway.

The fellahin produce the raw materials earning the nation its hard currency and making up most of its exports; and they get paid at reduced rates. The things they buy, though, have all gone up in the worldwide inflational spiral. It is as if there were a little third-third world within the country, an Egypt Egyptianized by Cairo the way the third world is Egyptianized by the West. You grow cheap cotton, the cotton shirt you buy is expensive.

A fellahin saying, from way back: "We're like the needle. It clothes other people and itself stays naked."

In fact, there is a strange and almost colonial contradiction between the treatment of the land and the people on it. The land is precisely described; Dr. Hindi showed me with great pleasure meticulously drawn graphs of land surfaces and products, things he had done himself with colored pencils. The land use, like the distribution of water, is regulated by an army of clerks and inspectors. It would be unjust to call it an army of locusts; still, there's something unpleasant, to me anyway, in the spectacle of all those more or less clean-handed fellows breathing down the necks of the fellahin as they are breaking their backs on the sun-scorched fields.

But the people are rather less carefully counted and described. What else to say of the statistics in a country whose inhabitants aren't pegged within a precision of three million —that is, eight percent or so of the population?

Minimum-wage laws cannot have much meaning in such a loose setup. If you want to substitute social justice for the old tyranny of supply and demand, something more is needed than the printing of a decree. But there's an interesting new element. Just like such agricultural fat cats as rural France and Germany, Egypt has now a few spots where hidden and unhidden unemployment exists in combination with labor shortages.

"Yes," Dr. Hindi said, "yes, in some areas we have a shortage of field hands."

"Which means higher wages there."

"Of course," he answered. "It has also given new resistance of the land owners against general education. But you can't really stop education. And then there's the city. And there's abroad. There are ways out now."

The fellahin now do have a few ways out. A series of social processes has been set in motion, often willy-nilly. Schools have been built, and social clubs where the television sets show an undreamed-of, different world. There's Cairo, and the cities of Arabia paved with gold (that is to say, oil); and a bit of education is enough to bring these within reach. This happens at a time when the fellah at home is not really better off than before; in fact, according to most criteria, he's worse off now than twenty years ago.

And not only is he relatively poorer than he was, while he subsidizes the subsidies and the handouts and the holidays that keep the Cairenes going. Another specter is haunting his life. The new techniques of agriculture and the new water of the High Dam have brought an old, new plague to the countryside and to virtually everyone who works it: schistosomiasis.

TWENTY-SEVEN

Wherever you go in the Egyptian countryside, you see little children splashing in the irrigation ditches and looking very happy. But it is the new curse weighing on the nation that they pay for this pleasure, almost without exception, by getting infected with a crippling disease. This is schistosomiasis, or bilharziasis as it used to be called, after a Dr. Bilharz, who discovered it in the nineteenth century.

Any contact with untreated Egyptian water will do it, and the life of the fellahin is entirely in, near, and about water. They cannot possibly stay away from it when they irrigate the land and when they work it barefoot, even if their village now has a tap for washing and drinking water. A man who has trod in water all morning may indeed just as well use it for the ablutions needed for his prayer of *duhr* just before midday. Realizing all this didn't make it any less painful for me to watch those babies laugh delightedly in the coolness of the canal water—it was like watching them unknowingly stick long, thin knives into their bodies.

I spent some hours in the laboratory of Dr. Nesli Mansur, which is in the grounds of the Cairo Fever Hospital on the east side of town. Mansur, whose life work is on schisto, began by explaining to me one of those charts we used to be pursued with in our school days and which have always given me the willies.

At the top, you saw a peasant crouched near a canal, relieving himself. He had the disease, and in his urine or excrement were the (invisible) eggs of the parasitical worms in his body. There was an enlarged drawing of these, and an arrow showed how they got into the water, hatched, and set a stream of larvae free. The next arrow pointed from the larvae to a snail. If the larvae are to live, they have to find a certain freshwater snail which will be their host animal, and they have to find it within forty-eight hours. Within the snail, they multiply for four weeks, and then they're discharged back into the water. They're now called "flukes," or "flatworms." (The snail later dies.) The flukes have to find a human being, who is the next host in this chain, and they have to find one within a day or two or they die also.

The chart showed a woman getting infected by doing laundry, a man by washing his face in a stream before prayer. The flukes looked like nightmarish creatures, but, as Dr. Mansur reminded me, they are microscopically small. Any human contact with water is sufficient; they break through the skin, unnoticed, and enter the body.

Then we saw how within the body the flukes develop. They mate and settle in the veins of the bladder or the bowels. More arrows showed how they start discharging eggs and thus set up a new chain of disease. The eggs, on their way out, break through the tissues of the bladder or the bowel, causing bleeding. This goes on for years, causing painful, and in the end fatal, damage to the body.

The chart showed two separate chains of larvae and snails, and Dr. Mansur told me the bladder and bowel worms are two different species, needing different kinds of snails as in-between hosts. One is called *schistosomiasis haematobium,* the other *mansoni.* It was a devilish cycle, and I could not resist asking the doctor what purpose such creatures could have. He looked rather blank at that stupid question.

The next thing to know, he told me, was that there's no wonder drug to cure a diseased person. Various chemical treatments have been developed, but they are hard and have many side effects. They must be carried out in hospitals, and few patients sit out a full treatment. Even then, only sixty percent get cured, and it takes six months to be sure. "And for our peasants," he added, "reinfection is unavoidable."

Mankind is forever stumbling through its environment like Frankenstein's monster breaking the glassware in the laboratory. We are forever and hastily working our improvements on nature without enough study and enough humility, and ignoring our bleeding-heart environmentalists—which is now becoming a dirty word, as "peaceniks" once was. "Before the High Dam," Dr. Mansur said, "or to go back even further, before Muhammad Ali forced cotton growing, Egypt had basin irrigation. Once a year, the Nile in flood filled the basins. After harvest, the land dried up. This killed the snails, and the schisto infection rate was very low. With the first dams of the nineteenth century, it went up somewhat. But in the present, with the perennial irrigation, it has become bad indeed." (The Ross Institute of Tropical Hygiene in London now lists the disease in Egypt as "very highly endemic," its top rating.)

"The Nile and the canals have become a first-class habitat for the snails, which breed in slow currents and feed on vegetation. The Delta has both types of disease. Until recently, Upper Egypt only had number one [*haematobium*], because the *mansoni* snail cannot live in water that runs fast. But the Dam has slowed the current, and we find number-two snails traveling upriver. *Mansoni* has as of now reached the town of Beni Suef, eighty miles south of Cairo.

"Lake Nasser, the big reservoir, already has infected snails [*haematobium*]. It is an ideal breeding place, and as it's earmarked for fisheries, so we cannot even think of molluscicides [chemicals killing snails] which are dangerous stuff anyway, further disturbing the balance of life. . . .

"The new areas [those places I discussed with Dr. Hindi, Tahrir Province and the New Valley, which they wouldn't let me visit] are all sick. This *could* have been prevented if only peasants with a clean bill of health had been sent out to colonize them."

I asked why that hadn't been done. Had no one been aware of the danger? "Well, yes," Mansur answered. "Yes and no. There was no choice at the time. Under the circumstances it would have been virtually impossible to check them. There was no time, no resources, for that."

Mansur got half out of his chair and changed the subject. "I'll introduce you to some colleagues of mine now," he said. "They're concentrating on vaccinations. We are doing animal tests here; one day, immunization may provide the answer."

Yes and no. They knew and they didn't know that the new land would breed new schisto. Politics. Easy headlines. Welcoming committee for the one thousandth family to arrive. Speeches on TV. Thus the men who control our destinies, who change the land, color the food, fly the supersonic planes, know and don't know. Mansur was changing the subject. They had probably called him an alarmist when he warned them.

"I think those projects were carried out irresponsibly then," I said. "Do you agree?"

He sat down again behind his desk, but he did not answer directly. "There are a number of things we can do," he told me. "At least in theory. We can use pipes instead of ditches for the water. That kills the snails. It is also too expensive. We can clean all the vegetation out of the canals and keep it out. That would help. We can build sewers and latrines. If you do that, and the people use them, you break the cycle.

You can kill snails with molluscicides. You'll kill a lot of other things, too. They do these things in test projects, as in the Fayum."

"Ah yes," I said, thinking of my evening in Sanhur.

"There's always reinfection from elsewhere," the doctor half-muttered. "Therefore, in the end such test projects are useless. One sick peasant will reinfect the whole test area."

I asked him if the fellahin were aware of this fate awaiting them in their work. "Yes," he said. "They are. Specially since 1945. Certainly now. But what can they do? This disease throws its shadow over the country. It cripples people, it makes them invalids, say by the age of forty. And that's one good reason for the peasants to want more children. How can you talk about birth control then? Who'll take care of them when they have been debilitated by the parasites, if not their own children? In many areas, seventy percent of the population is ill."

I looked once more at that chart with those snakelike things on it. "Why seventy percent?" I asked. "If any contact does it, why not a hundred percent?"

"The remaining thirty percent are people who don't have to work the land," Dr. Mansur said. "Officials, merchants, and so forth."

I thought about that cruelly simple answer and said I just couldn't grasp this situation. I couldn't understand how the fellahin could put up with it.

"Indeed," Mansur said, "people are now leaving the land. There is a shortage of labor in places." I had heard that from Dr. Hindi, without this extra reason. "The real solution could only be through modern, mechanized agriculture," Mansur added. "Malaria, which is endemic in places, is also favored by the Dam. But it's under control. Insecticides are very much easier to handle than molluscicides."

Schistosomiasis is also endemic, to a lesser degree, in some other tropical and subtropical countries, and I asked Mansur if any had licked the problem.

"China!" he said. He smiled. "At least, that's what a Chinese doctor told me when we had a seminar on it. But I don't know if it is true, of course. I asked him how. His answer was, 'Just as we got rid of our flies.'" (No matter how boring those endless reports on China's flylessness may be, they are true all the same.) "A mass effort," the Chinese had said. Canals were dug in each affected area, parallel and very close to the infected ones. Then in one huge operation, everywhere at the same time, their earth was thrown into the infected canals. It killed the snails and the vegetation, and the irrigation water seeped through into the new canals. "It was all over then," the Chinese had stated. "True or not, you couldn't do that in Egypt," Mansur ended.

"No, I'm sure you couldn't," I admitted.

Dr. Mansur stood up and, as I had feared, led me through a glass door into his lab. It was full of hamsters, which are the guinea pigs for his work. They were everywhere, sitting in buckets half-filled with warm water and all trying to climb out. "They have their baths first," he said.

At a long table, assistants were working with test tubes and microscopes. I asked if the work was dangerous. "We've monthly checkups," Mansur said cheerfully. "We've been lucky so far."

He invited me to look through a microscope. After a moment I saw them. There they were, the second state, flukes swimming around, cercariae, deadly, just tiny worms jumping and wriggling. Dr. Mansur adjusted the glass container under the lens with his hand.

The container was wet and he got his hand wet. The assistant whose microscope we were looking through scolded him, and Mansur very calmly reached for a bottle of alcohol and sprinkled some on his hand. It seemed to land on his wrist. "I'm not going to shake hands with him," I said to myself as we left that room of horrors, I with my hands tucked under my arms like a freezing bather, and avoiding the eyes of all those hamsters vainly scratching with their paws against the sides of their buckets. But as we stood in the next room—and Mansur wasn't even quite finished yet with his explanations—I found myself holding out my hand to thank him. "He'd be offended otherwise," I thought.

A minute later, as I was standing outside, I was sorry, and furious at myself. I looked at my hand and visualized the cercariae creeping through my skin. I came out on the main road and almost immediately two men in an old car pulled over and offered me a lift back into town. But as soon as we reached a shopping area in the outskirts, I asked them to let me off and dashed into a pharmacy. "Medicinal alcohol," I asked from my pocket dictionary. They said they didn't have it.

I hurried on and tried another store, and finally a third. In this way I discovered that medicinal alcohol is not sold in Egyptian pharmacies, at least not to people walking in from the street.

"It's too late now anyway," I told myself, "better forget it." But I couldn't dismiss the pictures of those creatures from my mind, and going back into the last place where they had no alcohol, I bought a bottle of cologne instead.

To the surprise of the children in that street, they then saw a harassed-looking foreigner (me) sit down on the rear bumper of a car and pour out a whole bottle of cologne over his right hand.

However, more than half an hour had gone by. I wrote Dr. Mansur a letter later that week, asking him if he hadn't been running a bad risk with that wet container. He never answered. Not because he was worried, I'm sure. He was a very committed and brave man. He must have understood that my concern was a palpable fake and that I was worried about my own skin. I was, and I was ashamed of it. But at least it gave the chart and those figures a genuine immediacy.

TWENTY-EIGHT

I criticized those people in Cairo who called their shops or restaurants The Godfather and Lolita. But is their concept of our world, based no doubt on movies and television serials, further off than our mostly literary ideas of the East? Don't we look at it with some kind of vague, ingrained nostalgia, going back perhaps to man's having trekked westward ever since the dawn of history? Wars and confrontations have nothing to do with this; they take place on another level. On this New York winter's day I feel a nostalgia for Cairo. I hope, but I'm not sure, that it's at least partly distilled memories and impressions, and not ignored impressions, and a return to books once read that described a place that never was.

Big cities cast a spell, but it is their totality that does it. Nothing magical about a side street in Forest Hills, or about one in Garden City, Cairo. I can only describe fragments, but I can try and find some of the color of the whole in them.

I've written before that there were moments when "a bitter charm" came across. I remember one, when I was walking up Kasr el Nil early in the afternoon, a hot, dry day, on my way to Groppi's to buy a sandwich. A sort of gay mood was afloat, heaven knows why. Perhaps streets have moods like people. There was a live-and-let-live look to the place, which must be one of the essences of a real city. We weren't just in any city, though; it was Cairo, all right. For once the air was so clear that you could see the brown, bare hills of Mukattam, and such a thick layer of dust covered the sidewalk that it was like walking on a carpet. A feeling of being in the center of a world, and a moment of harmony between all those people finding themselves in this one street, Arabians from head to foot in white, Bedu in brown galabias, an almost naked Nubian workman, students in pearly-grey suits (from East Germany) and glasses.

But why something bitter in a street in the sunshine? Because it is never absent in Cairo, which exists of, from, and through its poor. Whatever there is of gaiety in Cairo is often directed at its own misfortunes. It is after all (and never mind the Security Council invective) a Semitic city.

Another such moment was more obvious, and it had the classic ingredients. I was standing on the Corniche in the evening rush hour and hoping to get a place in one of the taxis going by. Then I turned my back on them and sat on a bench. The sunset was very red, covering half the sky; a warm, hard wind was blowing from the river. One of the sailing boats that are rented to tourists was mooring, and a middle-aged man, a foreigner, but dressed like a businessman rather than a tourist, was standing alone on the aft deck while the boatsman tied up the ropes. A strange contrast. They nodded at each other and the passenger walked away. A girl appeared from under the quay arch and helped the boatsman roll up the flapping sail. Only a few rowboats remained on the Nile, which was now changing color by the second, from blues to reds to black. The ugly new hotels were still everywhere, and all the cars were still honking all their horns. But water can redeem any scene. The water looked lonely, and vulnerable, now.

I went to see the Nilometer at the southern tip of the island of Roda, because it's the oldest Islamic structure alive in Egypt. It was built not later than the year 861, and it has Gothic arches (*tiers-points*) three centuries older than anything found in Europe. It is a pavilion with a winding staircase and, in the middle, a vertical stone pillar on which the precise level of the Nile could be read. The Nile doesn't go up and down any more, the Nilometer stands dry, and it took me a while to drum up its guardian from a house nearby to unlock the door for a tip of ten piasters. Birds and bats fluttered around me as I climbed down to the three tunnels through which the river used to enter, and back up again.

The bridge from Roda to the right bank dropped me in Old Cairo, Misr al Kadima, which is not a tourist-map name but a precise district where three hundred thousand people live. It has a bit of cottage industry, but apart from that it's just a disaster area. I was in my rented car that day, a jalopy surprised at nothing, but after a few hundred yards even it had to give up. The streets were mostly dirt, and with such holes and ridges that the only way to get through was on foot. It wasn't medieval, it was Eastern medieval. I stood a while at a railroad crossing and watched some women, all in the uniform of the poor, that black tattered dressing-gown-type garment, buy cabbage. They were haggling with two men who had managed to get a cart loaded high with cabbages that far. One of the men was young, one old; they were barefoot and in rags. A woman who had argued a long time got her cabbage and put it in her shopping sack, and she paid the old man two piasters.

Beyond the railroad crossing stood a wooden shack. In it was a tap, and an old man was in attendance, sitting next to it on a chair and maintaining order. A line of the black women were waiting with jars and buckets to get water. The houses were the usual core of brick walls and roofs, with added do-it-yourself rooms of flattened cans, canvas, wood, and newspaper. Five hundred years ago, this area had been famous for its pottery, and—almost mysteriously—the roadside stands near the edge, at the farthest spot you could get to on wheels, all still sold pottery only. They were run by children.

I bargained a bit with three little ones, because it made them laugh very much, and bought from them a turbaned man of glazed clay, grey, six inches high, with a jar under his arm. They said first he cost thirty piasters, and then I got him for twenty. He is very pretty.

VICTORY GATE

The walled city of Cairo—El Kahira—had sixty gates, and a thousand years later three are still standing. One is called the Gate of Victory, one the Gate of Conquest, and the third is named Al Mitwalli, after a holy man supposed to be still alive within the woodwork. These gates are maybe thirty feet deep, and tramps sit, sleep, and cook in their shelter, where once the enemies of the state were nailed up, hung head down in chains, or otherwise made to die very slowly.

A child showed me that by walking through a carpenter's shop, crossing a weedy lot, and climbing a stone staircase, I could get to the top of Victory Gate, Bab el Nasr. (*Nasr* is victory, and the many place names containing this word have of course nothing to do with President Nasser. His full last name, Abdel Nasser, means "Servant of the Victorious One." The Victorious One is God, one of his ninety-nine names. This is a common way of constructing an Arab family name and the only permitted way to use the deity in naming a person. Abdul-Hamid, the famous sultan, was the "Servant of the Praiseworthy One.") From Bab el Nasr I looked out over a market and a cemetery. As is the custom, the graves had houses and pavilions on them. The Bab el Nasr cemetery was a very much better place to live in than Old Cairo, and it was used for that. Everywhere I saw people going about, women carrying water jars, children playing, men with carts and bicycles. There was a certain furtiveness about these activities. The dead, I am certain, had no objections to their presence, but sometimes the surviving relatives did. The families living in Cairo cemeteries are always ready at a minute's notice to pack up and come back after dark.

KASR ABDIN

The White House of this country is Kasr Abdin, Abdin Palace. It looks quite a lot like Buckingham Palace minus the grass and the tulips: a low, pale, shuttered building. It sits on an empty square where a few dead or struggling palm trees stick out of the baked earth. On one side are large stone barracks with infantry, protecting it and its occupants; across, on the sidewalk, is the workshop of a man who makes coffins. The elements for a Shakespearean setting. It is in the center of the city, ten minutes south of the Ezbekiya Gardens, but in a sort of backwater. Facing the square are two cafés, where taxi drivers off duty sit with pipes and coffees while their cars, the hoods up, are cooling off.

I went to the palace a number of times, for I had a really personal letter of introduction to Tashin Bashir, President Sadat's press secretary, and that seemed worth pursuing. It wasn't, for all I got out of Bashir was a speech about how the lotus in bud symbolized Lower Egypt, and the lotus in flower Upper Egypt, about Egypt being different, unique, oldest, nontribal, green and yellow, Pharaonic, Coptic, and Moslem, and yet one. It sounded nice, and Bashir, who was a short, very jolly and lively man, delivered it with great gusto. I wrote it all down dutifully, but when I looked at it later I found it hard to say what he had meant with it. I guess it was, as such, a fine example of a government press statement. Bashir once gave me a lift, too, when I was standing in the portico of the palace looking forlornly down the empty square as he emerged in his official limousine, but he was rather patronizing about that. I'm not sorry about my visits, though. The security was relaxed, and it was nice to wander down those corridors and vast vestibules and stately rooms, to sit in the slightly faded easy chairs where once the British and French consuls waited to tell Ismail Pasha he had to resign, and where King Farouk refused to interrupt his luncheon the day Cairo burned.

NASR CITY AND HELIOPOLIS

Cairo isn't all slum; it has much construction, and not only of new hotels. In the northeast, many apartment buildings were going up, expensive ones mostly. Here Cairo had a different face; it was neither an African Calcutta nor the Paris-super-imposed-upon-Calcutta it often seemed on busy evenings along Kasr el Nil. This suburb, Nasr City, looked international nondescript, with concrete towers finished and half-finished behind empty lots where sand and plaster sacks blew about. Wide, potentially ten-lane dirt roads led every which way.

I went to look at Nasr City because I had seen it on television. It had been the background of the October 6 Victory Parade. Now the Victory Monument was sitting by itself in the middle of an enormous space, all sand still, but no doubt one day to become a city square such as planners of all nationalities like to build, a place where pedestrians kill themselves walking from nowhere to nowhere. The Victory Monument was constructed of two intersecting triangles, an evocation of a pyramid, and was quite striking.

One step farther out is the other place where Cairo builds for (some of) its citizens: Heliopolis, a suburb dating from

1906 (not to be confused with ancient Heliopolis, the "On" of the Bible), set up by a Belgian baron and a British Sir Reginald, knight, or who knows, baronet. It was all European once and now it was all Egyptian, but it had kept its European face, the discreet charm of the bourgeoisie turned to stone. There were many movie houses, and, oh miracle, you saw genuine empty taxis cruising for passengers. Young men parked their cars on the sidewalks without worrying about pedestrian toes or their papas' tires, and furniture shops exhibited Bloomingdale/Habitat types of furniture. There were many café terraces, not on the sidewalk but elevated, as in old-fashioned European bathing resorts. That turn-of-the-century Scheveningen or Deauville effect was quite strong, and you would have expected boulevardiers to stroll by in panamas and Malacca canes. In Heliopolis they'd have to keep their roving eyes to the ground, though, or they'd break their necks in the sidewalk holes. The streetcars which, in 1906, had made Heliopolis possible, were still running and were less packed and hopeless than downtown. But even here the days were over when, as a Heliopolis lady told me with nostalgia, "They immediately used to get up and make room when I got on, when they saw you were a lady—and mind, I was a young girl; this was on the days the car couldn't come to pick me up at school."

But whatever there was left in Heliopolis of the terrible old days, it didn't reach down the side streets. Turn a corner and you were back among the little butchers with chickens and rabbits in reed cages, street lights that flickered or had given up the ghost altogether, stalls and smells, donkeys instead of sports cars and furniture shops with Biedermeier-Sadat instead of Bloomingdale. I priced one of those red and gold overstuffed chairs here; thirty pounds, the man said. Twenty pounds would have taken it away. That was cheap from an "international" point of view. Their manufacture is

farmed out; it's cottage industry. A few houses away, someone was making a chair just like it on the sidewalk.

LIBERATION SQUARE
Midan el Tahrir, Liberation Square, is the center of town
from the point of view of getting around. That's why the
British troops were once stationed here, strategically hovering
over the comings and goings of the city, and why on this spot
the Hilton now stands, which is an improvement, anyway.
The place's former name—obviously it had a former name—
was Ismail Square, so there was a change for the better, too.
(It was Churchill who objected so vehemently to countries
changing names all over the place. "Are we now to speak of
Ankara cats?" he once wrote to the Turkish ambassador. But
then Churchill wouldn't have known how it felt to live
among the names of one's former masters and conquerors.)
    The Hilton cuts off the view of the Nile, which is a pity,
and the square itself has been abandoned to cars. I've watched
them go round and round from up high in the Hilton. There
weren't actually that many (Cairo's two hundred thousand
cars compare to Rome's 1.5 million), but within this framework they were overwhelming. Pedestrians were punished
for their lowly status by a series of obstacle fences only the
fittest could climb over. The rest had to follow an iron circular overpass which had occasional staircases to street level;
with the cars below and the broiling sun above, you got a
foretaste of the fifth circle of hell. Some green, a little park
with a fountain and the garden of the Egyptian Museum, was
visible but not accessible. The Arab League Building looks
out onto Tahrir, and it had a stretch of trees in front.
    Late at night it was nice to walk here. With only a trickle
of cars, people strolled on the asphalt. From this wide open
space, there was a view then over to the Mukattam hills,
black against a blue sky full of stars. Water must have been

piped up to them, for those hills, dark and deserted since the beginning of Egypt, now showed blinking lights. A restaurant is sitting on one hill now and new houses on another. The touts and money changers based at the Hilton entrances were about to call it a day and were chatting with one another. Tahrir was cool and quiet.

The Hilton grounds come down in a couple of grass terraces with low stone walls. On the lowest wall a little girl had her spot, every evening till God knows what hour. You could hardly see her in the half-light. She had a sheet of paper in front of her on the stones, and on it lay the tiny self-made paper bags she was selling. Each contained five peanuts

Cairo is not a sensual town, though it subjects you to an assault on the senses.

Well, why would it be sensual? Most Western descriptions make it out to be. I mentioned the Victorians and their nights of Cairo; but it goes beyond that. The supposed licentiousness of Islam—four wives, as many concubines as you want—combined with the traditional invisibility of women within veils, shapeless garments, and harems, makes you think of overwhelming desire, painfully kept within bonds by severe custom (male desire, that is; female desire remains unmentioned). But Muhammad's rules were actually restricting the polygamous tribes of the desert, not giving them more leeway; and the issue, as everyone by now is thoroughly aware, is not one of sexuality, let alone sensuality, but of emancipation and women's rights.

In these matters, Islam is behind Roman and Anglo-Saxon law in much, but ahead occasionally. I've read a conversation in which an old-fashioned sheik, who did have four wives, complacently pointed out to a Westerner that these were all the women he had ever "known" (in bed, that is) and that they were all provided for against poverty and loneliness to the end of their days, whereas the American (or Englishman or whoever he was) had left a trail of abandoned girl friends plus one or two unhappily divorced wives behind in his life. The choice of words shows (as if we didn't know) that it's all thought up from within a purely male world in which women are property, albeit with certain rights. And, then, the morality appears to be the one most practical to desert and soldier populations, where the men are away from home for months and years—which is why it appealed so to the nineteenth-century English. In such a society, the death penalty for an adulteress is on the same practical level as the death penalty in America's West for a horse thief. It keeps life simpler.

Most Western countries are only now finding the courage to think sexual equality through to its logical conclusions. Islam in Egypt has but just started on that. A woman has had the power to initiate divorce since the year 1929, and the new constitution says her political rights are the same as those of a man, but that's all mostly theory. A fifth to a third of all students from grade school to university are now girls; this is recent, and it should eventually give a reality to a battle waged on paper. But more than with us, it's a rich people's game here. A woman of means and family has always had many ways to assert her rights in Islam, and only to a man of means would there be any meaning in the legal right to sleep with (plus clothe, feed, and house) more than one wife. A fellah and a fellaha are equal, all right; there is no need or time for veils or other games, and work, disease, and poverty combined will take care and more of any excess lust. (A government publication of 1975 had the nerve to announce as a "woman's victory" the fellaha who worked in the fields and did not wear a veil. Cairo's Ministry of Information carries Orwellianism *ad absurdum:* a publication on agriculture had on its cover a lady arranging flowers.)

Many years ago, shortly after World War II, I was in Istanbul when it had just been decided to open the old Sultan's palaces to the public. A guide, with much winking and grinning, opened some doors and took me to the harem. What a mess. Very different from the 1930's Hollywood image, it was just a square of nasty little cubicles around a courtyard, looking like dressing rooms in an old municipal bathhouse. Someone later described the scene for me when the Sultan was overthrown and the palaces cleared. Muhammad VI was over sixty by then, and as the harem ladies were brought out, it was seen that most of them were in their fifties and sixties, too. The populace, who had been standing around licking their lips and waiting to see all this licentiousness aired, went home disappointed. Muhammad VI had been a good Moslem if nothing else, and he had had to hold on to his entire aging deerpark.

We in the West have written plenty of sensuous and erotic literature but until recently it had to be kept hidden, or the dangerous passages put in French or Latin to keep them from the unenlightened. The East didn't have these tabus, and thus its books, from *The Thousand and One Nights* on, gave it a somewhat undeserved reputation. Of course, since about 1970 we have left them far behind, while Egypt has gone in the opposite direction. As was once the case in Hong Kong, Manila, and Saigon, its sin used to be unrestricted but almost exclusively for foreign consumption. You need a semicolonial setup for that, with foreigners more or less above the law, no recognized national pride, women and men ready to do anything for a buck, corrupt police, et cetera, et cetera. Cairo fulfilled all these conditions during the British occupation. The Ezbekiya area used to be thick with brothels for the British soldiers, while the more elegant establishments for officers and gentlemen were discreetly housed in mansions on quieter streets. The whores were mostly recruited from the refugees of Europe's various wars and depressions, with some famous Egyptian ladies at the top of the scale and very poor ones at the bottom: the "Bab el Luki," women who operated near

Bab el Luk station, two blocks from what is now the American University, simply standing naked in the alleyways. A profession for which no capital at all was needed.

All this went on until 1952, and under Farouk it reached its climax; as in Batista's Havana, you could go and see women make love with donkeys (fake love; donkeys are not excited by women) and all other conceivable combinations; belly dancing was then a performance at times dirty, at times very exciting (I've seen it the proper way in Istanbul). Cairo's fire of January 1952 was started by a belly dancer—in a sense. That day, the milling crowds found a chief of police in a bar with a belly dancer at eleven in the morning, and when he was berated for such behavior at a time of crisis, a fight started which sparked the increasing wave of violence.

Then, with Nasser, it was all over. Revolutions, even if they're half-hearted on socialism, are chaste. Those brothels are now little shops or coffeehouses; the staff (I hope) are happily married ladies, probably overweight. What's now called belly dancing is a kind of gyration that may remind you of the *Royal Canadian Air Force Exercise Plans for Physical Fitness* but definitely not of a woman's orgasm. It's performed in cover-charge hotel situations and on the decks of Nile cruisers, for captive audiences of tourists.

Of course, as in every city in the world outside China, you can still hire yourself a girl. In the Free Zones that is once more getting into the open; in Cairo it's still very subterranean. My apartment-mate used to stand on the balcony in Zamalek, hopefully staring at the girls walking by along the Nile across from us, and saying, "Do you think that's one? or that one there?" But if they were, they carried discretion to the point where it restrained trade.

That is the happy ending, then (I think it's happy), of ten centuries of Western fantasies, beginning with the Crusaders who, between bouts with the battle-ax, used to hold forth about the *princesse lointaine,* the faraway princess, waiting to be taken by them. Flaubert had to go up the Nile for his fantasy, for at the time, around 1850, all Cairo whores had been banned upriver. His travel letters and those of his friend Maxime Du Camp were published, at least in English, minus the naughty passages; and just recently here in the U.S. someone has published the naughty passages minus all the rest. There is a very vivid description of the night he spent with one of the well-known exiled Cairo whores, down to the details of how it felt inside her. Interesting, though you don't need to sail up the Nile to study the subject.

As for the other great romanticist of the East, Gérard de Nerval, who was in Egypt in 1843, he was a wilder and weirder man than Flaubert (he ended his life insane). I had often thought of his *Voyage en Orient* as a kind of example. Nerval arrived in Cairo with a little money hustled together from Paris publishers. He didn't want any part of the European scene in Cairo and left his French hotel after three days, to rent an apartment among the Cairenes. And when he was told his neighbors didn't like the idea of having a foreign bachelor in their midst, looking down onto their balconies, he went to the slave market and came home with a beautiful young Javanese.

This Javanese gave Nerval a hard time, as he couldn't talk to her without an interpreter and she refused to do almost everything except to lie on a couch and eat. The idea of a Christian with a Moslem slave didn't go over so well either. In the end he had to leave her in the care of a French school in Beirut, but by then she had been the heroine of most of his book. So much for his story. Generations of readers have been entranced by it, henceforth associating Egypt not with pyramids or Arabs but with the idea of going out in the morning and buying yourself a young Javanese woman.

However, it was my misfortune that someone sent me to

L'Orientaliste, one of the nicest bookshops in Cairo, on the Kasr el Nil. There I discovered a copy of a book I had never been able to lay hands on before, *Voyageurs et Ecrivains Français en Egypte,* a famous, scholarly, and boring study by Professor Jean-Marie Carré. And what did Carré do but show that Nerval never bought any slave (an acquaintance of his, an Egyptologist, did) and that he wasn't in the least the "wandering and lost vagabond" of the letters but a guest at the table d'hôte of the Hotel Domergue where he nightly tucked in his napkin for an honest French meal? Carré made a stab at keeping something going for Nerval by suggesting that the Javanese had shared her "catlike caresses" between him and his friend, but the careful reader gets the firm impression that there weren't any caresses for anyone, just a long-drawn-out hassle about law and money.

The only Westerners, then, who got away with that dream of sensuality for a while were those few generations of Europeans who lived here before 1939, when they were little kings and queens. They, and more especially their children, could among each other play out lives of self-indulgence, in a colonial style but closer to Europe's civilization, and in a decidedly better climate than Delhi or Madagascar. It was before my time, and I must quote James Aldridge on them as he describes it so strikingly: "Not only were the cafés and bars and cinemas and swimming pools and sporting clubs and theaters gaily and specially theirs, but in this climate, warm and sunny most of the year, the Cairo countryside itself became a fascinating playground and so did the desert. In the summer when they had finished work at one, they would sleep naked in cool sheets behind shuttered windows, in the buzzing heat. At five they would emerge into a warm bright evening to dance or swim or drink sodas and eat cakes in wonderful patisseries, and they would pack the restaurants, the desert, the gardens, the hotels. [There was] an almost erotic, fenced-in atmosphere of stricture and abandon, of moral dogma and moral evasion, and of that curiously intense delight in the subtlest and in some ways the most sensual byplay of sex which no girl in Europe would have understood."

They were luckier than Nerval, these girls and boys, for they could live out a fantasy he only described. But a fantasy it was, too, with no connection to the country that was the painted backdrop. Now it's all really over; unless you want to consider some lost soul from Houston or Hamburg—who nervously asks his hotel doorman, "Where . . . eh, can you find, you know . . . ?"—as the last in the line looking for the princesse lointaine.

I went to a reception given at his house by the second man of the American Embassy. His name was Frank Maestrone. Americans, bless them, don't make puns about names, and it was an unavoidable simplification of thought rather than a false effort to be funny that made everyone refer to him as Mr. Minestrone. Mr. M, like all U.S. diplomats and most businessmen, lived in Ma'adi, a suburb on the Nile some six miles to the south of Tahrir Square. The invitation came with a little Xeroxed map like the ones they use back in Connecticut and Westchester, and that was not the only parallel. Ma'adi is a true New Canaan on the Nile, with its winding, neat lanes, which, going Connecticut one better, don't have names but numbers. Cops everywhere to keep undesirables away, playgrounds, blond children, and not a dark face or galabia in sight.

It was after sunset when I arrived, which made the illusion complete: an upstate or New England summer's evening. Mr. M's house might have been flown in from New Canaan lock, stock, tables, glasses, and guests; the odd Egyptian took the place of the black men and women without whom no liberal cocktail party is complete: the servants were black-faced and white-jacketed; the discreet hum of the air conditioning was just like home; and as for the drinks and the snacks, they *had* been flown in from over there.

Not properly forewarned by this setting, I made an instant faux pas with the first guest I was introduced to. He was a banker for the newly opened, or reopened, Chase Manhattan Bank in Cairo, and as he was rather swarthy and I couldn't immediately place his accent, I assumed in the conversation that he was an Egyptian. "I'm a German-American," the banker said coldly, and stalked away.

European diplomats manage somewhat differently. They aren't roughing it either, but whereas Americans have these ultramodern inverse ghettos in the suburbs, Europeans choose mansions of former pashas or beys, in town. An EEC ambassador I got to know lived in a house like that, surprisingly sitting by itself on a busy and now run-down avenue. His wife complained that it was too small for diplomatic occasions but it was a gem of a place, with a garden sloping to the river and Art Nouveau halls and staircases. This ambassador told me that Egypt was on the Number 2 list of his country's aid program; that is to say, it got development aid but not of the first priority. "Small projects," he said. "Say, twenty million dollars. Still, we do our best to help." "Of course, there's a political advantage to the West in doing these things," I suggested. He looked surprised. "Advantage?" he asked. "No. What kind of advantage would there be?" His office, like those of the editors, was large, clean, and cool without machined drafts; a clipped lawn ended at a brick wall; life was orderly. His crackling phone was the only bridgehead of Egyptian reality.

The foreign correspondents reflected their national idiosyncrasies. Americans lived in smallish, air-conditioned apartments, Manhattan-style. The man from the Paris newspaper *Le Monde* had an old house built by an Egyptian architect in 1890 Paris taste with wrought-iron balconies. Here no maid or wife opened the door; a manservant led me to a drawing room and wheeled in tea in a silver set while I waited.

I think that in general and all over the globe, Americans blend in less with the local scene than people from other Western nations. Switzerland and Sweden now have as high a per-capita income; the dollar is no longer first, so that's not it. But Americans abroad (from a certain class) have an air of taking for granted that the U.S. life style is superior in each and every detail and that no other custom is worth a try. In Moscow, U.S. diplomats' wives buy their pickles (pickles, mind you!) at the commissary, imported from New Jersey. It is a kind of parochialism that sets them apart. That, plus an abundance of liquor and ice cubes, and a passion for bathrooms not seen since the Romans.

However, I'm not concerned here with the Ugly (but clean) American. I am concerned with the dichotomy between Egyptian reality, itself many-layered, and the residences and styles of our diplomats. I've mentioned that governmental never-never land, and how can you escape from it if every place in the world looks like New Canaan? "Field trips" won't help. You need to do a bit of struggling and sweating like the natives. It may be objected that rich local people live as well or better. But when they do, they damn well know Egyptian reality, because out of it they have squeezed the money to live that way. Even so, I wouldn't think such people were qualified to judge and report on their countries. The rich here are a nation of their own; and so, it could be argued, are all those English-speaking barmen and cab drivers whose opinions so often find a place in our news magazine columns.

One of the guests at that Maestrone reception in Ma'adi was a New York congressman. He was from Brooklyn and his district contained more Jewish voters than any other in the United States, which gave his visit a certain piquancy and importance. He was on a fact-finding tour of the Middle East

Chance included me in the party that took the congressman and his wife to dinner after the reception. The place picked was The Sea Horse on the shore of the Nile, the selfsame spot where that Fayum professor had wanted his cabbie to wait while he had his food.

Well, there we sat at a table on the river, in a soft breeze from the water, and ate the very expensive seafood cocktails the headwaiter had strongly recommended, while the congressman told us about an interview with Sadat and the facts he thought he'd find. In the background a soft rattle could be distinguished, and when I turned my eyes away from the brightly lit table, I discovered that beyond the fence of the restaurant, fishermen were working on their boats. Two men were rolling up a wet net. They were all naked; their wet bodies were just visible as brown shadows in the light reflected from the Nile. Then in another boat the sail was hoisted and it got under way, absolutely without a sound, gliding on the wind. Only my *New York Times* friend and I had seen it, but when he wanted to point it out to the company, no one paid attention.

"Yes, President Sadat has himself a sort of Camp David," the congressman said, "and when I—"

"Oh!" his wife interrupted him. On the table next to us sat a big reddish-grey rat, studying us quietly.

THIRTY-ONE

About prices. I've harped on the maldistribution of Egypt's income; it obliges me to say something sensible about its minidistribution, that is, prices. "Mini," for prices alone cannot cure a system based on the premise that the majority, the fellahin, serve the minority.

I'll peg the Egyptian pound in this chapter at $1.50, which is a bit less than the tourist rate, a bit more than the free rate. This is for reference only; it is a key which, of course, has no meaning for the people, who have no access to free currencies. Any meaning has to come from comparisons with wages and incomes. But here I am bedeviled by all the rules, regulations, and subsidies which make it hard to figure out "real" income. I once did these sums in China and it worked well, but in Egypt there is general agreement from everyone, except officials while speaking officially, that the rules are observed more in the breach than otherwise, which gives a very vague aura to any calculations. Thus you might figure that a country laborer has a family income of one pound a day: forty piasters for himself, forty for his wife, and ten for each of two children. This would be based on the law setting the minimum daily wage for adults at forty piasters; but, indeed, it is not a law that is obeyed. (And, of course, under certain circumstances a laborer may be able to demand more than the minimum.)

When a fellah is a tenant rather than a laborer and grows cotton, the government buying price is calculated on paying him his cost plus profit, set at £160 per acre. Of this, £100 is for labor, for fertilizer at the official price, insecticide, and so on; £30 is the land rent per acre per year; and the other £30 is added as his profit.

Clearly such figures hide as much as they reveal. They're based on average yield. They don't take into account that the fellahin grow some food for their own use and keep a cow and chickens, and that they build their own houses, such as these are. If you leave all that out, you end up with a very barebone profit of £30 for half a year, reckoning two crops a year. Add the money they get for their own labor, at the most half of the £100 for each acre, or £50. For a family working two and a half acres, you end up with £400 a year income, or a bit more than a pound a day, not very different from a laborer's family that works all year round. The only statistics I found, from an American Universities Field Study, indicated that half the population in 1975 had a yearly income of less than £1,000, and two and a half million (presumably families, not individuals) had less than £400.

Anyway, a fleshpot it is not. What my informants agreed on was that no one was starving in the countryside. That was the least one could say, they announced. Perhaps it is also the most: I've heard the statement doubted. Visibly, there is malnutrition—which causes deaths—but visibly, there are no people dying by the roadside of hunger.

In the very different world of the town people, civil servants are the largest single group. I was told Egypt was the country with the largest wage differential in the world between government employees. The minimum (in 1975) was £12 a month. The maximum no one knows, for it consists of money plus cars, servants, a town house and a country house, but it was guessed to be £2,400 a month (money only, apart from the fringe benefits), which seems conservative. That made a differential of two hundred times the lowest wage, indeed a gap ten times greater than exists between parallel American incomes, and forty times greater than those for a country like Poland. My spokesman in this was one of the top government archeologists. He was hesitant about discussing it and not out grinding axes for socialistic egalitarianism. I knew that once, under Nasser, a tax law had been written aiming at a maximum income for anyone of £5,000 a year (the kind of thing Franklin Roosevelt suggested during the war). But, the archeologist said, even if the will were there, Egypt had never possessed the means to control such a measure.

Every college graduate has a guaranteed civil-service job waiting for him. My archeologist did some off-the-cuff arithmetic for me. He postulated half a million students, of whom a hundred thousand were foreigners. That left four hundred thousand, and of these at least forty thousand would graduate each year. Straining one's optimism, one could hope that ten thousand would find jobs on their own with private firms. That still left thirty thousand new civil servants each year. "Three people share a desk, four do the work of one, income is low, morale is low." He gave one example: "Teachers and even university professors don't try to do a good job. On the contrary, they try to do a bad job, in order to get students to their houses in the evening for private tutoring. It's their only way to survive."

A high-school teacher in a town may get as little as £30, but a cab driver may collect £50, the same as an airport policeman. Less glamorous policemen, standing around in the street in white uniforms (instead of the more elect greys) get maybe half that much, and are corruptible at the bargain rate of 25 piasters per squashed ticket. An engineer I met in Aswan made £80 a month plus free room and board, but he worked for the best-paying firm in the country, The Arab Contractors.

An editor of the weekly *Rosa el Yussuf* made "between £100 and £150."

What about Cairo rents? At the very bottom, a few piasters get you a spot under someone's stairs or on his roof, but £1.50 rents a room for one month, in a slum, with no water or electricity. Those amenities, plus an outhouse, boost the price to an average £3 a month. At the opposite end of the scale, I saw an apartment for rent in Gezira that cost £1,800 a month. That's for oil men. The *Rosa el Yussuf* editor paid £7 a month, but he was lucky; that is, he had connections, for it was an old rent-controlled price. He had four rooms in a street in Heliopolis. His place was rather bleak, with bare light bulbs and no curtains, but with a bit of trouble it could have been made quite nice. He told me his landlord was getting increasingly itchy under this rent control, which dated back to Nasser, and that his luck was bound to end. The landlord had already built a whole new floor on top of his house, an enterprise that had driven all the old tenants out of their skulls. The new floor, being new, was uncontrolled and fetched ten times more than the old ones.

I was told the budget of a well-to-do businessman who owned a house in Heliopolis. He, his wife, and their four children spent £80 a month on their food, £3.50 on electricity, and £6 every three months on their telephone, which included 1,500 message units. That's less marvelous than it sounds, for the phone equipment is at least twenty years old and it may take an hour or a morning to get a dial tone. Still, like the gasoline price, it shows a tilting of price controls. I was told of a bank that got first-rate phone service by giving a £30-a-month bribe to someone in the phone company. I doubt the truth of it, since I visited a government minister and contractor, Osman A. Osman, and saw that his secretary's phone didn't work either.

My businessman kept a car, a Nasr, which is the Egyptian

Fiat. He mentioned the cheap gas and agreed that more tax could help improve public transport—or perhaps "restore" is the better word. In Nasser's day, you paid 265 percent tax on the purchase price of a car, but this has now been scaled down to 75 percent. His children's education was free. "Of course, the poor can't clothe their children for school," he said, "or buy the needed books, which may be £15 for one imported textbook—even if they can afford to do without the extra income they [the children] might make working, or scrounging. But gifted students can earn government stipends which run from £5 to £8 a month." The family kept a cook, who worked six days a week from before breakfast till late in the evening, with Fridays off. This man got £21 a month and lived in a room on the roof. His wage was above average; £10 will hire a servant. The cook also received £3 a month for his own food. I asked why he shouldn't eat a portion of what he had prepared, but was assured it was much better to keep the two things separate: "It avoids temptation." I found this to be general practice. The cook was a Nubian, like many Cairo servants, and his wife and child lived in Aswan. Another room on the roof was standing empty, but, "If we allow him to bring his wife and child to Cairo, we'd never be able to get rid of them later."

The businessman's family were fed at £13 a head a month, but the cook supposedly didn't go hungry on £3 a month. Food is, of course, the crucial item in the budget of almost every Egyptian, and the government, aware of tensions and dangers, has an elaborate system of subsidies and rationing. This system is under attack from both ends: the haves told me, "We can't afford this indefinitely," and, "The people have to learn to pay their way," and the have-nots complained bitterly about the waits, the corruption, the shortages, and the foul quality of their rations.

Bread, rice, and beans must keep the belly of Cairo filled, and of these, bread is the most important.

There is a preoccupation with bread and its price which reminded me of the chronicles of the French Revolution, when the radicalism of Paris went up and down with the price of the kilo loaf. The standard loaf in Egypt, flat, round, and very dark, is heavily subsidized and sold at half a piaster, and was quoted as the cheapest bread in the world right now. Those loaves are not all precisely the same, but the average weight was a quarter of a pound, which means a pound of bread for two piasters (say, three cents). The same loaf, white, cost one piaster. And, in the winter of 1975–76, the supply was abundant.

Rice, with equal price support, sold for five or six piasters a kilo, depending on quality, or a bit more than four cents a pound.

Other basic things: cooking oil, meat, tea, fish, and chicken, all had two prices. They were sold at subsidized prices from government "co-ops," and at higher prices in the open market. Thus, on your ration card, sugar cost 8 piasters a kilo, 3.7 piasters a pound. On the free market it cost three times as much. A family was entitled to nearly two pounds a month of the cheap sugar.

Those co-ops were well hidden. I didn't see my first one until I stopped over in a small Delta town, Kaliub. Its co-op was in a dark kind of hangar, and maybe a hundred women, all in the black of the poor, were crowded in there, standing in line or sitting on the floor, arguing, pushing, or quietly waiting. It was a miserable scene, and I was no longer surprised they kept the Cairo co-ops out of sight. You are told indignant stories about people coming into free-market stores to sell their rations back, but I'd say that after going through a wait like that, they had earned a profit. Apart from the more serious consideration that they might need the money more desperately than the rations.

Another co-op snag is that you need an identity card to get a ration card. An identity card, called *bita'a* (which just means "document"), is only for folks with real addresses, which rules out all wanderers and families hanging on at the fringe in cemeteries and under staircases.

Cheap fish and chicken came in irregularly; the meat ration was the most resented one. A family of four got five pounds of meat a month in my time, at thirty piasters a pound, while in the free market, meat fetched twice as much or more. But in the co-op, you had no choice, you just got a mixed bag of odds and ends that looked like scraps for the cat. "In other words," I was told, "they trim the meat and send the garbage to the co-op." Defenders of the system said that if it were that bad, people wouldn't stand in line for hours to get it. An argument, but only to those who've never gone hungry.

Locally manufactured goods were obviously cheap in terms of world prices (for instance, a cotton sun hat cost 25 piasters; a pair of children's shoes, £2.50; men's shoes, £5). To quote the inviting words from the Government Pamphlet on the New Foreign Investment Law No. 43: "There is an abundant supply of low cost labor. . . ." Yes, indeed.

As I always lose my comb, I became an expert in the pricing of pocket combs. The first I bought cost fifteen piasters. That one lost, I got an equally good comb for ten piasters. The longer I was in Egypt and the more I learned to sound like a nontourist, the lower the asking price dropped. On my next-to-last day, one more comb, bought on the corner of Kasr el Nil (so that I could be presentable for the airport police), cost me two piasters. I've now lost it, but it was a fine one.

THIRTY-TWO

The Tourist has been defined as a person who does not want to travel but only to have traveled. Thomas Cook was the first to realize this and to cash in on it. He came to Egypt in 1860 and immediately saw it was ideal: antique art and mystery, decorative and quaint Easterners, climate, and a colonial atmosphere which made it so natural and easy to almost-visit a country, to be there and not quite be there. Given the distances and the unspeakable, tyrannical misery in which Egypt was held, it is amazing to find how many thousands of ladies and gentlemen were whisked through each year or, rather, each winter season, for in those days the summer sun (even of Nice, let alone of Cairo) was avoided by anyone who didn't have to earn his or her bread working under it. The tourists were mostly English, but toward the end of the nineteenth century, the American share became large.

Things haven't changed all that much. You don't have to be nearly as well off as once (in relative terms) to go on an Egypt vacation, and with air travel everyone has time for it, not just the leisured classes, teachers, and churchmen. The list of sights is about the same, and so is the cushioned, isolated, and insulated approach. Perhaps tourists are even more screened from reality now, with tour buses taking the place of donkeys—and which modern tourist would dream of walking into the local bathhouse for a wash? Under the flag of a peace of sorts, Egypt is again tops with the travel agencies.

But no tourist goes to Egypt to see the countryside, and very few to visit the beaches. Tourist Egypt is a series of ancient sites and monuments which lie quite outside the life of the nation; and thus tourism has in this case hardly affected the country at large. Tourist Cairo and the foreigners' Cairo in general are there to see, but Cairo is so huge and so disorganized, and in its poverty so outside the West's ken, that these foreigners hardly make a dent on the real life of the town. This may change; the government is trying its damnedest to change it. The tourism developers may all have their various wicked ways, the foreign investors may be lured back in droves—if, for instance, Beirut turns out to have ruined its image as the Zurich of the Middle East. But the case of Beirut, at this moment (the spring of 1976) miserably falling into and emerging from civil war, proves how thin the veneer of the free-enterprise investors' prosperity is, even in Lebanon, how little filters down from it, and how harsh the reality can be, shining through the cracks. As of now, there is little depth to the foreign visitors' Cairene world, and its geographical area is the mile of east and west river bank where the new hotels are.

THE HOTELS

As the newer hotels are automatically full, it would be expecting too much of human nature to hope that they would trouble themselves much. They don't, and all except the Meridien have an unpleasant atmosphere. Maybe I'm too old-fashioned, though, to judge; the only hotel that appealed to me, seen from a distance, was the Cairo Semiramis. It was large but rather low, it fitted within the setting; it did not look like a barracks for spacemen. But when I made for it to have a closer look, I found that it was boarded up and marked for destruction. So much for my taste. The Meridien, although French, has nothing olde-worlde to it: its various apparatus makes so much noise that when you are out on one of its terraces, gazing, for instance, at the Nile in the moonlight, you get the sound effects of being on a motorboat. Who are these new men or women, who assume we don't mind? I suppose it's a conflict between two eras, shown neatly in Luxor where the Old Winter Palace looks out on a large, still empty, traditional garden with benches and statues, and the New Winter Palace, through its air-cond windows, on the tour boats with their Oriental tape music going.

The Omar Khayyam on Gezira is another old Cairo hotel in the process of being torn down. Once famous for its winding marble stairway, it was built for the Khedive Ismail, who used it to put up the Empress Eugénie (wife of Napoleon III) when she came for the opening of the Canal. That was at the very tail end of that French empire, and also of Ismail, whose palaces, including this one, were presently sold out from under him and his guests by his Anglo-French creditors. The Manyal in Cairo still looks like a palace or, better, fortress; it's completely hidden within walls and guarded to keep out Cairo or at least macro-Cairo, for last fall there was a mild panic when the hotel cat turned out to have rabies. Cairo's revenge.

Finally, the Hilton, which in a way symbolizes, and perhaps started, these hotels-of-our-days. Well, they do have a lot of towels and hot water, and when you wake up, you won't have to know where in the world you are, which may be desirable to many. The Nile Hilton had something called the Taverne Bar which was labeled, "La Belle Epoque, the Gay 90's," and where the waiters and waitresses were dressed in Toulouse-Lautrec outfits—a measure of cultural and general confusion that seemed rather staggering. They went, of course, through the modern ritual of you-can't-sit-here and you-can't-have-that, down to the point where their patisserie-shop lady told me I couldn't buy two croissants, the minimum was six. It's not the gravest problem for Cairo, admittedly, but something is terribly wrong in a place like that. The Hilton (and this amounts to genius) also manages to serve, from within this coffee civilization of Islam, vile-tasting cups of coffee.

These hotels charged £15 a night and up for one person, which was—given the pathetic wages and the various tax and land purchase fiddles they avail themselves of—expensive. You didn't find many Egyptians staying in them, but their bars and restaurants (especially those at the Sheraton) were the "in" places for the children of the new prospering classes.

THE RESTAURANTS
I had a book on Cairo that mentioned as "highly fashionable" a restaurant called the Casino des Pigeons on the Nile in Giza, but it conjured up such an alluring picture that I decided to go and dine there one evening in solitary splendor (like a man in a Somerset Maugham story).

The casino turned out to have become just an old garden, where the wind blew last season's leaves around and where one waiter with some bedraggled helpers brought out plates of sticky spaghetti topped by gristly entities which must have been the pigeons. The scattered guests under the dark trees were that same kind of people who spent their afternoons in the Ezbekiya Gardens, genteel old Cairo poverty. Here, not in the Hilton's Taverne Bar, was a genuine *fin-de-siècle* mood: not gay but of an almost unbearable melancholy. A grey-haired man in a neat and threadbare linen suit was slowly pacing the path between the gate and my table—waiting for who knows what? The pebbles and bottle tops crunched under his shoes. Over the gate, a flickering neon sign vainly beckoned the passing cars to stop. Why have these places from the past (for this was not the only one) gone to seed? I don't see why there was no return for whoever had invested his money in the Casino des Pigeons, though developers were falling over one another building claustrophobic little Hilton Tavernes. Are only cars to sit in the open air while people stay immured?

There is one survivor from the old days, Groppi's. Groppi's was set fire to, as a symbol of the hated West, on that 1952 Saturday, but it did not burn down and it has now found itself a place within the new Cairo. Groppi's runs a bakery and a large kind of lunchroom-tearoom; it is perhaps the one place where you can have sandwiches and coffee all day, or even beer, and eat ice creams (and go to a sit-down toilet), and still feel you're in Cairo and not on the international-nondescript fringe. Groppi's also still runs a foreigners' type of restaurant adjacent, which is always three-quarters empty and often closed. One night I met its headwaiter in the street, shuffling home or to the bus stop. His tuxedo looked yellow in the light of a shop window; there was powder on his neck where he had covered a sore or mosquito or flea bite. I had a vision of his coming home to a doubtlessly dark and miserable room or apartment, and washing under a tap, and brushing off that suit, after an evening of smiling and bowing. At such moments I wonder what cement of human kindness or maybe hopelessness keeps this disjoined world together.

But Cairo the city eats in food shops. "Food kitchens" conjures up a more precise image. Three or four dishes are available, and they're spooned up out of big pots. The clients eat standing up or sitting on a bench, inside or on the sidewalk. The two basics are beans and a mix of rice and lentils. The beans, called *ful*, are similar to lima or broad beans but smaller. A helping of either of these dishes, with two large, round pieces of bread, is a white-collar worker's lunch or dinner. The helpings are small, but the total price is below ten piasters. I shied away from these places for a long time, because once in Indonesia I had caught typhoid in a shop of that kind. Finally I agreed with myself that when in Cairo, et cetera. I made a note of one such meal: a little plate of beans with about five fried vegetable balls, an egg, and a sort of custard, plus a lot of bread, all adding up to thirteen piasters. The beans don't taste of much, and they're often eaten with these fried vegetables to pep them up.

Cairo drinks coffee morning, noon, and night, and tea with mint, lemonades, Pepsis, and every earthly fruit juice. Egypt also brews a local beer, in spite of the Koran's word (Verse 216 of the chapter "The Cow": "They will question you about intoxicating drink and about gambling. Say, 'There is great sin in both, and also some use for men; but the sin weighs heavier than the use.'"). The beer is called Stella, and at about thirty piasters a quart bottle, it's the cheapest bottled drink available. Still, even in Cairo I've rarely seen Egyptians order beer, unless they were obviously of Greek, Armenian or other non-Arab origin. Stella tastes, I'm afraid, of piss. Ever so slightly, but it does. In the old days, Bedouin children were trained to drink camel urine without vomiting it back up, to prepare them for the emergencies of the waterless desert. It could be that the Stella people are using an old Bedouin recipe.

THIRTY-THREE

There have never been better guidebooks than the pre-World War II Baedekers; and of all the Baedekers, the 1929 *Egypt and the Sudan* was the finest (Scribner's published it in the United States). Baedeker's completeness is baffling. I can only visualize squadrons of German professors swarming out over Egypt, sleeping in every bed, and sketching every pillar. To give an idea, Baedeker tells you that the streetcar ride in Alexandria from Muhammed Ali Square to Ramleh costs two piasters (the line is still running, with the same cars, at the same price). But Baedeker then adds that you can buy a booklet for fifty trips at the reduced rate of seventy-five piasters. Now very few foreign visitors can have taken fifty streetcar rides to Ramleh, and this added information may seem like pedantry. It isn't; it is perfection. Somehow the Baedeker family (which worked from Leipzig) found un-pedantic Germans to collect their stuff, in itself no mean triumph. Nor did they stick to streetcar and hotel data; the notes on art and architecture are impeccable, the maps lovely. Fifty years have gone by and you are better off in Egypt with the 1929 Baedeker than with any of the modern publications.

Of course, they shared the conceptions and misconceptions of their day. They told you not to lend your binoculars to a native lest you catch something from him, and in general to be wary of "intercourse with Orientals," which did not then mean going to bed with them. The ethnographical notes in the introduction have an unmistakable touch of pseudoscientific racism. But in all this the Baedeker family was of its time and place, and it would be unfair to be very surprised by it. I am not sure I like their * and **, the one or two stars with which they classified every great feat of nature and of civilization on earth, the way the *Guide Michelin* classifies soufflés and entrecôtes. But they didn't make too much of an ado about them.

The only modern guidebook on Egypt I could find in New York last year was the Nagel publication (done in Geneva). The Nagel people write of themselves, in their introduction, that here is not just a guidebook but an encyclopedia, approaching perfection as closely as possible; and there is even a patronizing bit of praise for Baedeker "in its day," partly, I assume, because quite a lot of the material and the maps have been, uh, borrowed from Baedeker without any credit. The Egypt Nagel is a slapdash book, full of mistakes, lapsed information, and inconsistent spellings. Dated 1973, it doesn't include roads built long ago, it doesn't take into account that the El Azhar mosque has ceased to harbor a university or that the Opera House has burned down. It shamelessly suggests, in lieu of good maps, that, "Visitors who want to take the fullest advantage of ther sightseeing trips are recommended to buy a detailed plan of Cairo (obtainable in shops and hotels)." Well, thanks. No such maps are obtainable in shops or hotels, of course. The Egyptian Museum in Cairo has changed its room classification from letters, as in Baedeker's time, to numbers; ha, I thought, here Nagel will finally come into its own. But whenever I wanted to identify an object, it happened to have been left out by Nagel.

Worse than the errors and the gratuitous bits of advice, there is a kind of leaden vagueness about those 815 pages which cost twenty-five dollars. The Nagel itineraries, bus rides, and walks all sound unreal. And then a suspicion arises. No less than twenty-six savants are credited with compiling this book, not counting the late French Arabist Gaston Wiet who is amply, and usually anonymously, quoted; but where did they do it? In the Paris Bibliothèque Nationale, I would guess, or maybe on the second floor of the Brasserie Lip. It doesn't read as if they had been in Egypt within their own living memory; the practical information has a taste of government tourist handouts. Nagel might have performed a service not to be found in Baedeker—for instance, giving the names of major towns in Arabic script for drivers who have to read road signs. No such luck. Nagel doesn't even give the Arabic numerals.

My own gratuitous points for Cairo visitors:

Get all the inoculations in the book. The world is not getting cleaner but dirtier, and Cairo is in the van of the development.

Take pleasure in tips to the lowly of Cairo. It is the only United States aid that will reach them.

Learn twelve words of Arabic; it will put you in a different class.

Visit places alone. Going with other people screens you from their (very breakable) reality. Going with one of the "licensed guides" turns the places into meretricious objects. Guides treat the Pharaonic past as a kind of brothel in which they act as pimps.

No nation loves or even likes another nation, no matter what they may say. It is a miracle if people like their neighbors. There is as little reason to smile on the Cairenes as on your fellow passengers in the Madison Avenue bus; do not act too flattered by their new affection.

Everyone makes himself or herself an image of what a place will be like. Here is part of my Cairo list:

Expected: a rabbit-warren city, with many little eating places and terraces, and cafés everywhere, a sort of Oriental Paris.

Found: plenty of alleyways, but nothing between the few insulated "European" places and the food stalls and kitchen chairs on the sidewalk. The chasm between the rich and the poor crystallized in the physical aspect of the city. No mixture.

Expected: I'd find an Egyptian boarding house where I'd take a room, or an apartment in the fashion of Gérard de Nerval, or what I then believed to have been his fashion.

Found: Egyptian boarding houses are too hard to take unless you're eighteen and a very, very, very sound sleeper. You might find your own apartment (I did, sort of), but it would be a Western one.

Expected: my letters of introduction to get me many invitations, and people eager to discuss Egypt's past and future, Russia and America and Israel.

Found: little interest in what a foreigner has to say; a rather tired silence on the subject of Egypt.

Expected: the government eager, in Chinese fashion, to take visiting writers around and impress them with plans and achievements and needs.

Found: the government neither willing nor able to do any such thing.

Expected: spiders, scorpions, terrifying insects, crocodiles.

Found: none. The deadly creatures of Egypt are invisible to the eye. The only crocodiles in Egypt are the three in the Cairo zoo.

Expected: the old Egypt, as described in Edward Lane's

famous book of 1835—with water carriers, dromedaries, dervishes, belief in the evil eye, peddlers with donkeys—gone and vanished.

Found: it is all still there, though not seen in tourist Cairo.

Expected: a former socialist city, still almost so, now in a curious state of transition.

Found: no such thing. "Socialist" only a word in government briefings. No sense even that Nasser's time left the poor lastingly prouder, or the rich more restrained in their ambitions.

Expected: nostalgia for Nasser as a man; at the least, lip service to his memory.

Found: as in the Italy of 1945, where you couldn't find a man or woman who had ever applauded Mussolini, there doesn't seem to be a Cairene who ever had an atom of sympathy for the man.

Expected: a sense of front-line adventure and danger, a sense of being in the news.

Found: nations are as fickle as women were once supposed to be. The "aware" public, the middle classes, that is, were as parochial as if they lived in the Middle West instead of the Middle East. A big burglary, a Yemenite in Cairo who had the tip of his nose shot off by a political rival—those were the topics of interest now.

THIRTY-FOUR

Lt would be easy enough not to say anything more about the great confrontation—precisely because almost everyone in Cairo avoids the subject with such ease. Any interest Americans have in Egypt, though, is by now based as much on its desert wars with Israel as on its pyramids. I don't want to shy away from the issue.

When upon return I told a friend something about the corruption and misery I had found, her reaction was, "Now go see Israel. You'll understand its attitude. You will be amazed by the difference." Here was a potential misunderstanding about this book I must dispel. Knocking Egypt did not mean praising Israel. Well-run nations have no higher rights than badly run ones.

The subject of the confrontation is an overwhelmingly emotional one, and emotion chokes discussion. To many, any discussion is basically like chatting at a memorial service for six million dead. I did not learn anything surprisingly new about the confrontation in Egypt, but some people reminded me of what I had known: that the six million were not murdered by Arabs. They were murdered by Europeans, and they died within the framework of a white-race civil war. I was asked, as a survivor of that civil war, to remind myself that the Arabs had a very much better record on the coexistence of races and religions than the white nations. And as the confrontation is tied in with the cold war (which is as real as ever), and has paralyzed so many American Jewish (ex-) radicals, I in turn want to remind them, my fellow letter writers to the *New York Times,* that no matter how brave we were in the U.S. and England, it was the Red Army that tore the guts out of the German Army (to quote Churchill) and thus saved the lives of the many Jews, French, Poles, Dutch, and others hanging on by their nails at the time; and that in the Arab countries only the Communists accepted the UN partition plan in May 1948, to be accused of treason by their compatriots. Have they forgotten the hope (and the fears in Washington and London) that the Jewish state would have an innate Jewish radicalism, which would crack the feudality of the Middle East and create a bond between Jewish and Arab left? (What a historical idiocy that Israel made a trump card out of its anti-Communism, while its opponent Nasser called on socialism. Will the Jewish state as such mean the end of the great contribution of Jewish reformers and rebels to radicalism and daring political thought?)

If the Arabs hadn't attacked in 1948 . . . but has any nation since, including the U.S. and Israel, ever accepted a UN decision it felt was directed against it? A decision, moreover, that fitted in our history as an act of atonement, but in theirs as the last move of their former colonial master? To those mourning their dead, the price will always seem too high, but Israel may not regret that events turned that way, for where is there any example in history of a nation not born in and through battle?

"No nation can count on anything for its existence but battle." I said that during a talk I had late one evening with a writer, in the drafty lobby of the building where he worked, on a dark little street behind the *El Ahram* tower. People kept interrupting and bumping into us, but I guess we both felt that if we went somewhere else, we would lose our feeling of contact and sympathy. We did have that, perhaps because he spoke such easy English and because we had started out discussing movies. He was leftish, not very adamantly so, and he worked in a publishing house. He had said that Egypt could not go on as a nation with an enemy presence in the Sinai, and that was what evoked my remark about battle. And he answered, "But then there is no further point in talking of right and wrong. And the justification for Israel was that it was to right a wrong. What other justification could there be?"

He went on, "I shouldn't even bring in moral or emotional arguments. Let's you and I look at it in the light of what is possible and not possible. Egypt had always been ambivalent about the confrontation. Yes, Nasser, too. In the early fifties, Nasser would have liked to present the world with a Mideast solution. Between him and Ben Gurion, there was just that chance. But the French were trying to keep Algeria down and they thought he was behind Algeria, and that way he became anti-French and the French pushed Israel. The West was afraid of his leftness, and they pushed Israel. Many in Israel pushed Israel. The moment was lost. Ambivalence? Yes, for the simple reason that we're an ambivalent nation, sometimes Arab and sometimes Mediterranean and Copt and who knows, thinking back to the Pharaohs and Alexander. The non-Arab part of our nature would like to forget the whole business; just give us back the Sinai. But we can't cut ourselves off like that, don't you see that? Without the Arab world, we are little and we have less. I think Sadat has already gone too far. Nasser didn't want to wage any holy wars! In '67, he was saber-rattling in Cairo, not in the Sinai."

"It's a pet remark of mine," I said, "that our press personalizes history to a fault. To them, Egypt became Nasser and Nasser became Hitler. I know he was no Hitler."

The writer said, "We're not a modern state, and he wasn't

a modern statesman. Look, even in Farouk's days Egypt sent in its army, in the 1948 war, and those were the days of the old upper class. They thought of themselves only as Mediterraneans—no, even stronger, only as Europeans. Even they couldn't cut themselves off from the Arab world. How could we now? And how could we survive without Saudi and Kuwait?"

"Suppose," I asked, "that Sadat gets the Sinai back, with American help, and makes peace. How would the people react?"

He looked around in the hall with a certain irritation. "The peace agreement wouldn't bring the people out into the street," he said. "The misery would, if the oil-money subsidies were cut off. The scandal would, if Israel waged war on Syria or Lebanon and we stayed neutral. That would bring the army out, and with popular support, too. On the plus side: Sadat ended the confrontation, which was ruinously expensive. Think of the bomb damage, the closed Suez Canal. He could do it, but only because the '73 war had taken the sting out of our great loss of face."

"The Israel trauma," I said, which is what people had called it to me.

"It was a trauma. Now on the minus side: the U.S. help is supposed to get things better within the country. No sign of that yet. Israel was to avoid moves that manifested aggressiveness—like new settlements in the occupied lands. No sign of that either. It is a tightrope Sadat is on, and no net."

"Are you pessimistic?" I asked.

"Yes. Totally."

And if Sadat is on a tightrope, perhaps the world is up there with him. The dangers are great, and how easily the West, in its unshakable self-esteem, forgets that most of the political miseries of our time, here as in Latin America as in Ireland as in black Africa, are but the heritage and hangover of cen-

turies of Western conquest and occupation! How unhumble
we are, how readily holding forth about our Democracy and
our Rights and Needs.

It should not be thought there was anything typical about
that lobby conversation of mine with the writer. It was un-
typical. Typical would be a tired resignation to "the mess, to
the presence of a country imposed upon our region by the
United Nations but which now itself flouts the United Nations" (Dr. Philip). Or, even more frequent, a shrug, and
nothing but a gut-level resentment of Israel's discrimination
against the Arabs within its borders, a political discrimination
perhaps, but felt as a racist slur. I should write "tribal slur,"
though, for after all, Israelis and Egyptians are more or less
the same race, insofar as the word has a scientific meaning—
there is no personal anti-Semitism in Egypt in our sense of the
term. The wife of a newspaper editor here was Jewish, and I
would never have guessed; there was nothing like "let's tol-
erate her" about it, it was no issue. But let us not think there
are "enlightened" or "Western" Egyptians around who are interested in peaceful coexistence per se or who have any positive feelings about Israel. Those days are over, for a long time
anyway. Almost everyone wants peaceful coexistence, but only
if it's for good reasons of national and Arab logic.

"Egypt hasn't forsaken Arab solidarity," Mr. Haikel told
me. He was a man I met at the Arab League. Their building
on Tahrir Square, with much security outside and much luxury
inside, gave the immediate impression of a temple of orthodoxy, with no wishy-washy Westernness. Even the clocks
avoided European numerals. And Mr. Haikel, in his conservative business suit and tie on a hot Sunday morning, radiated
a kind of power and self-assurance which made me think that
he was no Egyptian but an Arab from one of the oil states.

But it turned out he was a Cairene; it was the League that gave him that aura.

"Egypt's Arab solidarity goes in cycles," Haikel said. "And the pendulum will swing back. Islam is socialist, and Egypt is socialist." When I expressed surprise, he went on, "Islam is the one civilization that wasn't based on exploitation of the lower classes. The nomads of Arabia didn't provide their sheiks with income, only with some men and some camels. The wealth of Islam came from trade. We were the great middlemen between Europe and India and China and Africa. Your wealth, which you extracted from your serfs, fed Islam. And when those trade routes withered, our decline began. Now the trade is reborn, and instead of tea or silk it is oil. You can see we will take care it won't wither away again, not in our lifetime or in our children's lifetime."

He had said all this quickly, having said or thought it often before. "But Egypt," I said, "hasn't Egypt been exploited for a thousand years?"

"The wooden swords in the mosques of Cairo . ." Haikel answered. "The Imam used to hold up a wooden sword at the service. Symbol that this was a conquered country. We found the peasants here, they were the legacy of the Byzantine past."

"*We?*" I asked with what I hoped was a disarming smile.

"Wherever there is Islam, we can use 'we,' " Haikel said.

THIRTY-FIVE

It was hard to believe from within Cairo that as soon as you crossed the Bulak bridge, you were in the country, in Africa. Along some of its approaches Cairo spilled over, into shantytowns and cemeteries sheltering squatters, but if you crossed the Nile up in its northern section, there was a clean break. That bridge was a metal crossbeam structure, with trucks, horses, and donkeys sharing one lane while the old, windowless trains went by in the middle, and below, on the Nile, passed the silent sailing boats, the feluccas.

After the bridge, a right turn took you straight into the Delta fields. It was a forbidden turn: Cairo, amidst all its chaos, has been seeded with "No Right Turn" and "No Left Turn" signs by some traffic expert back from a visit to maybe Vienna or Moscow, where they're also crazy about that sort of thing. By chance I ran into a policeman there who shouted at me for a long time, until I shouted back, pointing at myself, *"Deef! Deef!"* which (according to my dictionary) meant "Guest!" The policeman got off his stand, came around, and patted me on the shoulder through my car window. A bit of desert tradition re-emerging.

Then I was surrounded by silence, and back into the colors of Egypt: the azure of the Nile, the painful green of the fields, and along the roads stacks of reddish palm branches full of orange dates, being loaded on donkeys. All that, and the sky, and the white triangular sails of the feluccas. The fields were empty, with low stalks of corn, and very soon there was hardly any motor traffic left. The only life was the donkeys and their drivers loading dates and, along the embankment, more donkeys and occasionally a dromedary being loaded with bricks, which stood to dry in long rows along the river.

I followed that road until I came to the Barrage. The Barrage was a famous sight in pre-High Dam days, and it was once one of the largest dams in the world. Muhammad Ali started it, but it was finished only at the end of the nineteenth century by European engineers. It served to keep the irrigation waters of the Delta flowing and to keep the Nile navigable. Now it was but a second or third defense line of a system controlled near where it entered the country at Aswan. It was still heavily guarded by military posts, and across the Nile floated those strings of empty barrels connected by chains, to keep off any mines that enemy planes might drop. Egypt is terribly vulnerable in its water works; according to Mohamed Heikal's figures, seven million Egyptian pounds were spent just on those simple, improvised barriers of barrels. The Barrage itself, disappointingly, looked like nothing more than one of the arched stone bridges you see in France, with a kind of Moorish castle stuck on top. I drove across and right back again, which odd behavior caused a military post to haul me in and check me.

They weren't nasty, and presently I continued south, making a half-circle around the city, and found myself in an industrial section with many small factories, while across the river genuine smog hung over the chimneys of the new plants in Helwan. The road was now a four-lane highway, and on the side was the old sand road for the carts drawn by horses and donkeys, with their drivers, if that is the word, usually asleep amidst their cargo. That road continued south through all the valley, past Luxor to Aswan and on to the High Dam—precisely, for there all roads ended, and only a plane or a boat (or a camel) could get you to the border of the Sudan. My route lay inland, though. Across from Helwan there was a fork in the road, and a narrow, asphalted lane turned west and entered an area of palm woods (not groves, but palms so closely together that nothing grew in between, as in a pine forest). A strange landscape, almost somber in its sudden exclusion of the overflowing sunlight.

To my right lay a tiny mud-brick village, with donkeys parked under the palm trees and a one-story-high mosque. Across from it in the weedy grass of an open spot, bits and pieces of statues were scattered, and there was a small sphinx. Two young men in green galabias (a very unusual color) stood around waiting for tourists. Here, fallen on his back, lay a very large stone king, legless now but with a beautifully carved head, Ramses II, Ramesse, the Colossus of Memphis. An open stone house had been built around him. On the fence of a little café with a garden hung a sign saying in English, "Memphis Cafeteria."

For all this was the last visible presence on earth of the onetime capital of Upper and Lower Egypt, the great and famed city of Menfe, called Memphis by the Greeks, founded at the very beginning of Egyptian history. I went into the café, to drink coffee in Memphis, but there were neither guests nor landlord. A flyblown picture on the wall showed a movie-studio-type re-creation of the city, with white and golden pillars and golden banners. This was the place founded by Menes, the first king of "Both Egypts," five thousand years ago.

Three centuries later, forty-seven hundred years back in time, his successor Zoser built his own tomb nearby, and that tomb is the Step Pyramid of Sakkara, the oldest human structure on earth. Within those three hundred years the Egyptians had found copper in the Sinai, and with bronze, they had learned to build in stone.

I had no roadmap, but as I continued the palms thinned, I could see fields and canals, and then, unmistakably, the top of the Step Pyramid was visible in the distance above the trees, flat, dark, alien to the landscape. I steered for it almost as by compass, following narrow dirt roads. I went through hamlets of a few huts, a well, brick walls and straw roofs, indistinguishable from the way black Africa lives in its remotest corners. Women were washing clothes in the streams and going by with jars on their heads, some with a sleeping baby flung over one shoulder. A little child walked by with a glass bottle balanced free and untouched on top of her head, and looking very proud about that. I bounced across a bridge and drove through an open market where dense clouds of flies and wasps darkened the baskets of dates and other fruit. It was very hot, as if it were midsummer instead of late fall. The Step Pyramid was to my right now, behind a row of fields. I followed the embankment of an irrigation canal, very calmly, to give the dogs, geese, and goats time to step aside. A blindfolded donkey was turning a waterwheel, and a small child, all alone in a vast dark-green field, was slowly turning the handle of an Archimedean irrigation screw.

Then the dirt road sloped upward, and I was back on asphalt. A road led straight out to the desert, which began no more than two hundred feet from there. I passed a gate with a guardhouse, and I was on sand, on the plateau of the Sakkara city of the dead.

The Step Pyramid is less than half as high as the great one of Giza, but that still means two hundred feet. It goes up in six steps of about thirty feet each, as for a giant to walk up on. And without consulting any books, you accepted that this construction went back beyond prehistory, to the very dawn of civilization. It looked so ancient in its clumsiness that I thought Giza must have looked upon it as we do upon Giza. I know it was built not very long before the Great Pyramids, but perhaps the unrecorded time of that age of myth ran longer than ours, just as a child's day is so much longer than a grownup's.

The Giza Pyramids are buildings, precisely as ours are in the year 1976. The Step Pyramid of Sakkara is but one remove from the cave and the rock.

I drove around on a road that was just a track in the rocky and sandy soil, with a high flag of dust behind me, all alone. When I got out, I was again in the desert stillness, and a warm, clean wind was drying me off.

Rounding a hillside, I came upon a human being. A man was sitting in the shade of a wooden shack. He came toward me; it turned out he was the guard of a new excavation being done by the University of Pisa. He was a nice old man, very different from the Cairo guides, and he opened a gate and let me look into the entrance to a tomb. The team, which would be back in winter, had got as far as the tomb door, which was now protected by a wooden screen and padlocks. He pulled a canvas cover off a wall, and there was the name of a king. Kings' names in hieróglyphs are always set in a ring, called a "cartouche"; it was thought this king had lived in the XXVIth Dynasty, which ruled about 600 B.C. His name was

That is a bird with a large craw on top, and the creature at the bottom, he told me, was a snail.* Each sign presented a consonant, and these would spell, B-k-n-r-n-f. All this had been buried in the sand until it was uncovered in 1974. He allowed me to climb down to the door of the tomb, and when I started slipping and sliding, he came along and held on to me, for he was very much more agile than I. It was a tricky business, he said, for we looked up into rock and sand seemingly hanging free over our heads. I peered through a crack into the darkness of the tomb. A ray of light entered and seemed to end in midair: the first light after twenty-five centuries.

Hieroglyphs started as word signs, of course (like Chinese), with, for instance, a circle with a dot meaning "sun." Gradually some of them became phonetic signs representing sounds, the words as spoken, and now they could be used for many things at the same time, and not only homonyms—for in hieroglyphics, no vowels were used (as is still the case in Hebrew and Arabic). To help the readers out of this confusion, the hieroglyphs combined word signs and phonetic signs, plus, often, a "determinative" as a clue to the meaning. Here is an example, taken from Alan Gardiner's famous Egyptian grammar:

"To drink" was, in speech, something like *sowr*. Writing this required an *s*, a *w* and an *r*. For the *s*, a purely alphabetic sign existed: ∏ . The *w* and *r* originally had one sign to-

* Actually, it is a horned viper.

gether, the swallow:  . This consonantal skeleton later fitted many different meanings, the most frequent one being "great," and the need was now felt to add a phonetic sign to help its pronunciation. In the case of "to drink," a phonetic *r* sign, ⌒ , was added. "To drink" had now become .

There was still need for a determinative, to show that here was some kind of action connected with the mouth, and the figure chosen was a man with a finger on his mouth. "To drink" finally read

The story of the deciphering of the hieroglyphs, beginning with the Rosetta stone and its text in three languages, is told to every schoolchild, or at least it used to be. But look at this "to drink" in its innocent elaborateness, and at the long, long way humanity had to go to learn writing and reading.

The following morning I went to the Egyptian Museum. I had often gone by it, and numerous people, including even the President's pressman, Tashin Bashir, during our short car-ride together, had eyed me with dismay when I had had to admit I hadn't been in it. But I had always lacked the courage to join the quatrilingual line of tourists. I had dutifully seen the Egyptian collection of the Metropolitan Museum in New York many times, and it had seemed of a tiring and deadly remoteness. But after Sakkara I thought it would be different here. Sakkara's remoteness was alluring and haunting. I wanted to see what had been saved from the grave robbers and the Western thiefs and brought to this museum.

The Egyptian Museum was put up by a French Egyptologist, Auguste Mariette, to have at least some of the newly dug-out treasure stay in its country of origin. It served that purpose, and during the century it has now existed, it has been filled with an enormous art collection. Those who rush through, though, or who let themselves be rushed through by one of the guides (who make things more interesting with anecdotes about Ramses II and Moses and what they said to each other), will be disappointed. It takes a kind of dreamy patience to overcome the museum's handicaps and not let these spoil the beauty of its contents.

The museum has guards, many of them. They're in white uniforms with dark berets, which gives them the appearance of the policemen in the backgrounds of those turn-of-the-century photographs of presidents and politicians, and they are just as immobile. It has any number of sweepers and other manual help, and it has workmen who, according to some desultory plan, are forever patching up its most dilapidated parts. The workmen with their well-heralded Pharaonic tools are the most real: they're doing a job. The sweepers, and the occasional guard who bestirs himself, are forever—again, just as in Pompeii—propositioning the visitors, although in lieu of dirty wall-paintings all they have to offer is mummies. You are looking at a statue, and suddenly you hear, "Psst! Psst!" and a man comes up and says, "Tutankhamen?," leering and winking like a demon. It is disheartening.

I tried to dodge all these people, and whenever one beckoned, I fled. Of the many objects, I tried to look at only a few, but for a long time. There was a vast amount of articles from daily life, furniture, combs, chairs, whips, bows and other weapons, jewelry, toys, and everything else once buried with the dead to allow them a continuation of their favorite pastimes—those dead now all waiting in eternity with empty hands. Cairo also had much more art of later periods than the Metropolitan. This was different from what we expect of Egyptian styles. It was less severe and formalized, softer. The distance from Greece and Rome was less. The women had become tender and desirable.

I wrote down the text from a stone tablet addressed by a king to his workmen: "Heavier are the provisions I give you than the work itself. No one sighs with poverty." Those were the days.

After some hours the museum began to weigh me down. There was no big difference from New York after all. The statues and obelisks did not seem more natural here, they had that same taste of loot. They were almost as much out of place as on Fifth Avenue. They looked painfully wrong indoors, as they do under a New York sky: they only look right, as I later found out, in their natural places. They were designed for the air and the colors of the desert. They represented death here, not immortality.

I hastened away from its half-lit and unlit corridors and out into the square. But the melancholy of the museum is not just that it has tamed, and covered with dust, objects of worship and exaltation. It is also full of a more recent melancholy.

Those yellowed French captions still glued to showcases, those dusty busts, peering from the corners, of European "pashas" who had been the museum's benefactors, even the hustling and the guides' terrible jokes—they made the museum a monument not to the Pharaohs, but to a melancholy, washed-away past of genteel European science, and patron age, and theft, and patronizing oppression.

THIRTY-SEVEN

The day train to Luxor left at half-past seven in the morning. It was not a windowless wreck, but neither was it outside Egyptian life, like the Rapide from Alexandria to Cairo. The carriages were Hungarian-built and had seen their best days. They were hot, the toilet stank, and there were flies and cockroaches; but there were also two waiters who brought dishes of marvelous food from beyond a little door—eggs, broiled meat with rice at midday, and coffees and teas without end. At nightfall, I had run up a bill of a dollar. We kept on time, too.

The station signs are now in Arabic only, but occasionally I could just make out the traces of the erased European name (in French transcription), and once I saw an untouched "Ladies Waiting Room" on an entrance. Beni Suef was the first town of some size, and facing the station still sat its Semiramis Hotel, which must be about a hundred years old, with a faded *"Tous Conforts"* sign still on the wall and its six little windows tightly shuttered, hiding nameless horrors of bugs and smells. After that, vast fields of sugar cane stretched to the horizon on both sides, interspersed with walled fruit gardens, and sticking out over the palm trees were chunks of stone, remnants of ancient tombs and temples, as different from the mud brick of the present as glass and concrete would be.

We stopped at El Minya—baskets of fruits on the platform, people getting off the train to relieve themselves at the side of the track, clouds of flies over everything, and the houses of the town, of yellowish brick, some of them five or six stories high, all with blinds down against the sun that poured over everything. A strong feeling of traveling south now and inland, farther and farther away from what you knew and understood. Above Asyut, you could see the hills of the desert on both sides of the valley; looking out of the windows on either side of the train, you looked from one end of the country to the other.

This narrow land, all visible from a train, was worked over as painstakingly as Asia's plains, and more backwardly than in Asia now. The people in the fields here had nothing but hoes, and the plows were pulled by dromedaries. Dromedaries also turned the waterwheels, and outside every village were the partly opened little round towers which the peasants built to dry their bricks.

Asyut is very old and was once famous and infamous. In the nineteenth century, it was the terminal for the slavers' caravans from the Sudan, who stopped here to turn the boys selected for that role into eunuchs. As two out of three died in the process, this was more economical than feeding them till Cairo. Annie Quibell, writing around 1920, thought Asyut was a pretty and modern town then. Asyut has not changed. We have. Even sixty years ago, such a place, almost carless and with many dirt roads rather than paved streets, was comparable to a small Western town. Now it seemed out of another world.

Asyut is Upper Egypt, and here began a new change in the landscape. It was more primitive, less formed. The houses had mud walls rather than brick or mud brick. But in spite of that, the villages were cleaner and more appealing. The peasants looked less victimized. The train crossed the Nile on an iron bridge; until then we had followed the west bank, but from now on we would stay east of the river. "Different people here," a fellow passenger said to me, "much more friendly." I asked him why that was. He answered, "It's black Africa—this is how far it reaches." (He was not an Arabian Egyptian, but a Nubian; he ran a garage in Cairo.)

Twilight fell. The tops of the hills were still in sunshine, but in the valley the villages huddled in a quickly darkening world. Mist spread over the fields. It was the coming-home hour—little animals following bigger ones, little children following big children, grownups trotting on donkeys (and no creature trots like a donkey), all heading for their village in the soft light.

And then it turned out that this remote scene was quite near a town, for suddenly we passed a radar mast, and telegraph wires, streets, a few lights, and a lit-up café garden where a group of people were watching television. After that we were back in a countryside with not one light, not even a lamp behind the door of a hut. An hour of darkness, and then, when we stopped, we were in Luxor.

Luxor's name, in spite of its classical sheen, is derived from the Arabic, El Kusur, which means "the castles," a somewhat heavy and ignorant reference to its temple of Amen. Luxor was called No in the Old Testament, which is just "city," and the Greeks gave it the name Thebes. Homer and Herodotus celebrated it, and it was left to some Roman military lout to destroy it. I have a copy of a sketch Edward Lear made of Luxor from the river in the year 1867, and all that remained of Thebes, the hundred-gated, were the temple ruins with some makeshift dwellings on top of them, a cluster of palm trees, and a fisherman's hut and boat.

It is a tourist town now but it has a certain air, mostly because of its river boulevard, the tree-lined avenue which runs all the way to Karnak some two miles north, and of course because of the Nile itself, which dominates it. The tourists have brought in their wake the hangers-on, who hail you with cries of "mister, mister," or what sounds a bit better at least to non-French ears, "m'sieu, m'sieu." And since most tourists overpay when they get separated from their tours, they make it necessary for others to bargain for everything rather than pay the normal price as a matter of course.

The Amen temple is in the heart of the town, naturally enough, as not so long ago it was all that was left of the town.

☀ 229

There are fences and guards and signs, but if you try, you can wander in from many points, which takes the sightseeing curse off it. I came in along a causeway marked "Closed to the Public" and lined with sphinxes, lionesses all with the head of King Ramses II. (They looked like lionesses to me, that is, but Baedeker says they're rams.) Ramses, the most (self-) publicized of Pharaohs, added many statues of himself to the temple, but it was built some one hundred and fifty years earlier, around the year 1400 B.C., by Amenhotep III. His god-like birth is chiseled onto the walls of one chamber, where Khnum, the ram-headed god, fashions him on a potter's wheel. I stood there and looked at that birth, and out to where two mangy dogs were sitting and scratching themselves and, in the distance, groups of tourists in their sports clothes made flecks of color and flesh against the granite. The weather, miraculously, had suddenly turned from the crushing heat of Upper Egypt to just warm and lovely. The Mosque of Abul Haggag, a holy man, which was built into a corner of the temple, stood out white and shiny against the crumbling ancient stones. All these discordant elements fused for a moment; there was a weird, dreamlike truth in that creation of life on the divine potter's wheel. When I came out of the temple, there were still two hours of light left, and I got a carriage to Karnak.

(The pleasure of carriages for real and not as a Central Park luxury stayed with me in all small towns, though I realized my motives contained a doubtful mixture of romanticism and environmentalism. But they were just a nicer form of transportation than hot, crowded service taxis. Luxor had a few cabs, but carriages were its main transportation. Here they weren't as nice, though. You had to haggle nonstop.)

The pleasure of guidelessness: I wandered onto the Karnak grounds, past a guard who was dozing on the ground and half-raised himself to take my money. I entered a court, looked at a little map I had brought, and thought, "This is the temple of Mut, wife of Amen." On a piece of column a scholarly-faced young man was sitting, and I asked him if this was Mut. He was an American; he said he had no idea. We laughed, and I said, "You're probably right, you don't have to know these things to look."

I walked on and suddenly found myself at the threshold of an enormous hall of columns. It was a place of more gigantic proportions than I had ever seen. We were not in the Mut temple; this was the great Karnak temple of Amen, built for him by King Thutmose III of the New Empire, in the year 1500 B.C. Thutmose made Thebes his capital, and Amen, who was now identified with the Sun god Ra of the Ancient Empire, his god. The temple proclaimed his decision to the world. This hall, to use an image beloved of guidebooks, is large enough to put Notre Dame of Paris in. It had over a hundred columns, of which many are still or again standing, and the tallest are eighty feet high. They were built of drums of stone so thick that "six men holding hands cannot encompass them." I have to give the figures but they are only a preamble to this: the hall, one of the wonders of the world, is so beautifully proportioned that it doesn't overwhelm its visitors. It was not built to overawe you but to pay proper homage to the godlike sun who (which) is the overwhelming reality of Upper Egypt. I hoped the young man hadn't turned around without getting to this point. We had been wrong; one should at least know why this was built. Tour groups came in but nothing changed; that space, shaped by man, was too vast.

I passed through two pylons, which are trapezoid walls. The first pylon of Karnak (I can't resist one more set of measurements) is 370 feet wide and 140 feet high, and its walls are 49 feet thick. Beyond the fourth pylon, I came upon my first real obelisk, in its own place, and it stood forth even in this world of giants. It was the obelisk of Queen Hatshepsut. Alterations and additions to the temple were continuous, and after her death, her brother put columns all around the obelisk to withdraw it from the view of the temple visitors. But time has avenged her and frustrated this spiteful trick. Her obelisk is rising free and dazzling against the sky. The hieroglyphics on it are as deep and sharp as if they had been cut recently, and when you look up along it into the blue, the effect is literally of almost infinite height, and it makes you completely dizzy.

I am assuredly not writing a guidebook, but I must mention the picture stories cut into the outside walls of the great colonnaded hall, what are called "historical reliefs." They show in picture-strip style the wars of Kings Ramses and Sethos in Palestine, Syria, and Libya: the Kings in their chariots, shooting arrows, leading sieges, and taking captives, and the natives fleeing, or dying, or asking for mercy.

Every figure shown in relief in Egypt is always shown sideways, in profile. But the Syrians fleeing King Sethos are shown full face, hiding behind trees. It may not sound like much of a thing to fuss about, but within this stylized art it was an enormous surprise, those round-faced, bearded fellows peeping out at you from between the tree trunks. No one knows the reason. I'd guess that full-faced pictures were considered demeaning, perhaps dangerous for the soul, and thus only to be used for defeated enemies. But it gives you a new idea about those profiles with their one eye. There was nothing primitive in them.

Sethos is also shown returning to Egypt with his loot and prisoners, and at the frontier the priests and nobles are welcoming him with little bouquets of flowers. The frontier, which is the border between Africa and Asia, is shown as a zigzag canal full of crocodiles. That was the happy-ending picture of one strip.

Within those pylons are staircases, but they are blocked now by doors. I passed one door with a broken padlock, however, and after making sure no guard was watching, I climbed up the stone stairs. They were perhaps a foot wide and very steep and sloping. My worry wasn't about falling but about scorpions or snakes, for it was very dark and the debris everywhere made me think no one had been there in a century or so. But I got up and out into the sunlight and looked over this mile-long temple field.

It was grandiose. As we make maximum war efforts, it was a maximum worship effort.

It was also frightening in many places: the kings with their swords and cudgels striking and killing their opponents and (perhaps as awful, to me anyway), the oxen being sacrificed. The temple pictures portrayed how one leg of an ox was bound up to his belly, and as he stood wobbling on three legs, he was pushed over and slain. The oxen are then shown on their backs, with their tongues hanging out in a frozen stone agony. The Syrian and Libyan captives are also shown as being dedicated to the three gods, but if that meant they were killed, too, the reliefs do not show it. Those three gods were Amen, Mut, and their son Khonsu, the peregrine-falcon god, a bird that flies straight up into the sun and thus shows it is the sun's child.

The portrayal of the sacrifices made to them was crueler than the act itself had been. It had the matter-of-factness of real cruelty, a curiosity about suffering which you also find in medieval woodcuts of torture.

There is no end to human cruelty, and I do not know where the love could be found to obliterate it. The monks who came here nineteen hundred years later painted saints over the hieroglyphics on the columns and defaced some of the gods, but that was not a victory of love over cruelty.

When I left the temple grounds, the sun was setting over the hills across the water. I went back down the street toward the river and began walking to Luxor.

Women were washing clothes, and a man out to his middle in the Nile was scrubbing a buffalo. A woman in black sat by the road with a baby. Its eyes were half-closed by pus and it waved at me with its fist. She smiled on it. Two posh beach houses were screened from the world by sheetrock walls which also closed off the embankment in front of them, and on each side a bored soldier stood guard. I passed many schoolchildren. Some were chatting among themselves and some jeered at me. An abandoned-looking villa bore a sign, "Arab Socialist Union."

Back in town, I saw hawks, or perhaps they were falcons, circling high up in the sky, a mile above the houses.

I came to a little café garden on a dark and silent stretch of the boulevard, and here a man in galabia, skullcap, and spotty apron cooked me a plate of rice and what I hoped was chicken.

THIRTY-NINE

The west bank of the Nile across from Luxor is the place where the dead kings of Thebes were buried and where the temples stood in which they were worshiped. It is the place of the most intense concentration of tombs, treasures, mystic art, and ruins in Egypt, and probably in the world. It is also a field of perpetual battle between the visitors and the men who feed on them.

Wise from my experience of the Pyramids, I went across very early in the morning, but the men of Thebes got up even earlier. One wicked old man obviously owned the ferry concession, for no matter which boat you chose, he got twenty-five piasters first. He screamed "money, money" till you paid. He did not give out receipts; that is to say, it was his own show. Then afterward, on the water, the boatsmen came around for tips. On the other shore, no pause for elevated thoughts about that sacred soil; I was pounced on, the way mosquitoes would pounce on a bather in a swamp. Ten to twenty men and boys tried to drag me hither and yon, to their cars or tours or buses. Everyone yelled and I yelled back and finally just went to sit on a bench with my eyes closed until they left off. Indeed, a conducted tour protects you somewhat against them; I met a BBC reporter in Luxor who told me he was going around in a tour, simply so as not to have to do battle. And there were some French students who came with bicycles, which also gave them a bit of protection. But be it known that when you watch those NET or BBC documentaries where a professor stands all alone on a rock against the sky and points out the marvels of ancient Egypt, off camera the scene is a free-for-all of chaotic greed, and it must take about a regiment of the Egyptian army to clear space for shooting those scenes. After a while, to get away from the landing stage, I found a taxi driver who agreed to take me inland as far as the Colossi for fifty piasters and who accepted that I did not want him to wait or anything else.

When he turned around and drove off, I stood alone in a stubbly field, at the foot of a stone statue sixty-four feet high. Another one sat on a throne beside it. They are called the Colossi of Memnon, a hero of the Trojan war, but they really are statues of a Pharaoh of Thebes, sitting in front of his temple, which is now gone. They're too battered to be called beautiful or ugly, but they are so huge, sitting in that sun-grilled plain, that they make quite a sight. One of them used to sort of peep or moan at sunrise—I guess because the warming air inside him expanded through a crack—and this phenomenon became one of the foremost tourist attractions of the Roman Empire: consuls and emperors came to Thebes to see if the statue would moan for them. Supposedly it was Memnon greeting his mother, Aurora, the dawn goddess, and the dew was her tears for him. All those visitors covered the feet of the statues with graffiti, but in the last seventeen hundred years he hasn't made a sound. Children were herding goats in his field, and presently they came closer and offered various pieces of stone for sale.

I got back onto the road and slowly walked north toward a little village at the foot of the hills. On my right were cane fields, at the left of the road the hills began, and the reflected heat from the sun on the rocks and sand was already tremendous. To be in the countryside and meet normal fellahin going by was nice. A child leading a buffalo across a little canal stood still and stared, and the buffalo started eating the sugar cane behind her back. I pointed at him, and she hastily pulled him away and smiled at me.

I climbed over a six-foot-high wall of rubble and dirt, and found myself in a temple courtyard. It was a lovely place—pylons, pillars, walls, half-standing and half-ruined. A vast area of grey and yellow stone against the blue, with grey-green cactuses and thorns growing between the paving stones, and everywhere birds nesting in the cracked columns. Not very much was left upright, but from what there was you could see how large the temple had been, and how it was surrounded by low brick buildings (storehouses for the temple people, I learned later). There wasn't a soul in sight, and I climbed up in all the corners and followed the walks through the pattern of sun and the cool shade from the thick stone. Then I sat on the empty base of a column and tried thinking how it once had been. My luck held, and only when I was climbing back out and standing on top of the rubble wall did a white-burnoosed man appear at the far end of the field, crying, "Mister, mister!"

At the edge of the village was a resthouse where sodas were sold, and here a very sober and untouristy landlord told me I had just seen the Rameseum, the mortuary temple of Ramses II—the place where after his death his relatives and priests were to come and pray. I've been back there with that knowledge, but never again was it like that first morning.

The resthouse landlord told me it was half an hour on foot, over the crest of the hill, from his place to the Valley of the Kings, along a path of white stone. But the air over it was vibrating with heat, and I hesitated cowardly. He then told me the man next door ran a taxi and I could also be driven up, for a pound.

The car road leads up to the valley in a wide hairpin curve, through a landscape of nothing but yellow rock, bare, angry hills. Then, at the tombs, was the usual shock of guards, fences, tickets, and arguments. It wasn't as bad as at the landing stage, because people who had gone this far on their own were very rare, but some blighted official had seen fit to spruce up the road from this point on. There were neat little banks of stones all the same size, and white gravel markings, and thus they had managed to make the Valley of the Kings look like a miniature golf course in New Jersey. In the middle of it all loomed large (it is hard to believe) Ye Very Olde Coffeeshoppe. Visitors were resting up in its shade from their cultural efforts while their guide, leaning on an Egyptian shillelagh, lectured them on the cultural oneness of Egypt through the ages.

The tombs, different from what I had visualized, are at the end of long corridors and staircases in the rocks, hundreds of feet from the surface. Most of them had locked gates which you had to tip your way past, but after that you were pretty much left to your own devices. The only exception to this was the tomb of Tutankhamen, where someone had cornered the market on pictures and guards were hovering to make sure no others were taken. Visitors with cameras had to leave these in the safekeeping of one of the men hanging around, and all in all it wasn't a very inspiring atmosphere around that gilded coffin with, Amen forbid, colored lights shining on it. That was rather sad, and a disappointment. I had seen the traveling exhibition of the tomb's treasures, and long before that I had read about the curse on the grave openers, and how the lights of Cairo had gone out inexplicably the night that the Fifth Earl of Carnarvon died there, one year after he had opened the tomb of the Prince, in 1923. It had all appeared so mysterious and exquisite then.

But other tombs, less public-relationized, were quieter and

very lovely, and most of all those of Amenhotep II and Sethos, him of the Karnak temple and the wars against the Syrians.

"Lovely" must seem an idiotic word for a tomb, but these deeply hidden burial rooms have walls covered with picture stories of great beauty. Extraordinary, for after the burial the corridors were filled with rubble, and no mortal eyes were ever meant to see them again. They weren't decorative art; they were there, literally, to save the souls of the kings.

The dead king traveled with the sun god through the underground of the night, and to do so without instruction would have been disastrous. He had to know about the way, about the guardian snakes and monsters, and about whatever happened at each of the twelve hours of the night. Texts, foremost the *Book of the Underworld*, told all this, and on the walls of the tombs the sculptors and painters turned these texts into a holy and mystical strip. The alabaster sarcophagi and the mummies of the kings have been scattered over museums and collections from Cairo to Boston; but the texts and pictures which they thought they needed in all eternity are here, and many of them look fresh and clean and as if just made. In the tomb of Sethos is a room where the pictures were sketched in only with red and black chalk, and somehow never finished; these were even finer, less naive, than the completed ones. (I stood there as a guide in an antichamber hollered, "That room not ready," and made his obedient tour pass it by.)

Sethos and Amenhotep have many chapters from the *Book of the Underworld* on their walls. One hour, "The Sun's Voyage Through the Third Hour of the Night," for instance, might take up a whole wall or more, perhaps a hundred square feet. On that wall was a haunting repetition of one motif—the god traveling, his followers and retinue, other gods and goddesses, every animal seen in Egypt at that time, servants, rowers, boatsmen hoisting the sails, the dead king sacrificing, demons, spirits, and mummies. A unity of life in which any animal might appear with a human head and any man or woman with an animal's head or wings. All this in Amenhotep's grave under a blue ceiling with yellow stars painted in.

Think of the men who worked here for years, with little oil lamps, believing they were engraving the very secrets of life and death on earth. And who are we to have ruled they weren't?

FORTY

My departure from Luxor-Thebes was a bit by way of being put to flight. One morning around eleven, I suddenly packed up and hastened to the station. I was going to the Aswan High Dam and away from the "This room not ready!" guides. And when I found out there was no train till evening, I recklessly entered into hasty negotiations with the cab drivers sitting around and took a taxi (agreed price, £15 for the 130 miles).

The road from Luxor to Aswan often runs through desert, but at times it is the precise dividing line between the lush, tropical land with its palms and fields, and the total, baking wilderness. So narrow is the life-sustaining ribbon that the villages have all been put across the divide, in the desert, to save acreage. They are nothing but long walls, with little sections roofed over by straw or baked mud with cane stalks. These villages lay naked to the sun. The heat was staggering in them; shade became the most precious commodity in the world. Electricity, though, had made its appearance: wires went to those baked-mud sheds.

The settlements here were mostly Nubian. The Egyptian fellahin this high up the river valley are almost as dark as the Nubians, but their features are different. So are their bearing and clothes. The Egyptian women we passed were all in the poor woman's black; the Nubians (not better off) had white scarves at the least. Most of them wore shiny dresses, often with gold, red, or white spangles. And after midday, we also passed flocks of schoolchildren. They were all in neat tan and blue school uniforms, and in these children I could no longer tell the two nations apart. To see them walk along the road in that wasteland was a happy sight.

The Nubians here were mostly resettled from where they had lived along the Nile, above Aswan, before the water backing up at the High Dam flooded their villages. Where Lake Nasser is now, between Aswan and the Third Cataract, each Nubian village once had its own particular style, tradition, and color of houses, and from each and every door you could see the river. Some sixty-five thousand people were moved in a great upheaval and cutting of roots, and many are said not to have survived it.

"One day," Dr. Philip had said to me in Cairo, "my barber suddenly started talking nonstop for fifteen minutes about the evils of the High Dam. And that evening in a governmental scientific committee, I heard exactly the same remarks." So concerted has the sudden campaign against the Dam become (linked, of course, with anti-Nasser and anti-Russian moves) that a writer, Philip Gallab, published a book in January 1975 called *Shall We Destroy the High Dam?* However, that was meant ironically. I had learned of the Dam and schistosomiasis; the Dam and the transmigration of the Nubians was a second point. I was not prejudging it, though.

Before leaving Cairo, I had gone to see Osman Ahmed Osman, Minister of Housing and Reconstruction and also the largest private contractor in Egypt. The sign of his firm, "The Arab Contractors," was—to say the least—on every second construction site in the country, and the press regularly called him "the greatest builder since the Pharaohs." However that may be, he was certainly the man to talk with about the Dam, which he helped build. I also thought that an introduction from him would be crucial on the spot in Aswan.

Mr. Osman was accessible. He prided himself on running a ministry without red tape, which surely seemed true, and with little or no corruption. He had a secretariat where important-looking Englishmen, Frenchmen, and other foreigners were waiting and making jokes in all languages with his private secretary (as I've said, she, too, had trouble with her phone), and when I was led into his private office, he was just having an overworked executive's meal of a glass of milk with cookies. He later told me that decisions within his ministry took an hour, and when he had to go to another ministry, it took three months.

The office had that silent coolness reserved for the VIPs of the country; there was a large conference area to the side, and two startling modern paintings were displayed on easels. No presidential portraits here or verses from the Koran. Osman was wearing an open blue shirt-jacket and, heavy, with a square jaw, he looked very Russian to me (he won't like that idea), but with dark Egyptian coloring. He told me he had graduated in 1940 and "all I had then in the world was an engineer's diploma." (His uncle was a contractor, though.) His first job was to build a garage in 1942, at a total price of £106, and now he had thirty-five thousand employees.

He accepted the High Dam job in November 1960, after he put in the lowest tender and when it had become clear that "nothing got done if the Russians employed Egyptians directly." Nasser nationalized his firm on July 22, 1961— Osman repeated that date a number of times while we were talking. "Yes, July 22, 1961," he would say, staring over my shoulder. However, he had kept a largely free hand because he had offshoot contracting firms in many other countries, and the hard currency he earned there gave him a lot of clout.

"I've always been against Nasser," he said to me, "always." After the October 1973 war, Sadat asked him to take the Ministry of Reconstruction. Was there no conflict of interest between being a minister and having a contracting firm, I asked. "No," he said. "I just want to get the work done."

"I wanted to build the High Dam," he told me. "Given Egypt's infrastructure, it was quite a job. But I did it." (To be precise, his firm built the body of the Dam, as I learned later, not the hydroelectric plant.) "The Russians," he went on, "sent equipment that was forty years behind the West. In the end, I had to import English and American stuff. Egypt built the dam, and the Russians took our money—just as with the rotten arms they sold us. Yes, I've never held a brief for Nasser. His policies started all this corruption. But we are socialists."

I: "How do you define your type of socialism, say, as different from U.S. capitalism?"

He: "It isn't. In the U.S., the government takes care of education, welfare, and all that, too. That is our socialism. We're open to all now. Come. We're in transition, but once that's over, it will be very good here."

We got talking, naturally, about the campaign against the Dam. "There I can't join the anti-Nasser bandwagon," Osman said, "because today the Dam would still be built on the same place and in the same way. It is not true that all twelve turbines are not working. They are all working. We just don't yet have use for all the possible electricity that can be generated. Not until the aluminum factory is ready at Nag Hammadi." (The faulty generators were one of the Cairo rumors. Others included that the Dam was the cause of the general breakdown in the telephone service and, even more surprising, that it was now shifting at the rate of one centimeter, or about half an inch, a year—toward Cairo, of course.)

"The Dam project had been around since the 1930's," Osman added, "and the final project was first approved by the U.S. and the U.K., and then later by the Russians. That's a rare phenomenon."

Actually, the Russians had first suggested scattered barrages and industries, as Gallab, the author of that blow-the-dam book, told me. Gallab, who had streams of figures at his fingertips, answered a number of serious objections I had heard raised. "About the Dam stopping the silt," he told me, "in the past, sixty thousand tons of silt came with the river in flood. But of this, eighty-eight percent was lost in the Mediterranean, and only twelve percent stayed on the fields. Ten thousand billion gallons of water was lost in the Mediterranean each year." (This silt is the mixture of coarse clay and salts which the Blue Nile and the White Nile carry downstream from Ethiopia and tropical Africa. Room has been left in Lake Nasser, above the Dam, for five hundred years of silt. Gallab's use of the words "was lost" needs qualifying; it ignores the balance of nature in the Mediterranean.) "But," Gallab said, "to make up for the loss of silt, we need just thirteen thousand tons of nitrate fertilizer. We can produce that for less than it used to cost to clean the canals of silt." Of course I objected that artificial fertilizer kills oxygen, pollutes the water, and all that. "That happens everywhere," Gallab answered. "We can deal with it as every other country does. And there were a number of side projects, new drainage canals and new protection for the embankments, because the water without silt wears them down. We got the loans for these, but they weren't built. Can you tell me why not?" I couldn't. "As of now," Gallab said, "this black-sheep Dam has earned £320 million, and that is twice its cost. Almost a million acres under year-round irrigation. A million acres reclaimed. We've got ourselves 1.75 million kilowatts electricity, and it will be 2.1 million."

(That is *power*. The *energy* output is supposed to go to ten billion kilowatt-hours a year. Power is like, say, horsepower; in energy, there is a time element. A kilowatt-hour is one and a third horsepower during an hour. The Grand Coulee Dam has also about 2.1 million kilowatts.)

"The Rosetta sardines?" Gallab asked. "Oh yes, those famous sardines. We've got sixteen thousand tons of fish from Lake Nasser so far; 1972 would have been a disaster year of floods if it hadn't been for the Dam—we never noticed them now. Even Sadat commented on that. As for the Russians, they charge two and a half percent interest, which isn't usury."

"Specially as they aren't paid," I said.

He laughed. "No, I don't think they are."

FORTY-ONE

The seventeenth of June used to be called the Night of the Drop. During that night (found on the Coptic sun calendar), a miraculous drop was thought to fall from the sky into the Nile to cause its rise. For no one knew where the river came from, and no one could understand why in the hottest months of summer, when all streams and brooks in the Mediterranean countries dried up, it alone would rise and rise, through the torrid months of July and August and September. There was a functionary called "the Crier of the Nile" who would go through all quarters of Cairo every day and call out the rise in cubits, which is the length of a forearm, or twenty-two inches. The government always jumped the gun and cheated, because it was not supposed to start collecting taxes before the Nile had risen sixteen cubits on the Nilometer. The Arab word for "river" is *nahr*, but the Nile is called *bahr*, and that means "sea." In those days, and until May 15, 1964, when the High Dam was closed, the Nile at Aswan was a "surging rapid, pouring from the south, washing the granite islets a shiny black." But when I arrived in Aswan, its water was as calm as in Cairo. The island of Elephantine across from the town, far from being pounded by the Nile's surging, looked, with its little boats and colored lights, like the rock garden in the pond of an amusement park.

A message from Osman A. Osman had reached Aswan and had got me a security clearance for the Dam; it also brought to my hotel room someone who said he'd take me around. He spoke only a few words of English, and while I felt up to light Arabic conversation on coffee or the weather, I surely couldn't discuss kilowatts. However, we set off and drove to the old dam first, the one built by the British around 1900. This one is near the town, just above the First Cataract of the Nile. When the Nile was in its summer flood, all the sluices were simply opened, but afterward the dam served to fill a backup reservoir for the leanest months. It was a great work in its days, but now, like the Delta Barrage, it looked very small and gentle, just a low brick causeway. However, it had machine-gun posts all along its length, and our driver dashed across it at breakneck speed. I protested that I hadn't been able to see a thing, and so we went down a sand road on the other shore to have a look from there. But a soldier walking by with his clean laundry knew a spy when he saw one and ran up to us, so we raced off again. I said, "Okay, I've seen it," and we continued along the west bank to the High Dam, Sadd el Ali.

The west-bank road was well paved; the surrounding country was empty, bare, stone. Power lines ran every which way, and while these are usually a blot on the landscape, there was something nice in their presence here—power, life, in the midst of and across nothingness. We passed several road blocks and radar stations, and then the wide gateway to the Dam began. On the right was the monument dedicated at its opening, but my guide obviously had instructions not to stop anywhere, and we flew by. Beside the road now lay Lake Nasser, the reservoir filled by the Dam, running all the way to the horizon and far to the sides into the bare hills. It had just reached its fill—for whoever wants figures, that is 48,000 billion gallons. It is the third largest man-made lake now, covering 2,000 square miles, which includes those Nubian villages.

We went through a checkpoint and past a railroad platform and bumped down a sand road to a wooden shack. Here the Aswan director of The Arab Contractors had his field office. We shook hands and exchanged compliments, and he said he'd come and see me that evening to answer any questions I might still have. I thanked him and added that I'd very much want to see a bit more, and with an engineer. The director, who had the euphonious name of Abdul el Abas Abazil, was not too pleased with that, and a slight souring of the atmosphere took place. However, the distant eye of Osman A. Osman on me won the day, and eventually I went off in an old company car with a man of about thirty, a civil engineer whom I'll call Mr. Khazzan (he was outspoken, and I know it won't be remembered who went with me), and of whom I was to see a lot in Aswan.

Khazzan first, dutifully, took me to a little museum with a model of the Dam and various ugly drawings and photographs which bored me as much as him, and then we went back out and stood on the platform looking down on the power station. To the right stood the Dam, curved against the stream, lined with smooth concrete, and at its foot a little beach, lapped by a very still Nile. It gave an impression of enormous solidity; there was nothing "if it only holds" about it. (Its base is more than half a mile wide, and it has concrete curtains going down six hundred feet into the river bed.) That still water was where the old course of the Nile ran, and right in front of us was the power station, and the new channel, also smooth, but with a deep turbulence just surfacing. These notes need qualification of my point of view. I had a period in life when I was studying to be an engineer, but that was long ago; I don't like technical things and I hate "progress" between quotes, which is ruining the earth. That said, I must proclaim that our view was beautiful, and sort of incredible. The power station sitting high over the river was graceful, long, and low under its forest of electrical towers. The entire façade was glass with vertical stone louvers, slanted at an angle of about forty degrees to keep out the sun. It wasn't heavy and "Russian" at all, it had none of that solid stolidness we identify with Soviet industrial or any other architecture. It reminded me of some of the best things in Brasilia. There was such a sense of both power and modernity about it; it was very exciting.

The power station was constructed in Moscow and Leningrad factories, and it is the kind of thing the Russians excel in (though the latest U.S. dams, like the Cochiti in New Mexico, may well be more sophisticated in such matters as computerized controls). In spite of my security clearance, Khazzan said he couldn't take me inside, nor could he go himself. As a compromise, he agreed to visit the inlet channels, although one isn't allowed to stop and look at them either.

We walked down to a railing and watched the waters combining the Blue and White Niles, after their three-thousand-mile journey, vanish into six concrete tunnels. A sentry stared at us from high up, and we walked on. Khazzan said that four turbines were working just then, but the others were surely in working order; there was indeed no use for them yet. Of the power station's steel doors, only two were up, and in front of them was that deep stir within the river. I said, "Suppose those doors got stuck," but he assured me there were two sets of everything and it couldn't happen. The old 1900 dam had little sluices with handwheels, but the Sadd el Ali has steel doors with winches, together weighing ten thousand tons. That's my last figure. It was all quite staggering, though.

We drove across the gateway, and this time I managed to have us stop at the monument. It is a tower-high kind of open chapel built from five concrete fins which hold a cogwheel up some hundred and fifty feet in the air. It makes a lotus flower, but you have to watch from afar to see that. An airy structure, surprising and imaginative in its double and triple symbolisms. Inside are texts on the Russian-Egyptian collaboration, and a sculpted portrait of President Sadat. Nasser was there, but of him only the outline has been left, and the picture of Sadat is half superimposed over that silhouette. On another of the lotus leaves are the words from the twenty-first chapter of the Koran, "And from water, We gave life to all things."

Such is the Monument to Soviet-Arab Friendship. The elevator (in one of the petals) doesn't run any more, the tour buses don't stop at it any more, and in Cairo I was told that from the air you could see it is really a hammer and sickle (no way). "It's beautiful," I said to Mr. Khazzan. He shrugged. "It cost a million pounds," he answered.

Khazzan was a skeptical man. "Plans are drawn up now," he told me, "to build giant stirrer-uppers which will allow us to send some silt through, after all. That'll take care of many problems."

"Also," he said a while later, "we're working on prevention of erosion."

"But," he said after another pause, "we're very good in words."

He liked being with The Arab Contractors. "They're the best boss in Egypt. Hassan Alam is the other big one. They did the power part of the Dam, we did the barrier."

We were heading back to town now, on the east bank this time. The road was terrible, and we bumped up and down in our seats. "This is the road for the working people," the engineer said. "The other road, the good one, is for the minister and the directors. Whenever something is good in Egypt, it's for the big shots." He laughed. "Yes," he said, "we have this comfortable saying in Egypt, 'Anyway, here no one dies of hunger.'" "Isn't it true?" I asked. He sort of smiled.

"Now about this High Dam," I said. "Is it or isn't it? Is it good or is it bad? Did the Russians do a good job or a bad job?"

"They did a fine job," he answered. "They did what they undertook to do, what they were asked to do. What else could you wish? We're always griping, always blaming the others. We always depend on others. We should help ourselves. It is we—" he put his hand on his heart in a fine gesture from the Arab past—"it is we who are wrong and need redoing."

The wilderness we drove through on this side was more forbidding than west of the Nile. This was really the *la siwa hu* world, "nothing but he." It was a desert of greyish-black stones we were bumping through, with but little sand, and cut everywhere by irregular gullies and hills. It was so much more inimical, so much hotter and *deader*, than a sand desert. Indeed it was frightening. The air blowing through our car was the air out of a furnace, although it was November. We saw, on a dirt embankment in the distance, the little freight train go by, to the quarries at Shellal. Who had built those works, who had laid out this narrow road? And how did they once in antiquity quarry granite here? Were they killing people then by the thousands, or had the climate changed? I felt that a flat tire would be enough to kill us, that it would be impossible to change a wheel in that incredible heat.

This petrified furnace was Egypt without the Nile. As the Nile makes Egypt, when they dammed the Nile, they dammed, artificialized, controlled, or whatever the word is, the entire country. This wasn't a works in some remote mountain; it cut right at the root of the nation. It surely took nerve.

FORTY-TWO

On we bumped. As we approached Aswan, we saw a military zone on the left of the road. Behind the barbed wire sat some trucks, and there were radar masts and two sites mounted with surface-to-air missiles. We crossed the railroad and were in the outskirts of town.

A miserable row of apartment houses appeared, in sandy, grey squares with a few scrawny trees. The side roads were rutted and full of holes. Children were leaning against the house walls, in the strip of shade behind one of those blocks that some insane planner had lined up all facing south—this in Aswan, where "the night is a hot day, and the day metallic and inexorable." That development looked so awful, it was a relief to leave those modern boxes behind and find myself among the old-fashioned, brick and straw, one-story slums in the traditional style. Closer to the heart of town we passed the housing once put up for the Russian engineers. It was better than the apartments on the outskirts, but it was neglected, too; the air conditioners had been removed and the holes in the walls crudely stopped up with pieces of brick; the grass was long dead; debris lay everywhere. A semi-slum.

We turned onto the river boulevard and slowed down. To my surprise, I saw beggars here, an unusual sight now. In front of a closed co-op store, a long line in black was waiting.

Here also, empty building lots alternated with new buildings, already slightly seedy and set in the middle of sunbaked squares which no human being without a camel and a sunshade would cross voluntarily. I had expected that Aswan, where more electricity emerges than in the rest of Egypt combined, would have become all different. "A new city, humming with life and activity," a government pamphlet had said. Engineer Khazzan found this another occasion for a shrug. "There isn't much work any more," he said. "Old Aswan—new Aswan—it is a *face*." He spoke that word in italics. "Behind it is poverty."

We stopped at my hotel and drank coffees. "By the way, don't expect Abazil tonight," Khazzan said. "He won't come. He just said that, to say something." (He was right; Abazil didn't show.) We then talked about our lives. Khazzan was the man I mentioned before who earned £80 a month plus living expenses. He was unmarried and happy in his profession. It must be noted that, negative as his comments were, he was quite cheerful; he simply wasn't going to sit by while I was swallowing any government nonsense. He gave me a pile of official booklets, and when I asked if I should read them, he said, "Only the one on the Dam. The rest is just . . . oh well, you know, the usual stuff." He had been hired by The Arab Contractors straight from school—yes, he had had very good grades.

I think he must have been doing a very good job and not caring what people thought about his ideas. I asked him how he spent his evenings, for Aswan, as I had already seen, did not offer much entertainment. "We have a television room," he said. "I watch, with some of my colleagues." I walked him back to his apartment later. It was a fine building. "Yes, nothing but the best for The Arab Contractors," he said, laughing. He was a nice man.

It will be many years before any balanced judgment can be

given on the Dam, a judgment that takes into account everything from the parasites in the Nile snails to the electricity for the resettled Nubians. Perhaps such a judgment is per se impossible, for who can weigh one man's diseased body against another man's newly reclaimed farmland?

As far as the Russians are concerned, certainly they came in with the same kind of political motivation as we have with our third-world projects, but the suggestion that the High Dam would be in the seventies what the Suez Canal was a hundred years ago has proved to be nonsense. We don't live in that kind of world; no Russian high commissioner is sitting in Cairo to make sure the debts are paid, the way the English and French did it then; and no High Dam shareholders are collecting profits. The Dam has come under attack from the left as sharp as that from the right: Mahmoud Hussein, writing from his Paris exile, called it "a high prestige project that accentuates the concentration of economic power in the hands of a minority, that encourages the development of highly specialized technical cadres cut off from their social-economic environment . . . promoting a spirit of capitalist modernization, creating little islands of industrial production in an ocean of archaism. . . ."

Having duly noted all this, I must add that I thought it was pretty amazing nonetheless. The English built the little dam in 1900, and they were very proud of it. At that time, they controlled the country.

When Americans work in underdeveloped countries, they isolate themselves in their little Shangri-las, and when they come out in the morning, all freshly showered and shaven, they can smile upon the natives.

The Russians in Aswan were only one remove from the local misery. They found themselves in a climate that to them more than anyone must have seemed a pure slice of hell. They found themselves in a country where at the time they surely had influence and the ear, hand, and at least one foot of the President, but where they didn't run things and were anything but popular. That, plus the fact that even now, ten years later, a phone call to Cairo from Aswan takes up to three days to put through, that nothing really works, that in the New Cataract Hotel the johns are placed in the bathrooms in such a way that only a one-legged dwarf can sit on them—when you add all that up, it seems a holy marvel to me that they got the thing done.

There is not one picture postcard of the Dam for sale in Egypt.

Engineer Khazzan had recommended a restaurant, in a round little tower on the river. When I got there, I was told they had stopped serving meals a year ago, but I was happy to sit on the terrace with a soda and look out over the Nile.

I thought, that evening, that now for the first time I really understood the spell this river had had for so many years on so many people, the fantastic idea that no one knew where it sprang from, the adventure for those lucky men and women a hundred years ago who set out to find its source.

At the table next to me were some rich-looking teenagers, and presently the one nearest began to question me. He kept asking about "my income in Aswan," and did I have English or American friends in town. He studied in Switzerland, he said, and would go back soon. He was out to sell me some pounds for black-market dollars, but I pretended not to understand—not from excessive virtuousness, but because I didn't want any and because he was a snooty boy. He wore very beautiful Italian shoes.

It got dark. Across the water, neon lights sprang up on the new hotel built on Elephantine island. The hotel was Indian —a bit of a surprise that India now has excess capital looking for faraway speculative deals—and I was told it was the most expensive in the country. Neon lights also went on over the mausoleum built on the island, not long ago, for the late Agha Khan, the leader of the Ismailian sect of Islam.

The Agha Khan lived in Zurich for a while when I was a student there in the early years of World War II, and I had known him then. I used to hang out in a bar called the Schifflaende, nursing one Pernod for as long as possible, and he used to dine there. Butter was rationed, and his secretary would bring a big chunk of it in his briefcase. Then, after the Khan had been served, the secretary opened the briefcase, carefully unwrapped the butter, and placed it on his master's potatoes or rice. Here was a holy man who liked butter. The memory gave a new and somewhat disconcerting slant to other mausoleums I had visited that held the bones of sheiks from the past. Better not to know holy people personally.

The trimmings, the fringes of Egyptian life were changing, and perhaps the changes here were more startling than in the West, just by contrast. With us, car traffic superseded fine train traffic, but my one-hour taxi ride from Cairo to the Fayum had replaced a three-day camel caravan from Giza, and that only in the last thirty years or so. And why shouldn't a mausoleum have neon lights? That morning, I had seen an advertisement in *El Ahram* for the Mecca Continental Hotel —air conditioning and charge cards for the pilgrims of 1976. But underneath all that, Egypt seemed as old and as poor to me as ever. A poor society, and so screwed up by twenty-five hundred years of one kind of colonialism after another that there were no proper rules or traditions left for relationships. Islam filled many gaps, but Egypt isn't Arabia. Islam didn't help the jeering schoolchildren, or the boy with the Italian shoes who didn't want to come back from Switzerland, or the Fayum officials who appropriated the fertilizer. What colonialism leaves behind is a highly developed instinct for self-preservation, escapism, an urge to be happy as the former masters seemed to be happy, and according to their recipe. Once, at two in the afternoon, in front of the Immobilia Building in Cairo, I saw an army truck get stuck in the traffic. The escort, a man with a sten gun, jumped out and screamed at some other driver. The back of the truck was closed with wire mesh, an armed soldier was sitting at the rear, and the heads of prisoners standing up were just visible. The prisoners all started shouting, but no one in the street looked their way. Then the road was cleared and they drove on.

For a brief while, Nasser had appeared to come up with a new approach, a chance to identify with something—for the first time in many years. Probably it never quite was what it looked to be, and anyway, that was now old history. Nasser had been buried once more, and there were no four million mourners this time, there wasn't a one.

Then Richard Nixon appeared at the Nile, and again the crowds were out; cheering now, for no very thought-out reason, cheering because Egypt seemed to have changed sides from a severe and austere camp to the camp of "the rich people" (as that agronomist had put it to me). It would be very silly to think their cheer was "arranged"—no need for that, and anyway, Egypt isn't particularly good at arranging. It would be equally silly to think they had come to cheer for Western democracy or free enterprise (even Nixon can't have thought that); they were cheering for the change, for lightheartedness, for good gadgets that worked, for sexy movies, for TV dinners, for an easier, more glamorous life. Once more, others were to do it for them. Then once more, the streets emptied. In a way they may seem pathetic, these forever disappointed, childish hopes; but to me they also seem weak, sad, and dangerous.

The Nile, flowing by my Aswan café terrace, had just

emerged from six concrete tunnels designed by the Russians (and not yet paid for) but built, as everything is, by fellahin.

The river still carried the tropical rains from the mountains of East Africa to the fields of Egypt, as it had done for a long time. Reflected on its inky surface, even the neon of Elephantine didn't look too awful.

FORTY-THREE

Philae, the pearl of Egypt, little island south of Aswan, is closed to visitors. It's about to go under in the Nile. All that tourists are now allowed is to walk over the cofferdam surrounding it and look down.

But by great good luck I had one more of those letters of mine, this one to Abdis Siyan, director of Aswan antiquities. Mr. Siyan wasn't particularly jolly or happy to see me, but who needs jolliness? He was there, which was what counted, and he said that if I paid for a taxi, he'd send someone with me and I could cross on the work launch and go to Philae. And so we did. We took the boat, Siyan's man installed himself somewhere on the cofferdam with his cigarettes, and I climbed down an improvised wooden staircase onto the island. It was to be my happiest monument.

Philae lies above the old dam of the British, and every time the sluices in that dam were closed in winter, the Nile, backing up behind it, covered Philae almost to the rooftops of its temples. Then the following summer Philae re-emerged, the temples still standing, covered with slime. But Philae had been one large garden, and after some winters of this all vegetation died. It was no longer anyone's pearl but a bare rock carrying slowly crumbling buildings: the two pylons and the Temple of Isis, a kiosk built during the days of the

Roman Empire, and five small temples spread on it, the prettiest of them dedicated to Hathor. Hathor was the goddess of love and of ecstasy, the one who became Aphrodite in Greece.

Isis was the special goddess of Philae. She was the sister and wife of Osiris, god of the dead, and their son was Horus, who as a child is shown with his finger to his lips, the god of silence. The worship of these three marked the last blooming of ancient Egypt, here and over the entire Roman Empire. It was mystical and sensual, and it gave way only to Christianity, and that quite late. On Philae the Temple of Isis was used until the middle of the sixth century, just thirty generations ago. In its sanctuary stood her sacred boat, with a chamber on each side lying in darkness. Its Birth House showed the birth of Horus, and Isis in the marshes of the Delta, feeding the god at her breast.

The High Dam lies above Philae. The Nile no longer rises and falls, and Philae will now be covered by water, eight feet deep, all year round. As part of the Nubian temple-saving program, UNESCO came to help. The temples of Philae are being taken down, and they will be rebuilt on Agilkia, a neighboring island of like size and orientation which sits well above the new level of the river. It is rather sad, but better than letting Philae disintegrate into the waters.

The High Dam Civil Works Company has already flattened the surface of Agilkia with dynamite, and built the cofferdam and put in the pumps to keep Philae dry a little longer. In the meantime, the Condotte Mazzi Estero firm of Rome was taking everything apart and carrying it to its new place. Formally, it's all under the Cairo minister of culture and under Mr. Hanna Botros, the local official, who works from a prefab on the nasty strip of desert across from Philae where the work launch moors. But the Italians ignore the Egyptians, and no sooner had I made my appearance at the foot of the stairs, than their headman came up and told me to be off again, and never mind what Abdis Siyan or Botros had said. I persuaded him to let me stay, which was a struggle.

The Italians blended in nicely with the scene. The sun had darkened them as much as any Egyptian, and they were funny with their white shorts and sun hats and dangling cigarettes, measuring and hoisting and shouting. This was an awesome enterprise. Every bit of stone and statue was delineated. The angles of each item's position were drawn in with yellow paint lines, distances were noted down to a twentieth of an inch, and every piece was numbered and catalogued. The whole enterprise looked like nothing so much as a film location, but it was grimly serious, and a broken or lost figure could never be replaced. This operation would take two to three years in all.

It may seem odd that being there was a happy experience, but this wasn't destruction, it was salvaging, and with much loving care. And the monument being taken apart became more real in this workmanlike setup than temples and pyramids I've seen, roped in as they were by touts and peddlers and sold peep by peep to the poor tourists in their Bedouin headdresses. The Italians were drawing lines and attaching wires to Isis's temple, but they showed her every respect.

The cofferdam had kept Philae dry now for quite some time, and between the paving stones and in the cracked columns new plants were pushing up: grass and little thistles and dusty thickleaves. A green hue over the grey stone, and blue all over and around it: an Egyptian tricolor. I picked one of the plants as a souvenir, for time was running out on it all and this was their very last season. As I stood in the sanctuary, shouts and commands were exchanged outside, a ray of light appeared, and very slowly, a stone beam went up in the air.

They didn't want the bother if a column dropped on my

head, and I was asked to get away from there. I sat in the temple gateway, put the plant between the last pages of my notebook, and copied out some of the inscriptions. The gateway cuts through the temple pylon. It was built by a Ptolemy, the second successor to Alexander the Great, and it showed reliefs in which he was doing his things. Emperor Tiberius had put himself in there, too. It opened to the south, but the cofferdam cut off the sight of the river. The sun had got around to it and lit up the stone, coloring it almost white.

Facing the Ptolemy and Tiberius, on the east wall, was something much more recent: a long text in French. That sounds terrible but it was not. It was the last, and the last appropriate and fitting, of those heroic inscriptions there. It also celebrated an army of the last emperor in history who traveled and fought on foot and on horseback, and it was executed in a fine, simple script.

I am not generalizing: I know French travelers and tourists are as nice or as nasty as any others. But sometimes the French do have an instinct for things. Those words were chiseled in the stone by a sculptor, Jean-Jacques Castex; and which army but that Egyptian one of Napoleon had sculptors and painters in its train? They went along with the troops that chased the Mamelukes from Cairo to beyond the First Cataract, and they stopped to draw and paint between battles and had to be dragged away from temples as the cavalry charges began. Undoubtedly the Mamelukes were the bad guys, the greatest despoilers of Egypt of them all, and thus there is nothing to mar my sympathy for that expedition upriver and for those men who were really the first Westerners to see it all—at that time, you needed a whole army as an escort.

There has never since been anything made here to compare with their great atlas, *The Description of Egypt*, with all its temples, monuments, pyramids, birds, trees, and people—ten volumes of text, fourteen volumes of drawings and paintings. They were men of their time in that they were fearless in those surroundings; they were carried by the idea of their Republic.

On that Philae wall, Castex had engraved how, "In the Sixth Year of the Republic, an army commanded by Bonaparte, on the 13th Messidor," defeated the Mamelukes at the Pyramids, pursued them to beyond the Cataracts, and arrived here, *"le 13 Ventôse de l'An 7,"* which was, the third of March of the year 1799.

They were the first from the West.

And as, on my morning, Isis had her sanctuary taken down, I felt I was the last.

Back in Aswan, I was asked by the antiquities director to go and see the temple of Abu Simbel, which is, or was, a hundred and eighty miles farther upstream, just north of the Tropic of Cancer. Abu Simbel wasn't "constructed." It and the four gigantic statues in front of it were hewn out of the local mountain; the rock wasn't removed, it was shaped. And the temple was oriented in such a way that twice a year the rays of the rising sun shone straight down those long corridors and lit up the deepest chamber.

I didn't go and take the hydrofoil to have a look. For Abu Simbel, as it was, is under the surface of Lake Nasser. The temple and its colossi have been sawed out and carried up the cliff, where they are high and dry. I'm certain it is still a beautiful sight, but I didn't want to see it.

The architects of Ramses II who designed the temple and its guardians somehow overcame the impossible problems of this project. I have an old book on Egypt which says of them, "Giants themselves, they summoned those giants from solid rock. They took a mountain and fell upon it, they cut out four huge statues, with their faces to the sunrise. Two sit at the right and two at the left of the doorway—here to keep watch to the end of time."

But modern man keeps his own calendar, and at Abu Simbel the end of time had already come.

4200 901   5591

916.2
K   Koningsberger,
             Hans.

             A New Yorker in
             Egypt

DATE		

5-77

WILMINGTON PUBLIC LIBRARY
409 MARKET STREET
WILMINGTON, N. C.   28401

Ⓓ THE BAKER & TAYLOR CO.

W9-BKZ-413

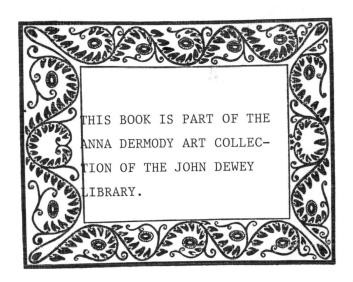

THIS BOOK IS PART OF THE
ANNA DERMODY ART COLLEC-
TION OF THE JOHN DEWEY
LIBRARY.

TURNER

LUKE HERRMANN

TURNER

Paintings, Watercolors, Prints & Drawings

John Dewey Library
Johnson State College
Johnson, Vermont 05658

NEW YORK GRAPHIC SOCIETY · BOSTON

459.2
T854
DH436t
C,2
80-3460

For Mark and Jeremy

Copyright © 1975 by Phaidon Press Limited

All rights reserved.
No part of this book may be reproduced in any form or by any electronic or mechanical means including information storage and retrieval systems without permission in writing from the publisher, except by a reviewer who may quote brief passages in a review.

International Standard Book Number: 0–8212–0657–5
Library of Congress Catalog Card Number: 75–9101

First published in England by Phaidon Press Limited
First published in 1975 in the United States by New York Graphic Society Ltd., 11 Beacon Street, Boston, Massachusetts 02108

Printed in The Netherlands

Contents

Acknowledgements

THE PUBLISHERS are grateful to the following for allowing works in their collections to be reproduced:

Bedford, Cecil Higgins Museum: 39, 80; Birmingham City Art Gallery: 101; Boston, Museum of Fine Arts: 148; Bury Art Gallery, Lancashire: 110; Cardiff, National Museum of Wales: 19; Cleveland Museum of Art, Ohio: 133; Edinburgh, The National Gallery of Scotland: 63, 149; Farnley Hall, Yorkshire, G. N. Le G. Horton-Fawkes: 70; Glasgow Art Gallery: 154; Indianapolis, Mr. and Mrs. Kurt F. Panzer: 3, 172; Indianapolis, Museum of Art: 23, 71, 73, 119; Lisbon, Calouste Gulbenkian Foundation: 32; Liverpool, Walker Art Gallery: 24, 160, 183; Lockinge, Berkshire, Christopher Loyd: 66; London, British Museum: 2, 9, 17, 25, 26, 29, 36, 37, 46, 47, 48, 50, 51, 59, 82, 87, 88, 91, 95, 96, 97, 98, 99, 100, 102, 103, 105, 112, 114, 115, 116, 129, 130, 131, 132, 135, 166, 167, 170, 171, 184, 185, 186, 187, 189, 190; London, Courtauld Institute of Art, University of London: 14, 60, 74, 104, 171; London, The Iveagh Bequest, Kenwood: 31, 85; London, National Gallery: 11, 27, 30, 77, 106, 107, 142, 146, 175; London, Royal Academy of Arts: 22; London, Tate Gallery: 1, 10, 18, 20, 21, 33, 34, 43, 44, 52, 53, 55, 56, 57, 58, 72, 78, 81, 83, 84, 89, 90, 108, 109, 118, 120, 121, 122, 124, 125, 126, 127, 134, 136, 137, 140, 144, 145, 147, 150, 151, 153, 155, 156, 158, 161, 164, 165, 170, 173, 174, 176, 177, 178, 180, 181; London, Victoria and Albert Museum: 15, 44, 138, 157; Manchester, Whitworth Art Gallery, University of Manchester: 16; New York, Frick Collection: 94, 117; Oxford, Ashmolean Museum: 5, 6, 7, 8, 12, 35, 67, 68, 75, 76, 92, 111, 113, 162, 163; Petworth House, Sussex: 42, 45, 54, 62, 64, 123, 128; Philadelphia Museum of Art: 141; Private Collections: 40, 139, 169; Reading, Ruskin Collection, University of Reading: 4; Sheffield, Graves Art Gallery: 41; Tabley House, Cheshire, Lt. Col. J. L. B. Leicester-Warren: 61; The Toledo Museum of Art, Ohio: 159; Toronto, University of Toronto: 28; U.S.A., Mr and Mrs Paul Mellon: 38, 69, 86; Washington, J. Biddle: 168; Washington, National Gallery of Art: 143; Windsor Castle, Her Majesty Queen Elizabeth II: 13.

Foreword

THE ILLUSTRATIONS form the core of this book. They have been chosen to provide a balanced visual survey of the work of Turner; at the time of writing this book provides the largest body of illustrations of his work yet published. Turner was one of the most prolific and varied artists that the world has known, and to achieve such a survey within the limitation of 190 plates was not easy. But Turner is an artist, as he himself was the first to realise, who must be looked at as 'a whole'. The plates are supported by the *Introduction*, which can be read as a running commentary on them, though in itself it furnishes a chronological account of the life and work of Turner. The essential 'catalogue' information relating to each work reproduced is given in the caption, and, where relevant, further points and references are to be found in the *Notes on the Plates*. The basic facts about Turner can be found in the *Biographical Outline*, while the selection of *Contemporary Reviews and Comments* will give the reader a fuller idea of the artist's character and reputation.

The sources of most of this material can be found in the *Bibliography*. It is at this point that I must acknowledge my indebtedness to all previous writers on Turner, notably, among my predecessors, A. J. Finberg, and, among my contemporaries, John Gage. I also owe much to those curators and private collectors in Britain and the United States who have assisted me in my studies of the art of Turner, many of whom have now generously granted permission for works in their museum or collection to be reproduced in this book. In the case of several items from private collections Evelyn Joll was instrumental in obtaining reproduction permission and providing photographs.

The illustrations for this book had been chosen and the bulk of the text written some months before the opening of the great Turner Bi-Centenary Exhibition at the Royal Academy in November 1974. Selected and organised by Martin Butlin, John Gage and Andrew Wilton, this presented a much larger survey of Turner than the present work could hope to do. However, the two surveys coincide at numerous points, especially in closing with a retrospective section devoted to Turner's depiction of Norham Castle on the Tweed. In the final stages of writing *Turner* I have been considerably stimulated by the Exhibition and its *Catalogue*, though they in no way affected the overall conception and realisation of my book. It has been most encouraging for a confirmed addict of Turner that the Exhibition has opened the eyes of a vast public to the wealth of treasure in the Turner Bequest. That paintings, drawings and prints have been available for study under the same roof has been especially welcomed by those who hitherto have had no idea of the unity of Turner's work. For nearly a century the housing of the Turner Bequest was a matter of recurring controversy, but in recent decades the present arrangements have been taken for granted. There is now again hope that a permanent Turner Gallery may at last become a reality; only then can full advantage be taken of the artist's unique gift to the Nation.

FOREWORD

This book owes much to a number of people at the Phaidon Press. Keith Roberts initiated the book and guided it skilfully through its early stages. Virginia Chapman devoted considerable time and energy to obtaining photographs and reproduction permissions. Susan Waterston has been a helpful and perceptive editor, and Jean-Claude Peissel an ideal designer who seemed to 'take naturally' to Turner. To all these I am immensely grateful. I must also thank Phyl Walker, who did the typing with great efficiency, though usually working against the clock. My final debt of gratitude is to my wife, Georgina, who exercised her editorial skills to excellent effect, even though, in this case, the author was prone to growl at her.

Clipston, 31 December 1974.   L.H.

TURNER WAS BORN IN LONDON, where he lived all his life. He was exceptionally endowed with the cockney qualities of curiosity and forthrightness. To these were added outstanding powers of observation, assimilation and expression. It was the combination of all these gifts that made him one of the most exciting and original of British artists. It is often the fate of a pioneering artist to be ignored in his own time and to achieve little material success. There was no period in Turner's long career of sixty years when he was not making money, and during the last fifty he was generally regarded by the majority of his fellow artists and by many critics and connoisseurs as the leading British painter of the day. During the final twenty years of his life he enjoyed acclaim throughout Europe, and since his death he has never lost his place on the list of Europe's greatest artists. What Shakespeare is in the realm of British literature, Turner is in the realm of art.

Both these great Englishmen were born on St. George's Day, 23 April. The year of Turner's birth was 1775; the American War of Independence had just begun, and the Royal Academy in London under the Presidency of Sir Joshua Reynolds was only seven years old. When Turner died, at the close of 1851, Napoleon III was seizing power in France, the Great Exhibition had taken place, and Sir Charles Eastlake had recently been elected the sixth President of the Royal Academy. In the year of Turner's birth the Norwich coach was waylaid in Epping Forest by seven highwaymen; by the time of his death the chief main lines of the modern railway system of England had been largely completed or authorised. In every sphere Turner's life-span was a period of tremendous change and development, and he is the only British painter of the time whose work truly reflected the spirit of progress of these years. In art the normal tendency was to look back to the past rather than to create a style in keeping with the advances in other fields; to this tendency Turner's work in the last twenty-five years of his life was a notable exception. Another such exception was, of course, John Constable (1776–1837), but in retrospect his advances in landscape painting appear more insular and limited than those of Turner. Constable's work exerted a strong influence on contemporary artists in Britain and France, which Turner's painting did not do, because it was too advanced and individual. On the other hand Constable never travelled abroad and even travelled relatively little in the British Isles, while Turner visited and drew in most counties of England, Wales and Scotland, and made numerous journeys on the Continent.

We do not really know Turner as a man, because both at home and abroad he kept himself very much to himself. Though he is two centuries closer to our own time the unresolved mysteries of his life are almost as great as those in the life of Shakespeare. Turner's withdrawn and introspective character is reflected in the obscurity of his own poetry and other writing, which usually add to the mystery rather than helping to resolve it. The same is true of much of his painting, especially in the second half of his working life. Many of his later exhibition canvases elude interpretation in anything other than abstract visual terms. There are also several phases in his development as an artist which defy confident dating and assessment, while in the explanation of matters of technique numerous paintings and drawings by Turner continue to defeat the experts. All these negative elements in the study of Turner are outweighed by the fact that the majority of his paintings and drawings provide sufficient visual pleasure and satisfaction to ensure our appreciation. This was the case in his own day when the much publicized adverse criticism was more than equalled by the writing of critics who were inclined to praise, though they too were often puzzled by what they had seen.

In modern times appreciation of Turner's work has changed quite considerably from generation to generation. It is only in relatively recent years that his late work, including the 'unfinished' canvases and watercolours not intended for exhibition or sale, has come to be valued as highly as the more traditional earlier Turner. For a time this change took place at the expense of the popularity of such earlier work, but today we have, perhaps, reached a stage when the art of Turner is looked at as a whole — a whole in which each phase of development plays an essential part. This is how Turner himself regarded his art and wanted it to be judged by posterity. Hence his elaborate plans, including the buying back of crucial canvases, for a Turner Gallery. These plans have never been fulfilled, but as more and more of the Turner Bequest becomes known to the public an all-round picture of Turner is at last a possibility. It is the aim of the present volume to provide such a picture in miniature, and every effort has been made to strike a balance between all the phases of Turner's output in all media.

Despite his greatness it is possible to be critical of Turner in a way that is not usually practised in relation to other great artists, such as Raphael or Rembrandt. Thus much has been made of Turner's apparent difficulties in drawing or painting human figures and animals. On rare occasions Turner succeeded in overcoming this weakness in a conventional way; on others he achieved convincing abstractions. He was no doubt aware of this weakness, but would not allow his art to be limited by it. As the variety of his subject matter shows Turner was far more than just a landscape painter. Apart from portraiture he tackled almost every aspect of painting known in his day, and in all of them he found material to enrich his art. The 'all-round' qualities of Turner's art have been too little appreciated, but such appreciation is essential if he is to be considered as a whole.

Turner's success as an all-round painter was based on two factors; his close study and recording of nature on the one hand, and his deep knowledge and understanding of the painting and drawing of earlier and contemporary artists on the other. These two factors, combined with his incredible visual memory and his inexhaustible imagination, lie at the heart of all his own work. It is the interaction between them that leads to the extraordinary dichotomy between the traditional and the revolutionary that is found in so much of Turner's work.

Turner's artistic training and early work were, however, wholly traditional. Warmly encouraged by his father, a Covent Garden barber, Turner had already been drawing for several years when he became a student at the Royal Academy Schools late in 1789. At about the same time he was also taking lessons from one of the leading architectural draughtsmen of the day, Thomas Malton, whose influence is much in evidence in works such as *The Pantheon, the Morning after the Fire*, which is signed and dated 1792 (Plate 9). He exhibited his first watercolour at the Royal Academy in 1790; this is a somewhat crude view of *The Archbishop's Palace, Lambeth*, in which, however, the young artist has mastered the complex problems of perspective which he set himself. In the Lambeth drawing the influence of Paul Sandby (Plate 13) can be traced; other artists to whom Turner looked at this time were J. R. Cozens and Edward Dayes. By adopting the standards established by such men, which had recently made the water-colour school a major element of English art, he quickly developed as a topographical watercolour artist of exceptional ability. In the 1790s Turner undertook sketching tours in many parts of Britain, and in the second half of the decade he already had more commissions for drawings of specific views and places than he could cope with, while he was also beginning to work for the engravers. Thus the pleasant view of *Chepstow Castle* (Plate 14) was engraved for the *Copper-Plate Magazine* in 1794.

At this time Turner was on very friendly terms with Thomas Girtin, his senior by only two months, who had also achieved a leading position among the topographical artists of the day (Plate 15). Girtin and Turner were often together in the winter evenings in London, working for Dr. Thomas Monro, who employed them to make copies of drawings by J. R. Cozens and others (Plate 16). In such copies and in other drawings of these years their work is often virtually indistinguishable; if it were not in one of Turner's sketch-books, such a study as '*Nunwell and Brading from Bembridge Mill*' (Plate 17) could well be mistaken for the work of Girtin. It is often said that in the later 1790s Girtin made greater progress in the development of watercolours than Turner, but at their best Turner's drawings of these years, such as the elegant *Transept of Tintern Abbey* (Plate 8), certainly equalled those of his friend. But while Girtin was content to devote himself entirely to watercolours for the rest of his tragically short life (he died in 1802), Turner also began to paint in oils. He was the more ambitious of the two, and he knew that he could only achieve the much coveted membership of the Royal Academy by exhibiting oil paintings; he showed his first, *Fishermen at Sea* (Plate 18), in 1796.

Apart from the work of the watercolour artists there was no strong current style in English landscape painting in the closing years of the eighteenth century. Thus for his oil painting Turner had to seek inspiration from earlier masters. At first he looked to such seventeenth-century Dutch marine artists as the Van de Veldes (see Plate 30) and Aert van der Neer, then to the first of the great British landscape painters, Richard Wilson, who had died in 1782, and finally, through the example of Wilson, to the leading artists of the classical landscape tradition, Claude and Poussin. Turner was never strongly influenced by the landscape painting of Thomas Gainsborough or his precursor Rubens, though he owed much to the similarly atmospheric landscape compositions of Salvator Rosa and Rembrandt. Rembrandt's influence may be detected in one of Turner's greatest early watercolours, the richly lit and evocative interior of *Ewenny Priory* (Plate 19), which he exhibited at the Academy in 1797.

Turner's early concern with the depiction of atmosphere is seen again in one of the four oil paintings that he showed in 1798, *Buttermere Lake with Part of Cromackwater, Cumberland, a Shower* (Plate 10). Each of the four paintings and one of the watercolours exhibited that year has an indication of time of day, season or weather in its title, and such indications were to be a constant feature of Turner's catalogue entries. In *Buttermere Lake* Turner has made full use of his powers of observation in the presentation of an English scene which he had visited, and recorded in his sketch-book, in 1797; in *Aeneas and the Sibyl, Lake Avernus* (Plate 20) which was also painted in about 1798, he has relied on another artist's drawing and on his imagination in effectively depicting an Italian scene some twenty years before his first visit to Italy. Here the influence of Richard Wilson is paramount (see Plate 21), and it is to be found again in the *Dolbadern Castle* (Plate 22), which Turner exhibited in 1800. In this emotive painting of a gaunt ruin in North Wales we witness the development from the picturesque qualities of works such as *Chepstow Castle* and *Buttermere Lake* to a vision that is already truly romantic. That quality is even more strongly displayed in Turner's first exhibited historical painting, *The Fifth Plague of Egypt* (actually the Seventh Plague), which was also shown in 1800 (Plate 23). Here again there are echoes of Wilson, but the most positive influence is that of Poussin.

The Fifth Plague was bought by William Beckford, the builder of Fonthill Abbey, of which Turner made a series of large watercolour drawings, four of which were also shown at the Academy of 1800. Turner's watercolours continued to be much in demand, both with patrons like Beckford and Sir Richard Colt Hoare of Stourhead, and with engravers and publishers, such as the Oxford University Press, who commissioned the first two of ten drawings for the headpieces of the *Oxford Almanack* in 1798. The first of these drawings, *South View of Christ Church, &c. from the Meadows* (Plate 12) was engraved in 1799. It shows Turner at the height of his powers as a topographical artist. His ability to use watercolour in even more ambitious ways was displayed by such forceful compositions as *Pembroke Castle, South Wales: Thunder Storm approaching* (Plate 28), shown at the R.A. in 1801, and *The Fall of the Clyde, Lanarkshire: Noon* (Plate 24), exhibited in 1802. In these relatively large works Turner is clearly trying to achieve the impact of an oil painting in the less respected medium of watercolour. He also continued to use watercolour in a more natural manner in on-the-spot studies like *Edinburgh from St. Margaret's Loch* (Plate 25), a page in one of the sketch-books used on his visit to Scotland in 1801.

A series of vivid studies made on the Scottish coast was probably to hand when Turner was at work on one of his first mature marine compositions, *Fishermen upon a Lee-Shore, in squally Weather* (Plate 31). He showed this in 1802, the year in which he was elected a full member of the Royal Academy, only two and a quarter years after he had been made an Associate. It will be remembered that his first exhibited oil painting was a sea-scape; the sea in all its moods was to remain one of Turner's most constant and fruitful themes. He found in it an absorbing subject for study; in addition to numerous Scottish shore sketches he filled two small sketch-books with pencil, pen and ink, and occasionally wash, drawings specifically connected with *Fishermen on a Lee-Shore*, such as that reproduced here as Plate 29. The best known major marine painting of the first decade of the century is *Calais Pier, with French Poissards preparing for Sea: an English Packet arriving* (Plate 11), which was exhibited in 1803. This, like *Fishermen on a Lee-Shore*, is concerned with an ordinary, albeit dramatic, occurrence at sea, which Turner himself had experienced at the end of his first crossing of the Channel in 1802, as opposed to the more traditional subject matter, in the Dutch manner, of the sea paintings that immediately preceded these, such as "The Bridgewater Sea-piece" of 1801. In these paintings of real happenings at sea, which culminated in the *Wreck of a Transport Ship* (Plate 32), painted in about 1807 and now in Lisbon, Turner shows his preoccupation with achieving vivid effects of light and atmosphere—raging sea and stormy sky are linked by the play of light on the boats and figures. In striking contrast with such dramatic scenes but equally atmospheric in its effect, is the calm of *Sun rising through Vapour: Fishermen cleaning and selling Fish* (Plate 27), which was exhibited in 1807.

In the summer after his election to the Academy Turner took advantage of the Peace of Amiens and made his first tour abroad, spending some five months in France and Switzerland. He was particularly inspired by the Swiss mountains; here he was in the midst of that grandeur and scale which his increasingly romantic outlook demanded. During this tour he used six sketch-books, in the largest of which he made several studies which he coloured (probably at his inn in the evening) such as the *Mer de Glace, Chamonix* and *The Old Devil's Bridge, St. Gothard* (reproduced as Plates 37 and 36). Here again Turner had moved away from recording topography and was preoccupied with achieving specific effects of light and tone. He used these studies to work up some of the most spectacular subjects for large exhibition watercolours. Despite their scale and degree of finish these achieve a remarkable feeling of immediacy; in *The Mer de Glace and Source of the Arveyron, Chamonix* (Plate 38) there is a sense of movement in the weather and the trees as there would be on a stormy day in the mountains. This is rendered by the skilful use of the pen or point of the brush, while the high-lights—the snow, the clouds and the goats—are achieved by leaving the white paper bare and by scratching out (scraping away the pigment to reveal the paper where a highlight is desired). Such a watercolour as *The Mer de Glace* demonstrates Turner's experimental methods, which were always most strongly brought out in his work when he was faced with a fresh experience, such as his first visit to the Alps. These same experimental methods were used to equal effect in *The Great Falls of the Reichenbach* (Plate 39), which was probably among the works shown by Turner in 1804 at the first exhibition in his own gallery, which had just been completed in Harley Street.

For his first oil paintings of the continental scenery Turner chose more placid subjects than for his watercolours. *Bonneville, Savoy, with Mont Blanc* (Plate 40), one of two versions of this scene exhibited at the Royal Academy in 1803, contrasts the dominating grandeur of the mountains with the quiet scenery at their base. The composition has strong 'classical' characteristics, and reflects the influence of such classical landscape painters as Poussin and Gaspard Dughet, whose work he studied in the Louvre on his return journey from Switzerland. While in Paris Turner spent much of his time in the galleries, making copious and detailed notes in two sketch-books in which he concentrated especially on matters of colour and light. Though these notes do not include any reference to the work of Claude it is most probable that he studied that master's canvases while in the Louvre. The impact of Claude, who was, of course, exceptionally well represented in British collections (see Plates 42, 79), is seen in another of Turner's 1803 exhibits, *The Festival upon the Opening of the Vintage at Macon* (Plate 41), a traditional 'historical' landscape distinguished by its magnificent rolling distance. The fifth canvas shown by Turner in 1803 is different again, and leans heavily on the example of Titian, whose work was particularly well represented in the

Louvre in 1802. This was the *Holy Family* (Plate 43), which one fellow-artist, Fuseli, called 'the blot of a great master of colouring'.

Understandably the majority of artists and critics were puzzled by the diversity of Turner's contribution to the 1803 exhibition, five canvases and two watercolours, of which five are reproduced here (Plates 11, 38, 40, 41, 43). This was the first exhibition for which he had been able to prepare properly since his election as an R.A., and the choice of works which he showed was certainly a deliberate one. The *Calais Pier* and the two watercolours illustrated his advances and aims in two aspects of his work already familiar to the public; the remaining canvases announced his ambition to rival the achievements and reputations of some of the greatest old masters. Turner was just twenty-eight when the exhibition opened, but his work was discussed, however critically by some, as that of an established master. In one paper it was reported that he had 'so much debauched the taste of the young artists in this country by the empirical novelty of his style of painting that a humorous critic gave him the title of *over-Turner*'.

Turner's first tour abroad had an immense effect on his work, but because of the continuing war he was not able to repeat the experience until 1817. It seems that he was not tempted to recommence his lengthy sketching tours in the British Isles and now undertook longer journeys only when commissions for paintings of specific houses were involved. In 1806 and 1807 he exhibited several canvases of scenes on the Thames, and the evocative painting of *Windsor Castle from the Thames* (Plate 45) is thought to date from about this time, though a date of about 1812 has also been proposed for it. In its execution as well as in its mood this formalised view of Windsor has much in common with *The Goddess of Discord choosing the Apple of Contention in the Garden of Hesperides* (Plate 44), which Turner showed at the first exhibition of the British Institution in 1806. In the bold masses that feature in both compositions the influence of Poussin can again be seen, and even the preparatory study for the *Windsor Castle* (Plate 46) has a peculiarly seventeenth-century feeling about it.

This comes as no surprise when it is remembered that in 1806 Turner launched on an enterprise which was his most obvious imitation of a seventeenth-century precedent. This was the *Liber Studiorum*, a series of engravings of which the first Part of five plates was issued in June, 1807, the fourteenth and final Part was published in 1819, making a total of 71 published plates in all. The conception and the execution were based on Claude Lorrain's *Liber Veritatis*. That book of drawings, which is now in the British Museum, was begun by Claude in about 1635 and continued until the year of his death; in it he made careful copies of his paintings in order to combat forgeries and imitations. The book reached the Devonshire Collection (where Turner may well have seen it) quite early in the eighteenth century, and achieved widespread renown with the

1. *(opposite) Self-portrait. c.* 1798.
Oil on canvas;
$29\frac{1}{4} \times 23$ in. (742×584 mm.)
London, Tate Gallery.

INTRODUCTION

publication of Thomas Earlom's striking engravings after all the drawings in the 1770s.

The drawings for the *Liber Studiorum* plates are usually in pen and brown ink and wash, and are often close to those of Claude both in feeling and execution, as can be seen in *Isleworth* (Plate 47), which dates from about 1815. From that drawing Turner executed an etching (Plate 48), which was then engraved in mezzotint by H. Dawe (Plate 49) and issued in 1819 in Part XIII of the *Liber*. The process from drawing to engraving can be studied again in the series of reproductions of works depicting Norham Castle (Plates 187, 188). As in the case of the *Isleworth* the majority of the plates were etched by Turner himself, and he also closely supervised the work of the engravers who completed the plates, many of which he published himself. Thus this series was very much Turner's own work, and differs from most of the other engravings after his paintings and drawings, for which he simply provided the originals.

It was planned that the *Liber* should have a total of 100 plates, but it was never completed. The series was divided into a number of classifications such as 'Mountains', 'Pastoral' and 'History', and the compositions range from country scenes in the manner of George Morland to landscapes in the grandest Claudian vein. Turner's aim was to display his mastery and versatility in the most popular traditional and contemporary modes of landscape and marine painting. This policy was clearly demonstrated by the five plates of the first part, which consisted of a simple pastoral scene, *Bridge and Cows*; a Claudian classical landscape, *The Woman and Tambourine*; an atmospheric shore scene, *Scene on the French Coast*; a townscape, *Basle*, and an historical landscape, *Jason* (of which he had exhibited a painting in 1802).

While the work connected with the *Liber Studiorum* was somewhat reprospective in character Turner was not neglecting that search for new material which was essential to the development of his art. As usual this advance is to be seen first in his drawings; in this case confident watercolour studies in a large roll sketch-book, drawn on the spot at various points in the Thames Valley. One of these, *Scene on the Thames* (Plate 50) illustrates his preoccupation with problems of masses and light. The watercolour has been applied with a dry brush in a technique close to that of oil painting, and it comes as no surprise to find Turner making similar studies in oils on paper at about the same time. There is a small group of these in the Turner Bequest, which includes the *Chevening Park, Kent* (Plate 51) with its lovely evening atmosphere. These studies probably preceded the well-known series of 'pure' landscape sketches in oils on thin board, of scenes on the River Thames between Walton and Windsor, and on the smaller River Wey, a tributary of the Thames. Many of them, such as *The Thames near Walton Bridges* (Plate 33) appear to be taken from a boat—on board which, as a keen angler,

2. *The Artist's Studio. c.* 1808.
   Pen and ink and watercolour;
   $7\frac{1}{4} \times 11\frac{3}{4}$ in. (184 × 299 mm.)
   London, British Museum (CXXI B).

3. J. T. Smith,
   Turner in the Print Room at the British Museum. c. 1825.
   Watercolour;
   9 × 7 in. (228 × 178 mm.)
   Indianapolis, Mr. and Mrs. Kurt F. Pantzer.

Turner probably also had a rod. In contrast to the breadth of the river scene is the more detailed study of *Tree Tops and Sky, Guildford Castle* (Plate 34), in which the movement of the sky and the trees on a windy day is strikingly conveyed. There is a similar feeling of immediacy in the *Willows beside a Stream* (Plate 53), though this much larger painting, on canvas, is unlikely to have been painted entirely on the spot. Nevertheless it certainly belongs to this period of *plein-air* studies in which Turner appears to have been on the path which Constable later made his own. While the dating of about 1807 proposed by Finberg seems generally acceptable for these studies, some more recent scholars have suggested later dates such as 1812 for some of them. It must be remembered, in favour of Finberg's dating, that Turner rented a house on the river at Hammersmith in 1806, and though he continued to use his studio and gallery in Harley Street, he lived in Hammersmith with his father. He almost certainly owned a boat or boats, and excursions on the Thames must have been part of his everyday life.

The calm of the Thames studies was repeated in the majority of Turner's exhibited works in the closing years of the first decade of the century. We have already noted this quality in the *Sun rising through Vapour* (Plate 27), one of the two paintings shown at the Royal Academy in 1807. The second was a placid rural genre scene—*A country Blacksmith disputing upon the Price of Iron, and the Price charged to the Butcher for shoeing his Pony* (Plate 52) which, in its execution, resembles two interiors sketched in oils on paper at Knockholt when Turner was on a visit to his fellow-artist and friend William Wells. In his own gallery that year Turner showed several restful river views and there were more in the following year, when *The Forest of Bere* (Plate 54) was also exhibited. This has a wonderful quality of inner light which renders, as one contemporary critic put it, 'the mild radiance of a warm summer evening'.

In the summer of 1808 Turner travelled to Cheshire to paint two views of Tabley House, Sir John Leicester's seat near Knutsford. The resulting 'house portraits', in which the actual house is a minor feature, are a pair of somewhat Dutch compositions entitled when exhibited at the Academy in 1809, *Tabley, the Seat of Sir J. F. Leicester, Bart.: Windy Day* (Plate 61) and *Tabley, Cheshire, the Seat of Sir J. F. Leicester, Bart.: Calm Morning*. The idea of such contrasting portrayals of the same seat was not a novel one—George Lambert and Paul Sandby were among earlier artists who had produced such pairs—but the views of Tabley were exceptionally well received, and their success led to further commissions for paintings of their houses from the Earls of Egremont and Lonsdale. *Petworth, Sussex: Dewy Morning* (Plate 62) is an evocative scene which convincingly depicts the harmony of the great house at Petworth and its beautiful park. The atmosphere of the more rugged Westmorland surroundings of the rather brash Lowther Castle (it was still being built at the time of Turner's visit in

1809) is also subtly conveyed in the mid-day and evening portrayals of that house, and in one of the three drawings connected with this commission which are in the Ashmolean Museum (Plate 35). In this preliminary study just enough watercolour is used in the distance and in the finely drawn thistle in the foreground to achieve this effect. The fine country house 'portraits' of these years, in which Turner displayed his understanding of the variations of the English countryside and weather, reached their climax with the well known view of *Somer Hill, Tonbridge*, which was exhibited in 1811 (Plate 63). Here the sheet of water in the foreground, reflecting the gentle lights in the sky, enhances an overall feeling of harmony and unity in the scene, into which the house fits with absolute naturalness.

In all these compositions water plays a vital role, as it does in the glowing Dutch landscapes of Aelbert Cuyp (Plate 64) which strongly influenced Turner at this stage of his development. This is most clearly seen in such a tranquil riverside scene as *Dorchester Mead, Oxfordshire* (Plate 65) which dates from 1810. A misty summer morning in the Thames valley is rendered with great skill, and, as in so many of Constable's slightly later Stour valley landscapes, the animals and figures play an essential role in achieving this effect of 'truth to nature'. Though they are smaller in scale, the same is true in the more classical *Whalley Bridge and Abbey, Lancashire: Dyers washing and drying Cloth* (Plate 66), which is based on a sketch-book drawing made on his way to Tabley House in 1808. The painting was exhibited at the Royal Academy in 1811.

Another influence on Turner was that of his neighbour at Hammersmith, the veteran fellow-member of the Royal Academy P. J. de Loutherbourg (1740–1812), who was the last survivor of the leading British landscape painters of the eighteenth century. In 1804 Loutherbourg had exhibited what was to become his best-known work, *An Avalanche in the Alps* (Plate 55), in which his experiences as a stage designer and as a landscape artist are combined to produce a truly romantic vision. Six years later, in 1810, Turner showed in his own gallery his *The Fall of an Avalanche in the Grisons* (Plate 56). In this somewhat smaller canvas the romantic drama of the scene is enhanced by the subdued and sombre colouring, and the whole composition focusses on the huge rock about to crush the cottage in its path. Nature is left to speak for itself—there are no figures.

In the caption for *The Fall of an Avalanche* Turner printed some lines of his own verse based on a passage from Thomson's *Winter*; for the vast historical landscape of *Apollo and Python*, which he showed at the R.A. in the following year, he produced his own paraphrase of some of the eighteenth-century translations of Callimachus's *Hymn to Apollo*. When he exhibited his great *Snowstorm: Hannibal and his Army crossing the Alps*

(Plate 57) in 1812 the title was accompanied in the catalogue by an eleven-line 'quotation' from his own manuscript poem, *Fallacies of Hope*. This was the first of many such 'quotations', for with his immense inventiveness Turner found it easier to create his own poetic captions than to hunt for suitable ones by established poets. As has been shown by several recent writers, Turner was deeply read in English poetry Milton, Thomson, Gray and Akenside being among his favourites. His own verse was usually stilted and pompous, relying rather on the sound of the words than their meaning. He considered the connection between painting and poetry to be a vital one, as he postulated in some of his lectures as Professor of Perspective at the Royal Academy. Having been appointed to that position in 1807 he did not deliver his first series of lectures until 1811. The surviving records and notes of these lectures, which he continued to deliver spasmodically until 1828, are confused and uncertain, and they have yet to be adequately deciphered and edited. However, for Turner the lectures were of great importance, as the long time of careful preparation he needed before giving the first course demonstrates. The period during which he gave these lectures was one of immense significance in Turner's own development as an artist, and if they can ever be intelligibly presented, the lectures should provide a valuable insight into that development. Unfortunately both Turner's prose and poetry prove that his skill with words left much to be desired.

While Turner certainly gained inspiration from reading poetry and even from writing his own poetry, the main source of his art was his constant study of nature. Thus the *Fall of an Avalanche* is yet another product—however indirect—of his visit to the Alps in 1802, while the conception of the *Hannibal* is associated with a severe thunderstorm he witnessed when on a visit to Farnley Hall in Yorkshire during which he was seen to be making notes; after the storm had passed he told his host's son, 'in two years you will see this again and call it Hannibal crossing the Alps'.

Having travelled relatively little for some years, Turner undertook another of his long sketching tours in 1811. He visited Dorset, Devon, Cornwall and Somerset, travelling over 600 miles in some two months and filling at least four sketch-books, with drafts of descriptive verse liberally interspersed among the drawings. The object of this journey was to collect material for a series of engravings to be published by W. B. Cooke, and it seems that Turner may have had the idea of also supplying a verse text for this publication, *Picturesque Views of the Southern Coast of England*. The forty engravings appeared at intervals (without the verses) between 1814 and 1826, and were the first of a considerable number of such topographical series which took up much of Turner's time and energy in the middle years of his career. These engravings quickly enhanced Turner's reputation with a public far wider than the London exhibitions attracted and the income they brought the artist provided the basis of his fortune. It is possible that he first undertook such work because of his need for money—early in 1811 he had made major alterations to his London house and gallery, including moving the entrance from Harley Street to Queen Ann Street West, and a few months earlier he had bought some land in Twickenham, on which he built an elegant small house of his own design, first called Solus Lodge and then Sandycombe Lodge (see Plate 7). Now in his late thirties, Turner was firmly established as a man of some means, and in the background he had his mistress, Sarah Danby, and her family, including his own two daughters, to maintain.

He made a second such sketching tour, to Devonshire, in 1813, and it was probably during this that Turner executed another of his rare series of oil studies from nature, of which this distant view of *Falmouth Harbour* (Plate 59) is one of the most successful. The paint is broadly and economically applied and the colouring is entirely naturalistic. The same somewhat dry technique is found in the watercolours of this period, such as *Sunshine on the Tamar* (Plate 67), which is based on a pencil sketch also made during the second Devonshire tour. Turner was definitely adapting his watercolour methods to suit the needs of the engraver working on copper. While more fluid and translucent watercolours and washes could be adequately reproduced in mezzotint or aquatint, for copper engraving somewhat firmer tones and outlines were desirable. That precision and firmness is seen in the foreground and middle distance of the watercolour of *The Junction of the Greta and Tees at Rokeby* (Plate 68). This was executed about 1816–18 and engraved in 1819 for Whitaker's *History of Richmondshire*, as was *The Crook of Lune* (Plate 60) in 1821. In both these fine drawings Turner has used an elaborate stipple technique in which the numerous strokes of the pointed brush are reminiscent of the small lines and dashes made by the engraver's burin. The colour schemes are subtle and harmonious within quite a narrow range, largely of yellows, greens and browns, which again coincides with the variations in tone available to the engraver. The same technique can be seen in the drawing of *Leeds* (Plate 69), dated 1816, though when this was reproduced for a history of the city lithography was used, perhaps because it was considered a better method to render the smoke shrouding the city in the middle distance.

The three watercolours which have just been discussed are all of Yorkshire subjects. From 1810 onwards Turner paid regular visits to the county, where he was a welcome guest at Farnley Hall, the home of his early patron and friend Walter Fawkes, whose first purchase of a work by Turner was the large Alpine watercolour shown at the Royal Academy in 1803 (Plate 38). Walter Fawkes, who was only six years older than Turner, was a man of advanced ideas who had read and travelled widely. He was an enlightened landowner, and took a particular interest in the breeding of cattle. Farnley

Hall is an attractive house, splendidly situated overlooking the valley of the Wharfe, and Turner was clearly at his happiest and most relaxed while staying there. The house was soon filled with his watercolours, and the lovely *Valley of the Wharfe from Caley Park* (Plate 70) is among those that are still there today. There is also an album of beautiful small watercolour studies of birds, which Turner drew for members of the family and in which he again proved his instinctive feeling for colour and texture. A few of the bird studies made at Farnley were dispersed, among them the *Sketch of a Pheasant* (Plate 76), which belonged to John Ruskin, and which he may have been given on his first visit to Farnley in 1851. Another Farnley drawing owned at one time by Ruskin, which in its meticulous detail contrasts strangely with the bold study of the dead pheasant, is *A Frontispiece (at Farnley Hall)* (Plate 75), which is dated 1815. This was drawn as a frontispiece for 'Fairfaxiana', a set of drawings Turner made of subjects relating to the Fairfax property which had come into Mr. Fawkes' family. Though damaged, the drawing still convincingly illustrates the absolute precision with which Turner could use watercolours.

Turner showed only two paintings at the Royal Academy in 1813—there had been some unpleasantness about the hanging of the *Hannibal* in the previous year. One of these two, *Frosty Morning* (Plate 58) was well received, though, like so many of Turner's paintings in these years, it did not find a buyer. In the following year Turner somewhat surprisingly submitted *Apullia in Search of Appullus* (Plate 72) as a candidate for the British Institution's annual premium for landscape painting. Here was an heroic landscape in the best Claudian tradition—a complete contrast to the natural simplicity of the *Frosty Morning*—but it did not win the prize, which was awarded to T. C. Hofland for a marine in the Dutch manner. One of the judges was Sir George Beaumont, whose violent criticisms of Turner's work reached a head in the following year. Turner had three canvases and five watercolours at the Royal Academy—of which four, one painting and three drawings, had been shown in his own gallery some years earlier. The remaining two paintings were *Crossing the Brook* (Plate 78) and *Dido building Carthage; or the Rise of the Carthaginian Empire* (Plate 77). These were widely praised by numerous critics and fellow-artists, and have always been recognised as Turner's outstanding masterpieces in his two Claudian manners. However, Sir George was reported as saying of the latter that 'the picture is painted in a false taste, not true to nature; the colouring discordant, out of harmony', and of *Crossing the Brook* that 'it appeared to him *weak* and like the work of an Old man, one who no longer saw or felt colour properly; it was all of *pea-green* insipidity'.

Despite its Italianate character *Crossing the Brook* is, in fact, based on drawings made in Devonshire in 1813, when Charles Eastlake was Turner's travelling companion.

Eastlake later recorded 'the bridge is Calstock Bridge; some mining works are indicated in the middle distance. The extreme distance extends to the mouth of the Tamar, the hills of Mount Edgcumbe, and those on the opposite side of Plymouth Sound. The whole scene is extremely faithful.' *Dido building Carthage* on the other hand, is an imaginary composition, closely related to Claude's *Seaport: The Embarkation of the Queen of Sheba* which was then in the Angerstein Collection in London. One of the many critics who praised these two paintings so profusely, wrote of the *Dido building Carthage*: 'the eye rests but a moment on this picture before its transcendent qualities completely occupy the mind, and it is felt to be one of those sublime productions which are seldom met with. . . . This is a fine work which, in grandeur and ideal beauty, Claude never equalled.' Turner was just forty years old, and judging from the general reception given to his Academy exhibits of 1815 there can be no doubt that he was considered not only the leading landscape painter of the day, but also an artist to be thought of side by side with some of the greatest of the old masters.

The Napoleonic wars had confined Turner to the British Isles since 1802, but he waited for two years after the Battle of Waterloo before crossing the Channel again in August 1817. This time he sailed to Ostend, and after a few days in Belgium, including a visit to the Waterloo battlefield, he spent just under two weeks exploring the banks of the Rhine from Cologne to Mainz. He then travelled for a similar period in Holland, sailing back from Rotterdam to Hull in the middle of September. Turner filled four sketch-books—three small and one large—on this tour with slight and rapid pencil drawings usually confined to the bare outlines of the scene he was recording, occasionally annotated with colour and other notes. Some two months after his return Turner arrived at Farnley Hall and brought with him the now well-known series of fifty-one watercolours of views on the Rhine which Walter Fawkes purchased for £500. Between landing at Hull and arriving at Farnley, Turner had visited Durham and other places in the North-East. He also spent some time at Raby Castle working on the commission for a painting of that house (now in Baltimore) for Lord Darlington. It was possibly while staying there that he worked on his Rhine watercolours.

These introduce a new element of confidence and fluency; the meticulous technique of watercolours made for the engravers is replaced in many of these Rhine drawings by a more fluid and luminous application of the medium. This is evident in the painting of the background hills of the *Marksburg* (Plate 73), in which the foreground details are however, still dryly painted and considerable use of body-colour is made. One important aspect of the Rhine series is the variation of technique and approach among the drawings as a whole; there is also considerable diversity of touch and method in many individual drawings, as can be seen again in the *St. Goarshausen and Katz Castle* (Plate

74), which is one of the most enclosed of these compositions. For Turner this large group of finished watercolours executed apparently without a positive commission in the space of a few weeks must have been in the nature of an experiment—an experiment which shows once again the impact that new visual experiences so often had upon this artist.

The few days spent in Holland had an even more spectacular result: the beautiful painting known as *The Dort* (Plate 86), which was shown at the Royal Academy in 1818 and also purchased by Walter Fawkes, this time for 500 guineas. While there is no doubt about the overall debt in this composition to Cuyp, who was a native of Dordrecht (see Plate 85), in detail it is based on a number of pencil drawings made in three of the sketch-books that Turner had used in 1817. These show once again Turner's acute powers of observation, and his ability to record with the greatest economy sufficient material to ensure accuracy in all aspects of such a large canvas as *Dort or Dordrecht: The Dort Packet Boat from Rotterdam becalmed*. As well as being accurate in its topographical and nautical details, this work is notable for the truth of its atmosphere and for the tones of sky and water. We have already had ample proof of Turner's knowledge of the different qualities of the ever-varying sea; his determination to be equally knowledgeable about the sky is shown by a sketch-book which he was using between about 1816 and 1818, and which he himself labelled 'Skies'. This contains over seventy watercolour studies of a wide range of sky effects, both by day and night, of which many are likely to have been made on the spot. There are numerous other watercolour studies of sky and weather effects in the Turner Bequest drawings, but this aspect of Turner's work has never gained the same attention as Constable's cloud and sky studies, the most important group of which dates from the early 1820s, some years later than the 'Skies' sketch-book. Near the end of this are two pencil drawings of the Fourth of June celebrations at Eton, which Turner is known to have witnessed in the company of the Fawkes family in 1818.

Further evidence of Turner's versatility in the use of watercolours is found in a strikingly different drawing, the well-known *A First Rate taking in Stores* (Plate 80). This is reputed to have been completed in one sitting between breakfast and lunch during his autumn visit to Farnley Hall in 1818. When breakfast was finished, we are told by the Fawkes' eldest son, Hawksworth, who witnessed the operation, 'Turner took a piece of blank paper—outlined his ships, finished the drawing in three hours and went out to shoot . . . he began by pouring wet paint onto the paper until it was saturated, he tore, he scratched, he scrubbed it in a kind of frenzy and the whole thing was chaos—but gradually and as if by magic the lovely ship, with all its exquisite minutia, came into being.'

Before this visit to Farnley, Turner had spent two or three weeks in Scotland to make studies for his illustrations for *The Provincial Antiquities of Scotland*, which was to be published by Cadell of Edinburgh with a text supplied free of charge by Walter Scott. Later the publisher presented eight of the finished drawings, including the *Roslin Castle* (Plate 71), to Scott, who had them all arranged in one frame made from an oak felled at Abbotsford at the time of Turner's visit there in 1831. In this drawing a variety of techniques has been used, including stipple and scratching out, and it illustrates the results of the various experiments which Turner had made with watercolours in the two or three preceding years.

In April 1819 the range and beauty of Turner's watercolours could be studied by a relatively wide public in London, when Walter Fawkes included over sixty examples in an exhibition of part of his collection of watercolours by contemporary British artists in his town house at 45 Grosvenor Place. As a Royal Academician Turner had not been able to join the Water-Colour Society founded in 1804, and he had long not shown more than a small group of watercolours in the exhibitions at the R.A. and in his own gallery. Turner's pre-eminent place among contemporary watercolour artists was clearly demonstrated by the Fawkes exhibition, and when Walter Fawkes printed a catalogue which included extracts from the many favourable press comments, he dedicated it to Turner (see p. 57). In opening his collection to the public Fawkes was probably following the example of Sir John Leicester, who, having just completed a new gallery at his house in Hill Street, opened it to the public in March. His well-known collection of British paintings included eight canvases by Turner, and the critics of this exhibition had also focussed their attention on his works. Thus Turner was already very much in the public eye when the Royal Academy opened its annual exhibition in which he had two large paintings, the *Entrance of the Meuse: Orange-Merchant on the Bar, going to Pieces* (Plate 81) and *England: Richmond Hill, on the Prince Regent's Birthday* (Plate 83). Notwithstanding its specific, narrative title the former is essentially a composition of sea and sky (reflecting the experience gained in the 'Skies' sketch-book), and the boats and ship play a relatively small role. Despite its Claudian character, the vast *Richmond Hill*—it was the largest painting that Turner exhibited—succeeds in conveying very naturally the mistiness of this breathtaking view of the Thames valley. It too was probably based on drawings made on the spot, of which the fine *View from Richmond Hill* (Plate 82) may have been one.

Early in August Turner crossed the Channel on his way to Italy—a few days before his departure Sir Thomas Lawrence had written to Joseph Farington from Rome; 'Turner should come to Rome. His genius would here be supplied with materials, and entirely congenial with it. . . . He has an elegance, and often a greatness of invention,

4. S. W. Parrott,
   Turner on Varnishing Day in 1846.
   Oil on panel;
   $10\frac{3}{4} \times 10\frac{1}{4}$ in. (273×260 mm.)
   Reading, Ruskin Collection, University of Reading.

5. Comte Alfred d'Orsay,
   Turner at a Reception. c. 1850.
   Lithograph;
   $12 \times 9\frac{1}{2}$ in. (305×242 mm.)
   Oxford, Ashmolean Museum (Hope Collection).

that wants a scene like this for its free expansion.' Turner spent some four months in Italy, touring most of the principal cities including Turin, Milan, Venice, Bologna, Rome, Naples and Florence. The initial impact of his first visit to Italy has often been exaggerated, and it took Turner several years to assimilate the wealth of his Italian experiences—it must be remembered that he was already in his mid-forties.

The immediate result of the Italian tour was twofold. He filled over twenty sketch-books, mostly with rapid pencil drawings, which became noticeably less detailed as he proceeded on his travels. Thus he recorded a wide variety of scenery in town and country and was at last able to familiarise himself with the landscape which had inspired Claude and Wilson. He also studied many of the masterpieces of earlier Italian painting, especially the warm and rich colouring of the Venetians. Turner tried to sum up all these experiences in a great public statement, the *Rome from the Vatican: Raffaele, accompanied by La Fornarina, preparing his Pictures for the Decoration of the Loggia* (Plate 84), which he exhibited as his only work at the Royal Academy in 1820 having executed it in the few weeks since his return from Italy. This vast composition, with its surprising allusion to Raphael as a fellow-painter of landscape, was not well received, and was particularly criticised for its gaudy colours.

Though Rome made a great impression on Turner, the impact of Venice was to have a more lasting influence. He spent over two weeks there, filling the larger parts of two sketch-books with pencil studies which clearly show how much he was attracted by the unique qualities of Venice (Plates 95, 96). The drawings in the second of these sketch-books are much less detailed than those in the first, a sure sign that he was now confident that the essential features of the city were stored in his powerful visual memory. He also used a few leaves of a much bigger roll sketch-book for a series of four superb watercolour studies in which he was principally concerned with recording the breath-taking light effects that can be experienced in Venice. In these he made full use of the white of the paper and of the translucent qualities of the medium to achieve his effects with greater economy than ever before. The delicate light of sunrise is the theme of three of these drawings (Plates 87, 88); the fourth, a close-up view of the Campanile and the Ducal Palace, features the strong blues that so often dominate the sky and waters of Venice. These few Venetian drawings are far in advance in technique and confidence of the other watercolours that Turner executed on his Italian tour, which are closer to those he had made of the Rhine and of English subjects in the years just before this. For his views of Rome (Plates 97, 98) Turner used grey tinted paper, on which the grandeur and solemnity of the city is seen to full effect. Naples (Plate 99) and Tivoli (Plate 100) are again drawn on white paper. In these direct and natural coloured drawings Turner was clearly working for himself to record the variations of light and

6. (*opposite*) George Jones, R.A., *Interior of Turner's Gallery: the Artist showing his Works.* Oil on millboard; $5\frac{1}{2} \times 9$ in. (140×228 mm.) Actual size. Oxford, Ashmolean Museum.

7. W. B. Cooke after William Havell, *Sandycombe Lodge, Twickenham.* 1814. Engraving; $4\frac{5}{16} \times 7\frac{7}{8}$ in. (110×200 mm.) Actual size. Oxford, Ashmolean Museum (Hope Collection).

colour, which he could not do in the numerous pencil sketches; he used few of them as the basis for finished watercolours for his patrons—he produced no more than a handful of Italian subjects after his return—but he certainly turned to them to refresh his memory when he began to paint Italian subjects more frequently in the 1830s.

On his return journey across the Alps Turner found that the Mont Cenis Pass was officially closed because of heavy snowfalls. However, he and a group of others decided to hire a private coach, and the hazardous drive went well until the top of the pass was reached. Here the coach capsized and the passengers had to proceed down the pass on foot. Turner recorded all this in several rapid pencil drawings; when back in England he executed a watercolour, *The Passage of the Mont Cenis* (Plate 101), for Walter Fawkes, which shows once again how fully Turner understood the moods and characteristics of mountainous country; his understanding of Italian scenery, on the other hand, took several more years to develop. After the disappointing reception of *Rome from the Vatican* Turner did not exhibit at the R.A. in 1821, and showed only one painting in 1822 and 1823. In the latter year he selected an Italian subject, *The Bay of Baiae, with Apollo and the Sybil* (Plate 89). Though still basically a Claudian composition, this does show, especially in the translucent qualities of the distant sea, the beginnings in an oil painting of that greater freedom and spontaneity which Turner had already developed in his watercolours.

For his painting in oils the mid-1820s were on the whole years of pause and reflection. In watercolours he was as busy as ever, mostly in work for the engravers, whose demand for drawings had increased with the introduction of steel plates which meant that many more impressions of each subject could be printed. In 1822 and the two following years, W. B. Cooke showed groups of the drawings that Turner had made for his publications in his gallery in Soho Square, and these were again well received by the critics. One of Cooke's publications was *The Rivers of England* for which Turner made sixteen drawings, including the lovely *Totnes on the River Dart* (Plate 102), of which the mezzotint on steel was engraved by Charles Turner (no relation of the painter) in 1825 (Plate 103). From the commercial point of view many of W. B. Cooke's publications were unsuccessful. In 1827 Turner started working for a new publisher, Charles Heath, who launched the ambitious *Picturesque Views in England and Wales*, of which 96 plates (engraved on copper) had been published by 1838. This again was a commercial failure (Heath went bankrupt), despite a successful exhibition of some of Turner's watercolours in the Egyptian Hall in 1829. The wonderfully atmospheric drawing of *Colchester* (Plate 104) was included in that exhibition; it had been engraved for this series by R. Wallis in 1827. Here Turner combines broadness of effect with minuteness of detail, and the composition is enlivened by the 'narrative' element of the hare being chased by the dog in the foreground, which also helps to draw it together. In the later *Richmond Hill and Bridge, Surrey* (Plate 105), engraved for this series in 1832, the jaunty figures play a similar role. No such gimmicks were needed in his 'private' and spontaneous watercolour drawings of this period, such as the bold *Storm Clouds: Sunset* (Plate 91), which is the sort of study on which Turner based his fine rendering of atmosphere in his finished compositions. Yet it is in itself a complete and balanced composition.

Though the series of British topographical prints were meeting with limited commercial success Turner was still kept busy with work for the engravers. In 1830 a new and luxurious edition of Samuel Rogers's poem *Italy* was published with a large number of vignette illustrations of which twenty-four were after drawings by Turner. This handsome volume was well received and its success launched Turner on a new aspect of his output for the engravers; he became one of the most sought-after illustrators of literary works and in the 1830s fine editions of the writings of Milton, Byron (Plates 111, 112), Scott and others were published with steel engravings after drawings by him. There were also to be one or two topographical series, among which *The Rivers of France* is pre-eminent. Published in three volumes in 1833, 1834 and 1835, these engravings and the outstanding drawings from which they were made, represent the apogee of this aspect of Turner's career. The bulk of the drawings connected with the series form part of the Turner Bequest, but there is also a fine group, which once belonged to Ruskin, at the Ashmolean Museum in Oxford, and a few more are dispersed in other collections.

Turner was in France on several of his journeys abroad between 1826 and 1833, and it is impossible to date the *Rivers of France* drawings at all precisely. Drawn on blue paper, which in numerous cases has faded to grey, these small and compact compositions combine a surprising amount of meticulous detail with a wonderful rendering of overall atmosphere. One of the most atmospheric is the *Scene on the Loire* (Plate 92), which was not engraved and which Ruskin described as 'the loveliest of all' the Loire series. Here, as in many of these drawings, body-colours and watercolours are used together, and large areas of the paper are left untouched, to render the misty effect of the calm of evening. In the *Château of Amboise* (Plate 113) black ink is used to strengthen the details of the bridge, the castle and other features; these details have naturally become rather more precise in the engraving after this drawing (Plate 114), which is on a considerably reduced scale. Despite this the engraving succeeds in retaining the atmospheric qualities of the drawing. This was happily the case in most of the 61 *Rivers of France* plates, of which twenty-one are devoted to the Loire and forty, in two volumes, to the Seine. In some cases the engraving even adds to the effect of the drawing; in the

Rouen, looking down River (Plate 115), for instance, the indefinite white streak in the sky on the right has become a rainbow in the engraving.

The three volumes were planned as the beginning of a large series devoted to the great rivers of Europe, but in the event they were the only ones published. But it should be remembered that the majority of Turner's *Rivers of France* drawings are rapid studies probably made on the spot and not prepared for engraving (Plate 116). In addition to the coloured drawings there are in the Turner Bequest over a hundred pencil and ink drawings, again on blue paper, connected with this series, to which Turner clearly devoted a great deal of hard work. This kind of work reaped its rewards not only in financial gain but also in a great boost to Turner's reputation. When Dr. G. F. Waagen, Director of the Berlin Gallery, wrote of his first visit to a Royal Academy exhibition in 1835, he records that he made a point of 'looking for the landscapes of the favourite painter, Turner, who is known throughout Europe by his numerous, often very clever, compositions for annuals and other books, where they appear in beautiful steel engravings'. Without the engravings Turner could not have achieved the international reputation that he enjoyed in the later years of his life.

Having again sent no works to the Royal Academy exhibition in 1824, Turner showed a painting and a watercolour in the following year. The former, *Harbour of Dieppe (changement de domicile)* (Plates 93, 94), was given a mixed, but on the whole adverse, reception. One critic described it as 'perhaps the most splendid piece of falsehood that ever proceeded from the brush of Turner or any of his followers'; another called it 'a brilliant experiment upon colours, which displays all the magic of skill at the expense of all the magic of nature'. For the artist this canvas represents a turning point. The composition continues to bring to mind an old master precedent, the harbour scenes of Claude. The execution is entirely 'different'; in its beautiful rendering of a busy scene in clear morning light it achieves on a greatly magnified scale the atmospheric effects of the watercolours of this period, and it does so by adapting in oils some of the methods that he had developed in watercolour. To the modern eye all seems real and alive in this scene, from the fine details of the household goods in the right foreground to the lovely blue grey effect of the distance. The *Harbour of Dieppe* heralds the fifty-year-old Turner's maturity as a painter in oils, and shows that the few years of reflection he had allowed himself since his Italian visit had been used to excellent effect.

In 1826 he showed four oils, including a companion piece for the *Dieppe, Cologne, the Arrival of a Packet Boat, Evening*, which is also in the Frick Collection in New York. Another of that collection's outstanding group of Turners was also exhibited in 1826; this is *The Seat of William Moffat, Esq., at Mortlake. Early (Summer's) Morning* (Plate 117).

Again the composition of this exquisite Thames-side scene is a conventional one, but its colouring and tones are Turner's own, as they are in the companion evening view shown in the following year and now in Washington. In 1827 Turner was tempted to practise his new oil painting methods in one of his rare series of on-the-spot studies in that medium. That summer he spent several weeks on the Isle of Wight as the guest of the architect John Nash at East Cowes Castle. His visit coincided with the Regatta, of which his host commissioned him to paint two pictures. As usual Turner made numerous preparatory pencil drawings, concentrating particularly on the yachts under sail. It seems probable that these pencil studies preceded the oil sketches. Of these Turner made nine, using a six by four foot canvas cut in two, with each part divided into four and five respectively; they were not cut up and put on stretchers until 1906. Six of these vivid direct studies can be connected with the two paintings of the regatta which were commissioned by Nash. Thus *Yacht Racing on the Solent, No. 1* (Plate 118) has several features, including the guard ship in the centre, in common with one of the two finished canvases, *East Cowes Castle, the Seat of J. Nash, Esq.; the Regatta beating to windward* (Plate 119). In this, like in its companion, a placid sunset scene showing 'the Regatta starting for their moorings', the architect's remarkable neo-Gothic house is seen in the distance on its hill above the river.

Though he made no oil studies of the house, Turner made a considerable number of drawings of it and its grounds on blue paper, mostly in pen and ink with white chalk. The Castle features prominently in *Boccaccio relating the Tale of the Birdcage* (Plate 120), which, like the two regatta scenes, was shown at the Royal Academy in 1828. Here the white castle in the background adds greatly to the mystery of the Watteau-esque figures in the foreground, which re-echo some of the figure drawings that Turner made inside and outside East Cowes Castle. The direct oil sketches also include one remarkable figure study, *Between Decks* (Plate 121), in which a group of sailors and their girls are shown casually seated around a gun-port on board a man-of-war. It has been suggested that Turner painted the oil studies of the Regatta from on board a boat or ship; *Between Decks* would seem to confirm this supposition, and together with the figure drawings made during this visit to the Isle of Wight it heralds the remarkable interiors with figures drawn and painted at Petworth a year or two later.

Walter Fawkes had died in 1826, and with his death Turner's regular visits to Yorkshire came to an end. It has usually been surmised that several years elapsed before the place that Farnley Hall had played in his life was taken by Petworth, the Sussex home of the Earl of Egremont, who had, in fact, commenced his patronage of Turner slightly in advance of Fawkes. However, it now seems probable that Turner's regular and frequent visits to Petworth had already begun by 1827. A recently recognised passage in the published correspondence of Thomas Creevey recording a visit to Petworth in August, 1828, refers to Turner's paintings of Petworth Park already hanging as part of the decoration of the panelled Grinling Gibbons Room, which was then used as a dining room. Having described some of the great portraits in this room Creevey continued: 'Immense as these pictures are with all their garniture there are still panels to spare, and as he [Lord Egremont] always has artists ready in the house, in one of these compartments, you have Petworth Park by Turner, in another Lord Egremont taking a walk with nine dogs, that are his constant companions, by the same artist'. The mention of the dogs means that *Petworth Park : Tillington Church in the Distance* (Plate 108) is here being referred to. This is one of the so-called 'sketches' in the Turner Bequest for the four well-known elongated views of Petworth Park, Brighton and the canal near Chichester, which are still at Petworth today. It now seems probable that the 'sketches', or at least two of them, were hung first in the Grinling Gibbons Room, and were later replaced by the slightly smaller and considerably altered versions still at the house, such as *The Lake, Petworth: Sunset, fighting Bucks* (Plate 123). How much later it is impossible to tell, but the newly discovered evidence does provide a *terminus ante quem* of the summer of 1828 for the commencement of this series, hitherto usually dated *circa* 1830.

In style and technique the Petworth 'sketches' follow on naturally from the studies made on the Isle of Wight, and from the watercolour compositions of the mid-1820s. *Petworth Park: Tillington Church in the Distance* is a bold and simple composition of the sweep of parkland on to which the great west front of the house faces. This is given complete cohesion by the running dogs on the left and the feeding deer on the right, and, of course, their shadows. That cohesion is not so successfully retained in the less broad version of the same view with the fighting bucks on the right and the cricket match on the left. In the *Chichester Canal* (Plate 109) Turner uses the dark silhouette of the ship to achieve another perfectly balanced composition despite the unprecedented freedom of technique.

With this great series of Petworth compositions we witness the first full flowering of Turner's own personal style as a painter of landscape, and it is now clear that this point had been reached *before* the artist set out on his second visit to Italy in 1828. On this occasion he spent most of his time in Rome, where he took a studio that Charles Eastlake had found for him. However, it took him nearly two months to reach Rome, during which he filled a number of small sketch-books with pencil drawings of scenes in the South of France and Northern Italy. On arriving in Rome Turner wrote to George Jones, one of his closest friends among fellow-painters: 'Two months nearly in getting to this Terra Pictura, *and at work*; but the length of time is my own fault'. His real object on this second visit to Italy was not to collect more material, but to do some painting, beginning with a major work for Lord Egremont as a companion to his Claude. The resulting canvas was the *Palestrina* (Plate 122), which in the event did not enter the Petworth collection. In a letter written to a friend not long after Turner's departure from Rome in January, 1829, Charles Eastlake stated: 'he worked literally day and night here, began eight or ten pictures and finished and exhibited three, all in about two months or a little more. More than a thousand persons went to see his works when exhibited, so you may imagine how astonished, enraged or delighted the different schools of artists were, at seeing things with methods so new, so daring, and excellences so unequivocal.' The three exhibited paintings, which it is reported that Turner framed with a rope nailed round the edges of each, were painted with considerable freedom, but retained, and this especially in the case of the *Regulus* (Plate 126) and the *View of Orvieto* (Plate 124), a strong element of Claudian classical precedent.

While in Rome Turner also painted a number of oil sketches, some of which were probably done on the spot. These latter, painted on board, are small semi-classical compositions with very misty tones and muted colouring, such as the *Coast Scene near Naples* (Plate 125). Another group of seven larger and more colourful studies, among them the *Ariccia?—Sunset* (Plate 90), was painted on one huge canvas, perhaps so that they would be more easily transportable back to England. Most of these also have an overall classical character, and it seems clear that Turner's deliberate plan to paint in 'the light of Rome' confirmed his life-long allegiance to the basic formulae of classical landscape painting. In the setting and atmosphere that formed the art of Claude and Wilson, Turner did not forget his discipleship of these masters; this was, indeed, an influence that Turner did not lose entirely at any stage of his career.

Much to his dismay Turner's exhibited and other paintings completed in Rome did not reach London in time for the Academy exhibition of 1829. However, he showed four works, including the spectacular but basically classical *Ulysses deriding Polyphemus* (Plates 106, 107), which, in its rendering of light and colour, illustrates the full effect of the months spent painting in Rome as the culmination of the advances made on the Isle of Wight and at Petworth in the two preceding years. Turner had had this great composition in mind for some twenty years, for there is an outline drawing for it in a sketch-book that he was using in about 1807. The next known stages in its development are two of the seven oil studies painted in Rome on the one canvas (which he must have had rolled up in the baggage that he himself brought back with him). The exhibited painting was certainly executed in the few weeks between Turner's return from Rome and the opening of the Royal Academy. Its reception was mixed, though *Ulysses deriding Polyphemus* has come to be regarded as one of Turner's greatest imaginative masterpieces. Another painting shown at this exhibition which has gained similar

35

reputation for its painter is Constable's dramatic *Hadleigh Castle*, now in the Paul Mellon Collection. Both these works represent a vital stage in the development of their artists, for in each there is a wholly successful fusion of nature and imagination which marks the achievement of full maturity. For Constable, who died in 1837, *Hadleigh Castle* was near the end of the road; for Turner *Ulysses deriding Polyphemus* marks the beginning of the full flow of his later masterpieces.

At the R.A. exhibition of 1830 Turner chose once again, as he had done in 1803 and 1815, to demonstrate his versatility. He showed seven works—more than in any year since 1815—including one watercolour, a large 'sketch from memory' of the funeral of Sir Thomas Lawrence, which is so free in technique that Finberg listed it in his *Inventory* in that all embracing category of 'Colour Beginnings'. Three of the paintings were ones that he had worked on in Rome—*Palestrina* (Plate 122), *View of Orvieto* (Plate 124) and *Jessica* (Plate 128). This, which was acquired either by gift or purchase by Lord Egremont, displays a considerable debt to Rembrandt, as does *Pilate washing his Hands* (Plate 127). The remaining two paintings—and they were the ones that gained the most general approval—were peaceful shore scenes, *Fish-market on the Sands—the Sun rising through Vapour* and *Calais Sands, low Water, Poissards collecting Bait* (Plate 110). The latter, with its beautiful rendering of the reflection of sunrise light on wet sand, perhaps records the memory of a scene witnessed during a brief trip to Northern France in the late summer of 1829. Turner had intended to return to Rome—indeed he had kept on his rooms there—but he changed his plans probably because of the poor health of his father, who died on 21 September, not long after his son's return from France.

Turner's relationship with his father had been a close one. The older William had always encouraged his son, and shown great pride in his achievements as an artist. After the death of his wife in 1804 he went to live with Turner and he came to play an important part in the running of his household, studio and gallery. It is understandable that Turner was reported as being 'fearfully out of spirits' after his father's funeral, but some authorities have made too much of the long-term effect of his death. It is certainly difficult to see 'a poignant note of sorrow' in the *Calais Sands*, as Finberg does. Indeed this is one of the most peaceful of Turner's later works, in which all the hopes and imponderables of a new day can be sensed.

In the next few years Turner spent much of his time in the congenial surroundings of Petworth, where the elderly and eccentric Lord Egremont kept open house. His guests —and there were generally some artists among them—were free to come and go as they wished and were in no way curbed by the social conventions of the time. Every part of the huge house (except the room set aside for Turner to paint in when he was there) was open to all, and there was a convivial atmosphere of ease and spaciousness. This was an ideal setting for Turner, and he felt completely at ease. There was agreeable company when he wanted it, but he could always escape to his painting room or to his favourite pastime of fishing, in the lake. In these surroundings his art gained a new dimension, for it is at Petworth that he produced his greatest works as a painter of figures and interiors. The Turner Bequest includes a group of some hundred body-colour drawings on blue paper of scenes in the house, the church and the park. Similar in technique and character to some of the unengraved 'Rivers of France' drawings, these are mostly studies of light and colour. The sombre form of a wooded slope in the park seen in evening light is rapidly scratched onto the paper (Plate 129); the luminous grandeur of one of the state rooms with sun light streaming in through the windows is recorded with detail yet also with economy (Plate 130). Many of the interiors are peopled, as in *The Artist and his Admirers* (Plate 135), in which the figures are boldly set against the bright light of the window, and *Playing Billiards* (Plate 131), where the figures and the table are diffused in the smoky atmosphere of the room. The scale of the rooms at Petworth was certainly important for Turner. They were large enough for him to be able to get away from the subjects he was depicting, though there are also some drawings in which the figures are seen quite close to.

From these small and attractive visions of light, colour and form Turner moved on to a series of large canvases based on Petworth interiors. With reds and yellows predominating these are much less positive than the drawings, and achieve a still greater subtlety of light, tone and form. In the modern idiom these could be described as 'mood' paintings, and their special quality is that they do not impose their mood but provide material for the viewer to create his own interpretations in accordance with his state of mind. *Music Party, Petworth* (Plate 137) could be considered gay with its reds and the gleaming light in the centre, or serious with the dark dress of the pianist and the shadows in foreground and background. In *Interior at Petworth* (Plate 134), which is generally considered the masterpiece of this series, the forms have become even less definite. This distillation of light is skilfully achieved with a limited range of colours, for when the eye looks directly into light, colours and shapes become dissolved. In such private paintings Turner left all conventions of style and technique behind him. In the history of art he is breaking new ground here, and the term 'Impressionist' has often, but mistaken-ly, been applied to these canvases, which certainly seem to foreshadow the interiors of Vuillard and Bonnard of some seventy years later. Much has been made of Turner's role in the development of Impressionism, but more research is needed before this can be properly assessed.

Except for the 1810 view of the house (Plate 62), which was shown at the Royal Academy, Turner never used a Petworth subject directly for an exhibited or engraved work. However, in 1831, when he again showed seven works at the Academy, he made indirect use of his deep study of the interior of Petworth in two subject pictures, painted on small panels. In the first, an historical scene of the time of the Gunpowder Plot depicting *Lord Percy under Attainder*, the richly furnished room is reminiscent of Petworth, and one of the three women in the room is actually based on a Van Dyck portrait which hangs there. The second, *Watteau Study by Fresnoy's Rules* (Plate 136), brings to mind several of the Petworth drawings, though there is no direct connection with any one of them. This was one of Turner's most didactic works, and it can be argued that he was more successful as an instructor with paint than he was in his lectures with words. Even in the latter, the numerous specially executed illustrative drawings played a vital role. The primary lesson of the *Watteau Study* was in the use of white, as indicated by the quotation from Fresnoy's *Art of Painting* printed in the catalogue:

'White, when it shines with unstained lustre clear, May bear an object back or bring it near.'

This was the period when Constable was being attacked by several critics for the use of white on the surface of his paintings, which he claimed gave them a quality of 'dewy freshness'. It may be that with the *Watteau Study* Turner was coming to the defence of Constable; too little is known about the relationship between the two artists for this to be more than a very tentative surmise.

Turner's admiration and respect for the paintings of Watteau—feelings which we know that Constable shared—had already been shown in earlier works (see Plate 120), but it is generally thought that in these the influence was an indirect one which came through the work of Thomas Stothard (1755–1834), a senior fellow-Academician who specialised in figure subjects in the style of Watteau. Stothard was also a successful illustrator and he had worked with Turner on the illustrations of Samuel Rogers's *Italy*, published in 1830. However, in Turner's painting of Watteau at work two of his canvases then in London are shown—*La Lorgneuse*, at the time in Samuel Rogers's collection, and (in reverse) *Les Plaisirs du Bal*, which was, as it still is, one of the chief treasures of the Dulwich Gallery.

Much can be learnt from the *Watteau Study* about Turner's sources, methods and aims, but the critics of the day were not impressed; one described the two figure paintings as 'caprices more wild and ridiculous than any other man out of Bedlam would indulge in'. On the other hand the same critics fully approved of another of Turner's exhibits that year, *Life-boat and Manby Apparatus going off to a stranded Vessel making Signal (blue lights) of Distress* (Plate 138). The setting for this dramatic shore scene is Yarmouth, where G. W. Manby, the inventor of the life-saving apparatus depicted here, was barrack-master. In 1831 he was elected F.R.S. for his services to life-saving, and thus the subject chosen by Turner was a topical one. All the details of the rescue operation are faithfully shown for the discerning eye, though the topographical features of the composition are not very precise. It is ironical that in later years—the painting forms part of the Sheepshanks Collection at the Victoria and Albert Museum—the topographical location, which had not been mentioned in his title by Turner, was remembered, while the rescue operation specifically referred to by the artist was forgotten. The use of such topical 'news items', quite common in his later exhibits, is comparable with his adaptation of specific personal experiences, as, for instance, in the *Hannibal* of 1812. Turner was fully conscious of the necessity for his exhibited works to have a recognisable subject, as demanded by the taste of the day. This was the great period of narrative painting in England, and to some extent Turner felt bound to follow the fashion of the time, though the technique and style of most of his exhibited paintings became increasingly individual.

In the summer of 1831 Turner set off somewhat reluctantly for Scotland to gather more material for a new illustrated edition of Sir Walter Scott's poems. The tour took some two months, and Turner filled twelve small sketch-books with pencil drawings. He thus made far more sketches than had been his wont on recent tours—he had filled only eight sketch-books on his much longer continental journey of 1828–9. His travels were extensive, ranging from Abbotsford to Elgin, and including Edinburgh and Glasgow, but the varied scenery that he saw did not seem to make a marked impression on him, for he made little use of these sketches in his finished work. Fifteen of the drawings which were engraved as illustrations for Scott's *Poetical Works* were exhibited in London by Messrs Moon, Boys and Graves in 1832 and 1833, and were considered at the time to be among Turner's finest achievements in watercolour.

One of Turner's six paintings at the 1832 Academy exhibition was a Scottish subject, based upon an experience at the close of his tour. He took a steamer from Tobermory to visit Staffa and Iona, but, as he himself wrote some years later 'a strong wind and head sea prevented us making Staffa until too late to go on to Iona. After scrambling over the rocks on the lee side of the island, some got into Fingal's Cave, others would not. It is not very pleasant or safe when the wave rolls right in. One hour was given to meet on the rock we landed on.' Turner certainly visited the cave, for one of his illustrations for Scott's *Lord of the Isles* is drawn from inside the cave, looking out through the entrance at the setting sun. It was then decided that the weather was too bad to proceed to Iona; 'the sun getting towards the horizon, burst through the rain cloud, angry, and for wind; and so it proved, for we were driven for shelter into Loch Ulver, and did not get back to Tobermoray before midnight'. *Staffa, Fingal's Cave* (Plate 139), seems to encapsulate this episode, but when exhibited in 1832 its title was accompanied in the catalogue by four lines from Scott's *Lord of the Isles*. Turner's own surprisingly graphic description of the event was not written until some years later, in a letter to Mr. Lenox of New York, who bought the painting on the advice of C. R. Leslie in 1845. It was the first of Turner's paintings to go to America, where there is now a considerable number of major works in public and private collections, though the *Staffa* is back in Britain.

For three consecutive years Turner did not travel abroad; the theory that he paid his second visit to Venice in 1832 has not been proved correct. A reason for that suggestion was that in the following year Turner showed the first two of a long line of Venetian subjects among his annual exhibits at the Academy. One of these was the *Bridge of Sighs, Ducal Palace and Custom-house, Venice: Canaletti painting* (Plate 140), which Turner referred to as a 'scrap' when it was purchased by Mr. Vernon, who was collecting British paintings for presentation to the National Gallery. There is no doubt that Turner could have based such a composition on the sketches and memories gathered on his visit to Venice some thirteen years earlier, but what is surprising is that this small and detailed panel is the first of Turner's paintings of which it was reported that he painted it almost entirely when already on the walls of the Academy, in the brief space of two days. That report was dismissed as 'absurd' by Finberg, but has been more sympathetically received by today's scholars, one of whom has also suggested that in showing Canaletto painting in the left foreground on a canvas already within a heavy gilt frame, Turner was demonstrating his own conviction that the frame is a vital factor in the total effect of a painting. The presence of the somewhat ludicrous figure of Canaletto may well have been meant as a gesture of respect for his greatest predecessor in the painting of Venice, which, if the conclusions formulated as a result of the most recent research into Turner's visits to that city are correct, he himself re-visited in the summer of 1833.

In each of the next two years he exhibited straight-forward topographical views of the city, which were followed in 1836 and 1837 by large compositions of Shakespearean subjects with Venice as their setting, somewhat surprisingly in the former case, where the subject was Juliet. Turner showed no Venetian paintings in the next two years, but from 1840 until 1846 there were two or more Venetian subjects among his exhibits every year. While there is still some doubt that he visited Venice in 1833, it is certain that he was there for about three weeks in 1840. Venice, the city of water, was an obvious source of inspiration for Turner. As Ruskin wrote in one of his most perceptive passages about the artist; 'At Venice he found freedom of space, brilliancy of light, variety of colour, massive simplicity of general form, and to Venice we owe many of the motives in which his highest powers of colour have been displayed.' Venice stands with Farnley and Petworth as one of the vital formative influences in Turner's art, but while he declined to make public the latter two, his Venetian impressions were an essential element of the public image of the ageing Turner. This was the time when Venice, with its Byronic connections, was steadily gaining popularity with British travellers and artists. Some of the most daring canvases that Turner exhibited in his final years were of Venetian subjects; as we shall see, there was also a private element in Turner's Venetian work, the scintillating watercolours executed on the spot during his final visit.

Soon after his return to England from a tour in France and Germany in 1834 Turner visited Petworth, from which he came back to London in time to witness the burning of the Houses of Parliament during the night of 16 October. On hearing of the fire he rushed out to record the scene from both sides of the river. He made nine rapid water-colour sketches on the spot that night (one is reproduced as Plate 132). These nine drawings were contained in a single sketch-book which was not used again, and which forms part of the Turner Bequest in the British Museum. In the following year (1835) he exhibited two oil paintings of the scene, both now in museums in America. The earlier version (Plate 141) was shown at the British Institution, and we have a vivid record, from the pen of the painter E. V. Rippingille, of how Turner completed this canvas on Varnishing Day. 'The picture when sent in was a mere dab of several colours, and "without form and void", like chaos before the Creation. The managers knew that a picture would be sent there, and would not have hesitated, knowing to whom it belonged, to have received and hung up a bare canvas, than which this was but little better. Such a magician, performing his incantations in public, was an object of interest and attraction. Etty was working at his side and every now and then a word and a quiet laugh emanated and passed between the two great painters. Little Etty stepped back every now and then to look at the effect of his picture, lolling his head on one side and half closing his eyes, and sometimes speaking to some one near him, after the approved manner of painters: but not so Turner; for the three hours I was there— and I understood it had been the same since he began in the morning—he never ceased to work, or even once looked or turned from the wall on which his picture hung. All lookers-on were amused by the figure Turner exhibited in himself, and the process he was pursuing with his picture. A small box of colours, a few very small brushes, and a vial or two were at his feet, very inconveniently placed; but his short figure, stooping, enabled him to reach what he wanted very readily. Leaning forward and sideways over to the right, the left hand metal button of his blue coat rose six inches higher than the right, and his head buried in his shoulders and held down, presented an aspect curious to all beholders, who whispered their remarks to each other, and quietly laughed to themselves. In one part of the mysterious proceedings Turner, who worked almost entirely with his palette knife, was observed to be rolling and spreading a lump of half-transparent stuff over his picture, the size of a finger in length and thickness. As Callcott was looking on I ventured to say to him, "What is that he is plastering his picture with?" to which inquiry it was replied, "I should be sorry to be the man to ask him." . . . Presently the work was finished: Turner gathered his tools together, put them into and shut up the box, and then, with his face still turned to the wall, and at the same distance from it, went sideling off, without speaking a word to anybody, and when he came to the staircase, in the centre of the room, hurried down as fast as he could. All looked with a half-wondering smile, and Maclise, who stood near, remarked, "There, that's masterly, he does not stop to look at his work; he *knows* it is done, and he is off".'

This well-known description of Turner at work provides a valuable insight into the unorthodox techniques which he used in his later years. These idiosyncratic methods were based on his mastery of the traditional rules of painting which he had painstakingly achieved during the first thirty or forty years of his working life. During these same years he had also constantly developed his skill in the use of watercolours and bodycolours, and, as has already been suggested, it was partially through the experience he had gained in these more fluid mediums that he was now able to revolutionise his methods in oils. Many of the details of how he worked during these later years are still a matter of conjecture. One unfortunate consequence of the unorthodoxy of his technique is that it has proved extremely difficult to preserve, clean and restore many of his late canvases.

Understandably the painting of *The Burning of the Houses of Lords and Commons* caused great interest, and on the whole its reception by the critics was favourable; 'Turner's picture transcends its neighbours as the sun eclipses the moon and stars', wrote the critic of the *Spectator*. 'The burst of light', he continued, 'in the body of the flame, and the flood of fiery radiance that forms a luminous atmosphere around all the objects near, cannot be surpassed for truth.' As this perceptive critic had realised, the event was far more than an emotional and historic occasion for Turner; it provided him with just that vital combination of vivid light and colour effects which were the central element of his painting. Turner produced another painting of the fire, seen this time from a more distant point on the Surrey side of the Thames, for the 1835 R.A. exhibition (Plate 133). This canvas also shows signs of having been rapidly painted, but there is no record of its having been completed on the walls of the gallery.

Another of Turner's 1835 R.A. exhibits, *Keelmen hauling in Coals by Night* (Plate 143), demonstrates his continued interest in the painterly possibilities of flames and smoke reflected in water. In this moonlit scene the flames add an element of foreboding to the ghostly appearance of the ships. That foreboding seems to be realised in the awesome *A Fire at Sea* (Plate 144), a painting which has been considered to be unfinished and which was certainly not exhibited. This composition must have been based on an event experienced by Turner, and in a sketch-book dated by Finberg to 1834 there is a small group of watercolour studies of a ship on fire. In *A Fire at Sea* Turner combines the impact of this experience with his deep existing knowledge of the sea and the sky, and uses all in a great swirl of paint that is almost as alive and dramatic as the moment he is portraying.

Water and the sea in particular continued as a focal centre of interest throughout Turner's life. In the 1830s and 1840s he painted many large and effective studies of waves and of stormy seas. Although it is tempting to think that some of these realistic canvases, such as *Waves breaking on a lee Shore* and *Breakers on a flat Beach* (Plates 145,170), were painted in the open, this is unlikely. However, in these studies Turner shows his complete liberation from the traditional concepts of oil painting. They were essentially 'private' pictures, not meant for exhibition or sale, though Turner may occasionally have used such a canvas as the basis of one of his 'public' compositions. The majority of these sea studies remained in his studio and are in the Turner Bequest, but a few are in other collections, including the lovely *Seascape: Folkestone* belonging to Lord Clark. It has been suggested that these may originally have been given to Mrs. Booth, and sold by her after Turner's death. Turner had lodged with Mrs. Booth at Margate, and later established her in a house at Chelsea where he spent most of his final years. While at Margate Turner certainly spent much time observing the sea, and what is probably his last sketch-book includes drawings of the town.

In 1837 the Royal Academy exhibition was held for the first time in its new galleries in the recently completed National Gallery building in Trafalgar Square. The exhibition was opened by William IV, and the Duchess of Kent and her daughter were in the audience. A few weeks later the King was dead and the Duchess's daughter succeeded as Queen Victoria; the Victorian Age had begun.

Turner was on the Hanging Committee of the 1837 exhibition, to which he contributed four paintings, two of which are now in America. *Scene—a Street in Venice*, in the Huntington Gallery, is a crowded view down the Grand Canal supposedly illustrating an episode in Shakespeare's *Merchant of Venice*. It is one of Turner's most gaudy paintings, and shows none of the subtlety which most of his Venetian canvases display. Its effect is in complete contrast with the dramatic *Snowstorm in the Valley of Aosta*, now in Chicago, in which the swirling storm is reminiscent of *Hannibal Crossing the Alps* (Plate 57) of some twenty-five years earlier. The inspiration for the Aosta composition certainly stems from Turner's visit to Switzerland in 1836, when he was accompanied by his new

43

patron and friend, Mr. H. A. J. Munro of Novar, but as that visit took place during the summer the artist could not have experienced such a storm on this occasion. The other two paintings in the 1837 exhibition also present a contrast, that of the serene calm of the *Apollo and Daphne* with the turbulent splendour of *The Parting of Hero and Leander* (Plate 142). Predictably Turner presents these two classical subjects in classical style, and both originated in his mind long before they were exhibited—indeed a drawing for the *Hero and Leander* is to be found in a sketch-book used some thirty years earlier. In many ways these works are backward-looking, though in their technique, especially in the complex light effects of the *Hero and Leander*, they display Turner's mature mastery.

He probably showed such compositions in an endeavour to combat the violent criticisms of many of his later paintings, which certainly riled him though they did little to affect his stature as an artist. Indeed it was in 1837 that he was represented for the first time at one of the 'Old Master' exhibitions at the British Institution. The painting shown was 'The Bridgewater Sea Piece', which had been exhibited at the Royal Academy in 1801. In this context it is interesting to note that the two 'classical' exhibits of 1837 remained unsold, while the *Snowstorm in the Valley of Aosta* was bought by Mr. Munro and the Venetian scene by John Ruskin's father. Turner was finding patronage among the rising number of middle-class collectors, and it is significant that the leading figure among his former aristocratic patrons, Lord Egremont, died in November 1837. Lord Egremont's death was a sad blow to Turner, who did not again find such a friendly haven as Petworth, and before that Farnley, had been for him. He himself was ill at the end of the year, and this may have persuaded him finally to resign as Professor of Perspective at the Royal Academy—he had given his last lectures in 1828.

The advent of John Ruskin in his life was perhaps more significant for Turner's posthumous reputation than it was for the artist during his lifetime. The young author had first made the acquaintance of Turner's work when he was given a copy of the fine 1830 edition of Samuel Rogers's *Italy* illustrated with Turner's vignettes. His 'love of Turner' developed rapidly, and in 1836, when he was only seventeen, he drafted a lengthy reply to the violent criticism of Turner's Royal Academy exhibits of that year published in the October issue of *Blackwood's Edinburgh Magazine* (see Appendix). Though approved of by Turner, the letter was not submitted for publication; it has been printed since and amply proves Ruskin's precocious understanding of his idol's work, of which he then knew only the more recent, or engravings. Defending Turner's use of colour, he wrote 'He can produce instantaneous effect by a roll of his brush, and, with a few dashes of mingled colour, will express the most complicated subject: the means employed appear more astonishingly inadequate to the effect produced than in any other master.... Turner thinks and feels in colour; he cannot help doing so. Nature has given him a peculiar eye, and a wildly beautiful imagination, and he must obey its dictates.' In 1837 Ruskin was given his first Turner drawing by his father, and this was soon followed by the acquisition of *Scene—a Street in Venice*.

Ruskin met Turner for the first time three years later. The relationship between the artist and his young critic never became a close one, but during the last years of his life Turner was a fairly frequent visitor at the Ruskin home in Denmark Hill, and he was one of the regular participants at John Ruskin's birthday dinner each February 8th. When Turner died in 1851 Ruskin should have been one of his executors, though in the end he refused to act because of the dispute over the artist's will. Turner became increasingly a recluse during the final decade of his life, and under these circumstances it is surprising that the precocious author became as intimate with the ageing Royal Academician as he did. It is also surprising that in his writings Ruskin makes little of his friendship with the artist; from them we gain a definite impression of worship from afar. At one stage Ruskin was planning to write a biography of Turner, but after Thornbury's publication he abandoned the idea. It is a remarkable and unfortunate fact that even today Turner still lacks a really satisfactory biography—no writer or fellow-artist has succeeded in doing for Turner what C. R. Leslie achieved so brilliantly in his *Memoirs of the Life of John Constable*. Much of Turner's life, especially the later years, is still shrouded in mystery. Modern research is beginning to fill some of the gaps; but there is little sign that one of the greatest needs, the provision of a full and reliable catalogue of the thousands of drawings in the Turner Bequest, will be supplied in the foreseeable future.

By the later 1830s Turner's work specifically for the engravers had almost ceased, as the demand for small books illustrated with fine engravings was ending. However, the fashion for large plates after individual paintings and drawings was gaining momentum once again, and, from 1838 until his death, some twenty such plates after works by Turner were published and proved popular. It is possible that Turner had such publication specifically in mind for a pair of canvases which he exhibited in 1838: *Modern Italy—the Pifferari* (Plate 154) and *Ancient Italy—Ovid banished from Rome*. Painted with overall freedom and luminosity both compositions also contain a wealth of figurative detail on a tiny scale. The *pifferari* (pipers) of *Modern Italy* are two insignificant figures in the left foreground, but their inclusion accords with the kind of genre subject that had become popular in the 1830s, partially through the influence of Wilkie. Indeed it is possible that in his *Pifferari* Turner was tilting at Wilkie's painting of that title, which he had exhibited in 1829, having already sold it to George IV. The Wilkie is a small figure painting and one of the few, rather disappointing, products of his visit to Italy in the mid-1820s. There are several accounts of Turner's jealousy of Wilkie, though other 'legends' record their warm friendship. Wilkie was frequently patronised by Royalty, and he was knighted in 1836. Turner only once received Royal patronage and was never knighted. There can be little doubt that he resented this, and it must have been a particularly cruel blow to him when the Honours announced soon after Queen Victoria's accession included a landscape painter, but not, of course, himself. The chosen artist was Augustus Wall Callcott, R.A., a successful but relatively minor painter who was a follower of Turner; they remained the best of friends.

It cannot really have come to Turner as a surprise that he himself was not selected, for he never made any pretence at being other than an eccentric, and only rarely made any allowances for the manners and fashions of his time. His character ranged from the gruff and harsh to the sympathetic and charitable, and he was never one to hide his true feelings. Ruskin, after their first meeting in 1840, described Turner a 'a somewhat eccentric, keen-mannered, matter-of-fact, Englishminded-gentleman: good-natured evidently, bad-tempered evidently, hating humbug of all sorts, shrewd, perhaps a little selfish, highly intellectual, the powers of his mind not brought out with any delight in their manifestation, or intention of display, but flashing out occasionally in a word or a look.' As Ruskin also wrote, Turner was generally considered to be 'coarse, boorish, unintellectual, vulgar', and he must have agreed wholeheartedly with the artist, George Jones, who wrote to him a few years after Turner's death, 'I am extremely solicitous about Turner, I thought so well of him as an artist and a man; his unpropitiating manner is more remembered by the world than his affectionate kindness to his friends.' As we see from the remarkable portrayal of the shabby and unshaven old man holding a tea-cup at a reception (Plate 5) Turner in his last years was far from being an impressive figure. Eugène Delacroix remembered him as looking like 'an English farmer with his rough black coat and heavy boots, and his cold, hard expression'.

Neither Turner's personal eccentricities nor the apparent eccentricities of his recent art had a fundamental effect on his position as *the* British painter of the day. This was shown by the immediate success and popularity of one of his 1839 Academy exhibits, *The Fighting 'Téméraire'* (Plates 146, 152). The critics were unanimous in their praise, though in *Blackwood's Magazine* that praise was presented with a touch of sarcasm; 'Here is genius . . . a work of great effect and feeling, worthy of Turner when he was Turner!' To modern eyes this ever popular canvas is an outstanding example of Turner's depiction of colour and light; to the public and critics of early Victorian England *The Fighting 'Téméraire' tugged to her last Berth to be broken up*, to give the painting its full title, was attractive largely because of its content. This was a subject picture, a painting with a story which provided a reminder of the country's glorious past. The great warship of 98 guns had been launched at Chatham in 1798 and played a distinguished role at the Battle of Trafalgar in 1805; Turner's portrayal of the last voyage of the heroic vessel evoked nostalgic feelings of patriotism. All this was brilliantly summed up by the young William Makepeace Thackeray, then a struggling young artist and art critic writing under the pseudonym of Michael Angelo Titmarsh, Esq., in *Fraser's Magazine*. Introducing it as 'as grand a painting as ever figured on the walls of any academy, or came from the easel of any painter', he continued, 'The old Téméraire is dragged to her last home by a little, spiteful, diabolical steamer. A mighty red sun, amidst a host of flaring clouds, sinks to rest on one side of the picture, and illumines a river that seems interminable, and a countless navy that fades away into such a wonderful distance as never was painted before. The little demon of a steamer is belching out a volume . . . of foul, lurid, red-hot, malignant smoke, paddling furiously and lashing up the water round about it; while behind it (a cold grey moon looking down on it), slow, sad, and majestic, follows the brave old ship, with death, as it were, written on her. . . . It is absurd, you will say . . . for Titmarsh, or any other Briton, to grow so politically enthusiastic about a four-foot canvas, representing a ship, a steamer, a river, and a sunset. But herein surely lies the power of the great artist. He makes you see and think a great deal more than the objects before you.' Thackeray ends his passage by predicting that 'when the art of translating colours into music or poetry shall be discovered, [*The Fighting 'Téméraire'*] will be found to be a magnificent national ode or piece of music'. No other painting by Turner ever aroused such widespread enthusiasm; Turner referred to it as 'my darling' and consistently refused to sell it.

Turner's three additional 1839 exhibits included another pair, *Ancient Rome* (Plate 153) and *Modern Rome*. Somewhat theatrical in character, these classical compositions are reminiscent of the crowded canvases of John Martin, who had begun exhibiting regularly at the Royal Academy in 1837. There must again be some suspicion that Turner was displaying his own ability to equal or outdo a potential rival who was gaining popularity. In contrast to such artificial works *The Ponte delle Torri, Spoleto* (Plate 155) represents Turner's more personal art at this period. Based on sketches made during the Italian tour of 1819, this large and delicate painting belongs to that category of 'unfinished' works which Turner on occasion submitted to the exhibitions and then 'completed' during the varnishing days. Fortunately a considerable number of such paintings remained in Turner's studio and in recent years they have been exhibited as an important part of the Turner Bequest. The essential element of *The Ponte delle Torri* is the diffused and misty glow of the Umbrian sunrise; in *Venice, the Piazzetta with the Ceremony of the Doge marrying the Sea* (Plate 156) Turner penetrates the secret of the deep and hot light of Venice in the bold blues of the sky and water. That Venice can also experience cloud and mist is seen in *Festive Lagoon Scene, Venice* (Plate 147).

It was when Turner succeeded in retaining these personal elements in his public pictures that he achieved his outstanding later masterpieces. *The Fighting 'Téméraire'* was one; another was the almost equally famous *Slave Ship* (Plate 148), exhibited in 1840. On that occasion its full title was *'Slavers throwing overboard the Dead and Dying—Typhon coming on'*, and the title was accompanied in the catalogue by seven lines from *The Fallacies of Hope*, of which the last two read 'Hope, Hope, fallacious Hope! Where is thy market now?'. The source for much of the gruesome detail can be found in some graphic lines in James Thomson's *Summer* which Turner had probably had in mind for years. It has been suggested that the immediate factor which moved Turner to attempt this subject was the re-publication in 1839 of T. Clarkson's *History of the Abolition of the Slave Trade* in which was told the dreadful story of the slave ship *Zong*, whose master, when an epidemic broke out among his cargo, threw the sick slaves overboard, as insurance could be claimed for those lost at sea but not for those who died from disease. Here again we have ample evidence of how carefully Turner assembled the material for many of his exhibited paintings. Yet there was, of course, the more important over-riding element of Turner's own experience and observation, in this case brilliantly summed up by John Ruskin in a famous passage from the first volume of *Modern Painters*, which was published anonymously in 1843. 'I believe,' he wrote, 'if I were reduced to rest Turner's immortality upon any single work, I should choose this. Its daring conception, ideal in the highest sense of the word, is based on the purest truth, and wrought out with the concentrated knowledge of a life: its colour is absolutely perfect, not one false or morbid hue in any part or line, and so modulated that every square inch of canvas is a perfect composition; its drawing as accurate as fearless; the ship buoyant, bending, and full of motion; its tones as true as they are wonderful; and the whole picture dedicated to the most sublime of subjects and impressions . . . the power, majesty, and deathfulness of the open, deep, illimitable sea.'

This moving passage is typical of Ruskin's prose at its best. But it is more than just a piece of fine writing; it shows Ruskin's deep feeling for an understanding of the art of Turner, and we should remember that these lines were written before their author owned the painting concerned; he was given the *Slave Ship* by his father in 1844. The first and second (1846) of the five volumes of *Modern Painters* are a monumental defence of the later work of Turner, and, until quite recently, much of the subsequent thinking and feeling about Turner has been strongly influenced by these youthful writings of Ruskin. Great enthusiasm and sincerity lie at the heart of *Modern Painters*, making its outspoken and often violent criticism tolerable. Yet when he wrote these confident passages Ruskin's knowledge and experience of painting—even of that of Turner—was relatively limited. This defect was more than made good by Ruskin's instinctive understanding of his hero's work, though Turner is reported to have said at one time that Ruskin 'discovered in his pictures things which he himself did not know were there'. Ruskin's authorship of *Modern Painters* became public knowledge in 1849, when his *The Seven Lamps of Architecture* was published as 'by John Ruskin, author of *Modern Painters*'. His reputation as the leading art critic of the day was immediately established. There is no doubt that Turner did benefit from the advocacy of this brilliant young man, who was at that time himself building up an unrivalled collection of Turner's drawings.

Turner showed as many as seven paintings at the Royal Academy of 1840. Two of these were of Venetian views, of which one, *Venice, from the Canale della Giudecca, Chiesa di S. Maria della Salute, &c.* (Plate 157), was bought by John Sheepshanks. Another of the 1840 exhibits, the lovely and intimate *Neapolitan Fisher Girls surprised bathing by Moonlight*, was acquired by Robert Vernon, though he sold it two years later at Christie's where it fetched only 55 guineas. The same collector purchased one of the two Venetian subjects shown in 1842, *The Dogano, San Giorgio, Citella, from the Steps of the Europa* (Plate 158), which was one of four works by Turner in the collection of British paintings which he presented to the National Gallery in 1847. The second of the 1842 Venetian subjects, the *Campo Santo, Venice* (Plate 159), was bought for 150 guineas by another of the 'new' collectors, Mr. Elhanan Bicknell, who assembled ten paintings as well as watercolours by Turner at his house in Herne Hill. He bought six of these direct from the artist in 1844, when he paid 1000 guineas for the *Palestrina* of 1828 (Plate 122).

Royal patronage, however, continued to elude Turner, who now renewed his efforts to achieve it. Queen Victoria had married Prince Albert in 1840, and his interest in art was well known. During his tour in Germany that year Turner visited Coburg, the Prince's birthplace. In the following year he exhibited *Schloss Rosenau, seat of H.R.H. Prince Albert of Coburg, near Coburg, Germany* (Plate 160), but, despite its sweet romantic manner, this did not enter the Royal Collection. Turner probably had similar hopes for *Heidelberg Castle in the Olden Time* (Plate 161), which dates from about this time though it was not exhibited. In its free technique this large canvas is once again reminiscent of Turner's use of watercolours, as comparison with the fluent drawing of Heidelberg (Plate 149) shows. It may well have been the way that *Schloss Rosenau* was painted that offended Victoria and Albert, whose taste in paintings at this time was for the precise and meticulous work of artists such as the Nazarenes or Landseer. Nor were the critics at all enthusiastic for the thick and solid paint of *Schloss Rosenau*, of which *The Times* wrote that 'it resembles nothing in nature but eggs and spinach. The lake is a composition in which salad oil abounds and the art of cookery is more predominant than the art of painting'. Again it was the Venetian subjects, of which there were three, that were best received at the 1841 exhibition, as were the two shown in 1842 (Plates 158, 159).

Little is known of how Turner himself reacted to the violent criticism so often thrown at his work. However, there is some evidence about this in the case of another of his 1842 exhibits, the dramatic marine composition, *Snowstorm—Steamboat off a Harbour's Mouth making signals in shallow Water, and going by the Lead. The Author was in this Storm on the Night the Ariel left Harwich* (Plate 173). On the day that one critic declared it 'a mass of soapsuds and whitewash' Turner was dining with the Ruskins. After dinner John Ruskin heard him 'muttering low to himself at intervals, "Soapsuds and whitewash!" again and again, and again. At last I went to him, asking, "why he minded what they said?" Then he burst out—"Soapsuds and whitewash! What would they have? I wonder what they think the sea's like? I wish they had been in it".' On the other hand we know from Turner's friend the Rev. W. Kingsley that when he told the artist that his mother admired the *Snowstorm*, Turner replied that he had only painted it because he 'wished to show what such a scene was like; I got the sailors to lash me to the mast to observe it; I was lashed for four hours, and I did not expect to escape, but I felt bound to record it if I did. But no one had any business to like it.'

Turner was then in his mid-sixties; several of his fellow-members of the Royal Academy had died in these years, including in 1841 his close friends Sir David Wilkie (also at times a competitor) and Sir Francis Chantrey, who were both younger men. Apart from the President, Sir Martin Archer Shee, Turner was the most senior Academician. For forty years he had been at the centre of the artistic world of London, and had been one of its chief ornaments. But a penalty of such early and continuous success was inevitably increasing loneliness and isolation. Something of this can be sensed in another of his 1842 exhibits, *Peace—Burial at Sea* (Plate 174), which commemorated the death of Wilkie at sea on the return voyage from the Middle East; but this dark and sombre composition seems to mourn more than the passing of one man—like *The Fighting 'Téméraire'* it symbolises the end of an era.

However unorthodox in technique, the 1842 exhibits still retained recognisable subject matter, but in the following year Turner showed a pair of compositions that were almost abstract. These were *Shade and Darkness—the Evening of the Deluge* (Plate 151) and *Light and Colour (Goethe's Theory)—the Morning after the Deluge—Moses writing the Book of Genesis* (Plate 150). Perspicaciously described by one critic of the day as 'two riddles that none but himself [Turner] can read', these pendant circular compositions have received considerable attention as evidence of Turner's thinking on theories of light and colour. The first English translation, by Turner's friend and fellow-artist Charles Eastlake, of Goethe's celebrated *Theory of Colours* (*Farbenlehre*) had been published in 1840. Though that publication may have revived Turner's interest, it seems probable that he had already been familiar with Goethe's thinking for many years, and these two puzzling canvases confirm the belief that Turner was not a man to be moved or influenced by particular theories. He was something of a scavenger, garnering material from every conceivable source, and re-using it in his individual way. *Shade and Darkness* and *Light and Colour* are prime examples of that individuality.

In the final decade of his life Turner continued to work prolifically in watercolour, and, as in earlier years, he made progress most consistently in that medium. During his last visit to Venice he used a roll sketch-book with relatively large sheets of white paper to make rapid on-the-spot watercolour studies, such as the magical views of the *Grand Canal* (Plate 162) and the *Riva degli Schiavoni* (Plate 163) reproduced here. In the Turner Bequest there are large groups of late Venetian drawings in watercolour and body-colours, some of them on grey and brown paper, which have yet to be firmly dated. It seems probable that the majority of these belong to the 1840 visit. In several instances one of these drawings was used by Turner as the basis of an exhibited Venetian oil painting, as in the case of the translucent *St. Benedetto, looking towards Fusina* (Plate 164), which was shown in 1843. There is a similar connection not previously recognised, between the drawing of the *Riva degli Schiavoni* reproduced here and the painting *Venice Quay, Ducal Palace* exhibited in 1844 (Plate 165). In these late drawings and paintings of Venice there is little to distinguish between Turner's technique in watercolour or in oils.

The full significance of Turner's later work in watercolour has yet to be elucidated. The quantity of drawings in the Turner Bequest makes this a daunting task, and when compiling his *Inventory*, A. J. Finberg listed hundreds of such drawings under the general heading of "Miscellaneous". The sketch-book study of *Ehrenbreitenstein* (Plate 167) is included in this category, as are other studies of this great rock fortress on the Rhine opposite Coblenz. It was one of the places which Turner visited several times on his travels and to which he devoted a number of drawings recording different effects of light and weather. In the present drawing, which is sometimes called the 'pink' Ehrenbreitenstein, the glowing sunset light is depicted in a variety of techniques, ranging from the use of a wet brush to that of his fingers and the tip of his brush handle. The last was also used to achieve some of the evocative and yet simple effects of the famous watercolour *Dawn after the Wreck* (Plate 171). Here the addition of the miserable dog shivering on the beach, adds to the poignancy of the whole. This drawing belonged to Turner's friend, the Rev. W. Kingsley, and it is possible that the dog was added as an afterthought to make this a more 'finished' subject rather than just an on-the-spot study, such as *River with Distant Castle* (Plate 166).

Turner's four final visits abroad, in the summers of 1841 to 1844, all took him to Switzerland; on these it was the lakes as much as the mountains that gave him material

John Dewey Library
Johnson State College
Johnson, Vermont 05658

for many watercolour sketches. On his return to England in 1842 Turner approached his dealer, Mr. Griffith of Norwood, with fifteen Swiss sketches from which he proposed to make ten finished drawings (of which he had already completed four) to sell at 100 guineas each. Griffith had considerable difficulty in selling these watercolours, but finally disposed of them at 80 guineas each to Mr. Munro of Novar, Mr. Bicknell and to John Ruskin, who has left a detailed account of this whole transaction. Ruskin considered these drawings as outstanding, especially *The Splügen Pass* (Plate 168), which Turner himself thought the finest of the group. This sombre composition executed largely in yellows, browns and greys, and with only small 'scratches' of colour, achieves a magnificent depth and breadth. There is something of the same feeling of infinity in *The 'Blue Rigi'* (Plate 169), in which the mountain on the Lake of Lucerne is seen 'floating' in the misty morning light. At Lucerne Turner stayed at *The Swan* inn, from the windows of which he could observe the constant changes in the tones, colours and surfaces of the lake and the mountain beyond it. Some of his rapid blot-like studies of these changes are in the 'Lucerne Sketch-Book' in the Turner Bequest, and there are many others among the miscellaneous late drawings. Six of the ten 1842 Swiss watercolours were of Lucerne and Rigi.

Turner again approached Griffith in 1843 with sketches for ten more Swiss watercolours on the same terms as in the previous year. On this occasion the dealer was only able to secure commissions for five finished drawings, of which two went to Ruskin and three to H. A. J. Munro of Novar. One of these three was probably another Lucerne subject, the *Lucerne by Moonlight* (Plate 180), which now forms part of the R. W. Lloyd Bequest in the British Museum, where it can be studied together with the original sketch (Plate 179). The haunting atmosphere of the sketch is somewhat lost in the firmer technique of the finished drawing, and to modern eyes some of the finished late Swiss watercolours are not as effective as the spontaneous studies on which they were based. Ruskin, on the other hand, considered the 1842 and 1843 watercolours to be among Turner's greatest achievements, and wrote movingly about them on numerous occasions. Turner executed another group of eight Swiss drawings for sale in 1845, and, as is proved by the recently discovered 1846 watermark on the *Lake of Geneva* (Plate 172), continued to do so in the following years. In the *Lake of Geneva* watercolours and bodycolour are used in a variety of techniques, including painstaking stippling; but much of the effect relies on leaving the white paper totally exposed, and this is how the distant snow-capped mountains are represented. This drawing proves beyond doubt that Turner remained the greatest watercolour artist of the day even in his closing years, though he himself never exhibited watercolours after 1830. He was not influenced by current fashions in his watercolours, except in his early years. Cotman, Cox, Varley and De Wint were among the numerous outstanding artists in this medium during the second half of Turner's life, but there is no sign of influence on Turner by any of them. On the other hand there was a considerable number of lesser watercolour artists who produced work in Turner's manner in the 1830s and '40s and later.

As a painter in oils Turner attracted fewer followers, though there were numerous efforts to produce fake Turners in the years immediately before and after the artist's death. It was largely the topographical works that attracted the attention of these artists, and no painter set out to rival or emulate such masterpieces as *The Fighting 'Téméraire'* or *Rain, Steam, and Speed* (Plate 175). The latter was one of seven paintings exhibited in 1844, its full title being *Rain, Steam, and Speed—The Great Western Railway*. It was another of Turner's symbolic works, painted at the height of the Railway Mania and recording with immense drama the effect that the 'omnipresent fiery monsters' must have had on the placid English countryside. Thackeray again wrote a perceptive description of this canvas, which closed by stating that 'the world has never seen anything like this picture'. This was entirely true, but there was no artist in Britain able to follow Turner's daring lead, though thirty years later some of the French Impressionists, particularly Monet, produced great paintings of railway trains and their surroundings. Once again Turner used a personal experience, described in several later apocryphal reports, as the basis of his composition. He completed the painting on the Academy varnishing days when he was watched by the nine-year-old G. D. Leslie, who himself became an R.A. many years later and who recalled: 'He used rather short brushes, a very messy palette, and, standing very close up to the canvas, appeared to paint with his eyes and his nose as well as his hand' (see Plate 4).

1845 was an active year for Turner, who celebrated his seventieth birthday that April. Owing to the illness of the President of the Royal Academy, Sir Martin Archer Shee, Turner acted as Deputy-President for a considerable period. Yet he still had the time and energy to prepare work for the annual summer exhibitions, showing six paintings at the R.A. in this and the following year. In addition he sent *The Opening of the Wallhalla* (originally shown at the Academy in 1843) as his contribution—by in-vitation—to the Congress of European Art in Munich in 1845. The painting was not well received by the Germans, and Turner had the additional annoyance of finding when it was returned that it was damaged.

Two of the Academy exhibits in 1845 were concerned with a new theme, the hazards and challenges of whale-fishing (see Plate 176). In the catalogue both paintings were simply entitled *Whalers*, but the titles were accompanied by specific references to Thomas Beale's *Natural History of the Sperm Whale*, which had been published in 1839. Turner was inspired by this book for his final great series, for he showed two whaling subjects again the following year. In that year he also showed one of his rare Biblical works, *The Angel standing in the Sun* (Plate 181), in which the all-powerful forces of sunlight are portrayed as the basis of the Apocalyptic catastrophe. In these late exhibits, Turner's principal subject was light, but in such works as *The Angel standing in the Sun* there is also a variety of symbolic content, which allows for an equal variety of interpretation. Ruskin dismissed these works as the product of a mind that was senile and unbalanced; others have seen them as indicative of overwhelming pessimism and gloom. There is little positive evidence concerning Turner's state of mind and way of life in his closing years, although the picture that has been built up is one of increasing eccentricity and withdrawal.

Turner lived in a cottage on the river at Chelsea, but he retained his gallery in Queen Ann Street until his death. As well as the painting by George Jones (Plate 6), we have several vivid descriptions of this during these years, including one written after a visit in May, 1846, by the authoress Miss Elizabeth Rigby, who was to marry the artist Sir Charles Eastlake a few years later. 'The door was opened', wrote Miss Rigby, 'by a hag of a woman, for whom one hardly knew what to feel most, terror or pity—a hideous woman is such a mistake. She showed us into a dining-room, which had penury and meanness written on every wall and article of furniture. Then up into the gallery; a fine room—indeed, one of the best in London, but in a dilapidated state; his pictures the same. The great *Rise of Carthage* all mildewed and flaking off; another with all the elements in an uproar, of which I incautiously said: "The End of the World, Mr. Turner?" "No, ma'am: *Hannibal crossing the Alps*." His *Battle of Trafalgar* excellent, the disposition of the figures unstudied apparently. Then he uncovered a few matchless creatures, fresh and dewy, like pearls just set—the mere colours grateful to the eye without reference to the subjects. The *Téméraire* a grand sunset effect. The old gentleman was great fun.'

Among the 'matchless creatures, fresh and dewy, like pearls just set' may have been such canvases as *Norham Castle, Sunrise* (Plate 177). It is impossible to date this and similar studies accurately, but it is certain that they are the work of Turner's old age, though, as the comparative illustrations (Plates 184–90) show, the *Norham Castle* is based on a life-long sequence of depictions of this subject. We see him here in the calmest of moods, his eye thrilled by the beauty of the sunrise which he had witnessed so often, for he was an early riser, his brush evoking it with a wonderful combination of colour and form and a full understanding of the problems of light involved. From such late masterpieces we can assume that Turner the artist was still very much alive.

As we have seen, he had already achieved the status of an 'Old Master', and Turner himself was definitely aware of the remarkable reputation which he enjoyed. In an early

Will he bequeathed two works to the newly formed National Gallery, to hang in perpetuity beside two paintings by Claude. In a later Will he devised an ambitious scheme for the formation of a Turner Gallery, and for the creation of a home for indigent artists, to which he assigned the bulk of his fortune, amounting to some £140,000. This Will was successfully disputed by distant relatives, who, though this was entirely contrary to Turner's wishes, received the money, while the contents of the artist's studio—some 300 paintings and some 19,000 drawings and watercolours—passed to the Nation, represented by the National Gallery. The housing and exhibiting of this vast collection was for many years a matter of controversy and there is still considerable room for improvement. A selection of the paintings is on view at the National Gallery, while a larger series is shown in a number of special galleries at the Tate Gallery. The drawings are kept permanently in the Print Room of the British Museum, though a selection is shown at the Tate Gallery. Thus thanks to his own forethought, England possesses a uniquely representative collection of the work of its greatest painter; what is surprising is that despite this, there are still such lacunae in our knowledge of Turner's life and work.

Having shown nothing in 1848 and only two early works in 1849, including *The Wreck Buoy* (Plate 183) after considerable alterations, Turner made a special effort for the exhibition of 1850, for which he painted four ambitious compositions, all of subjects taken from the story of Dido and Aeneas, and each accompanied by a 'quotation' from the *Fallacies of Hope*. These were the last paintings exhibited by Turner at the Royal Academy, and, though they are not among his greatest work, they are a remarkable achievement for a man of his age, combining his usual freedom of technique with grandeur of composition. *The Visit to the Tomb* (Plate 182) features a vivid evening sky with the sun setting in the centre of the picture, and was accompanied by the line, 'The sun went down in wrath at such deceit'. Another late sunset painting, *Sun setting over a Lake* (Plate 178), reminds us of the spectacular development of Turner's art from the proficient topographical watercolours of his teens to the fluent and courageous visions of light and colour of his seventies. This canvas brings to mind the description of Turner's last moments in his home at Chelsea as recorded by W. Bartlett, the 'Surgeon Dentist and Cupper', who attended him in his final illness: 'it was very dull and gloomy, but just before 9 a.m. the sun burst forth and shone directly on him with that brilliancy which he loved to gaze on and transfer the likeness to his paintings. He died without a groan.'

Biographical Outline

1775	23 April. Joseph Mallord William Turner born at 21 Maiden Lane, Covent Garden, London, the eldest son of a barber.
1787	First signed and dated drawings.
1789	Probable date of earliest sketch-book from nature. Admitted student at the Royal Academy Schools, where he studied for four years. Also studying under Thomas Malton during this period.
1790	First exhibit, a watercolour, at the Royal Academy.
1791	First sketching tour, at Bristol, Bath, Malmesbury, etc.
1792	First visit to Wales.
1793	Awarded the 'Greater Silver Pallet' for landscape drawing by the Society of Arts.
1794	Publication of the first engraving after one of his drawings. Probably first year in which he spent the winter evenings copying drawings for Dr. Monro, often together with Thomas Girtin.
1795	Shows eight watercolours at the Royal Academy.
1796	Exhibits his first oil painting at the Royal Academy.
1797	First visit to the Lake District.
1799	Elected an Associate of the Royal Academy. Takes lodgings in Harley Street.
1802	12 February. Elected a full member of the Royal Academy. First journey abroad, to France and Switzerland.
1804	Death of Turner's mother. First exhibition at his own gallery in Harley Street.
1806	Takes a house on the river at Hammersmith.
1807	First part of the *Liber Studiorum* published. Elected Professor of Perspective at the Royal Academy.
1810	First recorded visit to Walter Fawkes at Farnley Hall in Yorkshire, where he was a frequent visitor until 1824.
1811	Delivers first lectures as Professor of Perspective. Starts building house at Twickenham. Alterations to his Gallery; the entrance is moved to Queen Ann Street West.
1815	Turner's R.A. exhibits violently criticised by Sir George Beaumont.
1817	Tour of the Netherlands and the Rhine Valley.
1819	Highly successful exhibitions of his works at the London homes of two of his patrons, Sir John Leicester and Walter Fawkes. In August sets out on first visit to Italy.
1820	Returns from Italy in February.
1821	Major alterations in house and gallery at Queen Ann Street West (formerly Harley Street) completed. Visit to France.
1822	Series of watercolours made for engravings ex-hibited in London by the publisher W. B. Cooke. Further exhibitions in 1823 and 1824. Visits Edinburgh, going by sea up the East coast.
1823	Commissioned to paint the *Battle of Trafalgar* for St. James's Palace. Sketches on the south-east coast.
1825	Tour of Holland, the Rhine and Belgium. Death of Walter Fawkes.
1826	Visits the Meuse, the Moselle, Brittany, and the Loire.
1827	Stays on Isle of Wight as guest of John Nash, the architect. Probable beginning of regular visits to Petworth, as guest of Lord Egremont.
1828	Last lectures as Professor of Perspective. Second visit to Italy; exhibited three oils in Rome.
1829	Visit to France. Death of Turner's father, who had long been living with him.
1832	Exhibition of engraved watercolours at Messrs. Moon, Boys and Graves, London; also in 1833 and 1834.
1833	First Venetian subjects exhibited at the Royal Academy. Visit to Paris and Italy, including, probably, Venice.
1834	Visit to France and Germany.
1835	Visit to Italy.
1836	Visit to France and Switzerland.
1837	Represented in British Institution's 'Old Masters' Exhibition. Death of Lord Egremont. Resigns as Professor of Perspective.
*c.*1839	Takes a cottage on the river at Chelsea.
1840	Visit to Italy, including Venice.
1841	Visits Switzerland, and again in 1842, 1843 and 1844.
1843	Anonymous publication of first volume of Ruskin's *Modern Painters*.
1845	Represented at the Congress of European Art in Munich. Acts as Deputy-President of the Royal Academy during the President's illness; continues with these duties in 1846. Two short visits to French coast, his last journeys abroad.
1848	Painting hung in the National Gallery to represent the Vernon Gift. No exhibits at Royal Academy.
1849	Two early works shown in the British Institution's 'Old Masters' Exhibition.
1850	Last exhibits (four oils) at the Royal Academy.
1851	19 December. Dies at his home in Chelsea; is buried in St. Paul's Cathedral on 30 December.

In what may be termed the view department Mr. Turner steps before his brethren with gigantic strides; he looks at nature with a penetrating and discriminating eye, and arranges her representations with exquisite taste, aided by a powerful genius. He has in our opinion more of that sublime faculty which we denominate genius than any other of the pictorial claimants; and could be another Claude or Vandevelde if he thought it expedient; but it is necessary for the dignity of the British School that he should be the father and founder of his own manner.
Morning Post, 1802.

We hasten, while we have yet room in this, to congratulate the country in having to boast of work which will carry down to posterity the date of the present time and cause it to be named with honour by those who are yet unborn. Contemporary criticism seems puny, and almost irreverent when applied to productions whose flourishing existence, when criticism is hushed and critics are no more, is secured by the eternal laws that regulate the moral nature of man. Wilkie's *Distraining for Rent* (118), and Turner's *Crossing the Brook* and *Dido building Carthage* are of this high class, and one almost shrinks from discussing in a newspaper paragraph achievements that raise the achievers to that small but noble group whose name is not so much of to-day as of all time.
William Hazlitt, in *The Champion*, 1815.

Sir George Beaumont called & sat a considerable time. He had just come from the Exhibition at the Royal Academy. He had again attentively considered Turner's picture of '*Dido* building Carthage'—so much cried up by Artists & newspapers. He wished to satisfy Himself that He was not mistaken in the judgment He had formed upon it:— He felt convinced that He was right in that opinion, and that the picture is painted in a false taste, not true to nature; the colouring discordant, out of harmony, resembling those French Painters who attempted imitations of Claude Lorrain, but substituted for His purity & just harmony, violent mannered oppositions of Brown and hot colours to cold tints, blues & greys: that several parts of Turner's picture were pleasingly treated but as a *whole* it was of the above character.
Of His picture 'Crossing the Brook' He sd. it appeared to Him *weak* and like the work of an Old

man, one who no longer saw or felt colour properly; it was all of *pea-green* insipidity.—These are my sentiments said He, & I have as good a right & it is as proper that I shd. express them as I have to give my opinion of a poetical or any other production.
The Farington Diary, 5 June, 1815. Reproduced by gracious permission of Her Majesty the Queen. James Greig edition, vol. VIII, 1928, p. 5.

To J. M. W. TURNER, ESQ., R.A., P.P.
My dear Sir, The unbought and spontaneous expression of the public opinion respecting my Collection of Water Colour Drawings, decidedly points out to whom this little catalogue should be inscribed.
To you, therefore, I dedicate it, first as an act of duty, and secondly as an Offering of Friendship; for, be assured, I can never look at it without intensely feeling the delight I have experienced during the greater part of my life from the exertion of your talent, and the pleasure of your society.
That you may year after year reap an accession of fame and fortune is the anxious wish of your sincere friend,
WALTER FAWKES
Dedication of the Catalogue printed after the Exhibition of the Fawkes Collection in London in 1819.

Having touched every natural key in the scale of art, Mr. Turner is determined to become attractive by the violence of his powers: yet, amidst all this glitter and gaud of colours, it is impossible to shut our eyes to the wonderful skill, and to the lightness and brilliancy which he has effected: so that had the subject been a fairy scene, we should have regarded it with admiration, nor, as now, lamented that it was anything but natural.
The Literary Gazette, 1826.

I have fortunately met with a good-tempered, funny, little, elderly gentleman, who will probably be my travelling companion throughout the journey. He is continually popping his head out of window to sketch whatever strikes his fancy, and became quite angry because the conductor would not wait for him whilst he took a sunrise view of Macerata. 'Damn the fellow!' says he. 'He has no feeling.' He speaks but a few words of Italian, about as much of French, which two languages he jumbles together most amusingly. His good

temper, however, carries him through all his troubles. I am sure you would love him for his indefatigability in his favourite pursuit. From his conversation he is evidently *near kin to*, if not *absolutely*, an artist. Probably you may know something of him. The name on his trunk is, J. W. or J. M. W. Turner!
Letter from Thomas Uwins (quoting an anonymous source) to Joseph Severn, dated Naples, 3 February 1829 (Mrs. Uwins, *A Memoir of Thomas Uwins, R.A.,* 1858, Vol. II, p. 240).

This celebrated artist stands unrivalled; a perfect master of his art. In his innumerable works he has produced almost every effect of light and shade of which the face of landscape is susceptible. His pictures are full of truth and poetry, and he seizes with a masterly hand the most sublime features of nature. There is so much genius and knowledge of art in his pictures, that his engravings from them have become works of reference to many of his contemporaries. Mr. Turner may be said to have founded a new school of landscape painting; a school superior for its brilliance and originality to any other in the world.
The Gallery of Modern British Artists, 1834.

Turner reminds us of the story of the man that sold his shadow, and that he might not appear singular, will not let anything in the world have a shadow to show for love or money. But the worst of it is, there is so great a submission to Turner's admitted genius, that his practice amounts to a persuasion to hosts of imitators to reject shadows, find them where they will. They would let in light into Erebus, and make 'darkness' much beyond the 'visible' point. Turner has been great, and now when in his vagaries he chooses to be great no longer, he is like the cunning creature, that having lost his tail, persuaded every animal that had one, that it was a useless appendage. He has robbed the sun of his birthright to cast shadows. Whenever Nature shall dispense with them too, and shall make trees like brooms, and this green earth to alternate between brimstone and white, set off with brightest blues that no longer shall keep their distance; when cows shall be made of white paper and milk-white figures represent pastoral, and when human eyes shall be happily gifted with a kaleidoscope power to patternize all confusion,

and shall become ophthalmia proof, then will Turner be a greater painter than ever the world yet saw, or than ever the world, constituted as it is at present, wishes to see. It is grievous to see genius, that it might outstrip all others, fly off into mere eccentricities, where it ought to stand alone, because none to follow it.
Blackwood's Edinburgh Magazine, October, 1836.

Not only in truth to nature, but in all other points, Turner is the greatest landscape painter who has ever lived. But his superiority is, in matters of feeling, one of kind, not of degree. Superiority of degree implies a superseding of others; superiority of kind implies only sustaining a more important, but not more necessary, part than others. If *truth* were all that we required from art, all other painters might cast aside their brushes in despair, for all that they have done he has done more fully and accurately; but when we pass to the higher requirements of art, beauty and character, their contributions are all equally necessary and desirable, because different, and however inferior in position or rank, are still perfect of their kind; their inferiority is only that of the lark to the nightingale, or of the violet to the rose.
John Ruskin, *Modern Painters*, Vol. I, 1843.

Whatever hesitation might have been felt by the mass of those who gazed on the later efforts of his brush in believing that he was entitled to the highest rank in his profession, none of his brethren seems to have any doubt of his decided excellence, and the best of them all have ever readily admitted his superiority in poetry, feeling, fancy, and genius. Long ere his death he had the felicity of knowing that his name and his works were regarded with that reverential respect and estimation which is given to other artists by posterity alone, and his earlier productions have been placed among the classical ornaments of our choicest collections and galleries for many years. Even those who could only sneer and smile at the erratic blaze of his colour . . . lingered minute after minute before the last incomprehensible 'Turner' that gleamed on the walls of the Academy, and the first name sought for upon the catalogue by the critic, artist, and amateur . . . was his also.
The Times, 31 December, 1851.

Turner's conversation, his lectures, and his advice were at all times enigmatical, not from want of knowledge, but from want of verbal power. Rare advice it was, if you could unriddle it, but so mysteriously given or expressed that it was hard to comprehend—conveyed sometimes in a few indistinct words, in a wave of the hand, a poke in the side, pointing at the same time to some part of a student's drawing, but saying nothing more than a 'Humph!' or 'What's that for?'. Yet the fault hinted at, the thing to be altered was there, if you could but find it out; and if, after a deep puzzle, you did succeed in comprehending his meaning, he would congratulate you when he came round again, and would give you some further hint; if not, he would leave you with another disdainful growl, or perhaps seizing your porte-crayon, or with his broad thumb, make you at once sensible of your fault. . . . The schools were usually better attended during his visitorships than during those of most other members, from which it may be inferred that the students appreciated his teaching. . . .

His lectures on perspective, after he was elected to the professorship, were, from his naturally enigmatical and ambiguous style of delivery, almost unintelligible. Half of each lecture was addressed to the attendant behind him, who was constantly busied, under his muttered directions, in selecting from a huge portfolio drawings and diagrams to illustrate his teaching; many of these were truly beautiful, speaking intelligibly enough to the eye, if his language did not to the ear. As illustrations of aërial perspective and the perspective of colour, many of his rarest drawings were at these lectures placed before the students in all the glory of their first unfaded freshness. A rare treat to our eyes they were. Thomas Stothard, the librarian to the Royal Academy, who was nearly deaf for some years before his death, was a constant attendant at Turner's lectures. A brother member, who judged of them rather from the known dryness of the subject, and the certainty of what Turner's delivery would be, than from any attendance on his part, asked the librarian why he was so constant. 'Sir,' said he, 'there is much to *see* at Turner's lectures—much that I delight in seeing, though I cannot hear him.' . . .

In person Turner had little of the outward appearance that we love to attribute to the possessors of genius. In the last twenty years of his life, during which we knew him well, his short figure had become corpulent—his face, perhaps from continual exposure to the air, was unusually red, and a little inclined to blotches. His dark eye was bright and restless—his nose, aquiline. He generally wore what is called a black dress-coat, which would have been the better for brushing— the sleeves were mostly too long, coming down over his fat and not over-clean hands. He wore his hat while painting on the varnishing days—or otherwise a large wrapper over his head, while on the warmest days he generally had another wrapper or comforter round his throat—though occasionally he would unloose it and allow the two ends to dangle down in front and pick up a little of the colour from his ample palette. This, together with his ruddy face, his rollicking eye, and his continuous, although, except to himself, unintelligible jokes, gave him the appearance of one of that now wholly extinct race—a long-stage coachman.
Samuel and Richard Redgrave, *A Century of British Painters*, 1866.

The Plates

WITHIN THE LIMITATIONS posed by matters of design and production the plates are arranged in a chronological sequence. Each caption includes a date; if this is preceded by '*c.*' this indicates that it is an approximate date, usually based on comparative or stylistic criteria; if by 'R.A.' or 'B.I.' this means that the work was exhibited at the Royal Academy or British Institution in that year.

In all measurements height precedes width. In no case is the reproduction of a work an enlargement; in a few cases drawings are reproduced actual size, and this is indicated in the caption.

For drawings in the Turner Bequest, deposited in the British Museum, the relevant *Inventory* references are given at the end of the captions.

(Plates 1 to 7 will be found in the text)

8. *(opposite) Transept of Tintern Abbey, Monmouthshire.*
R.A. 1795.
Watercolour over pencil, with pen and ink;
14 × 10¼ in. (355 × 260 mm.)
Oxford, Ashmolean Museum.

9. *The Pantheon, the Morning after the Fire.* 1792.
   Watercolour;
   $15\frac{1}{2} \times 20\frac{1}{2}$ in. (394 $\times$ 520 mm.)
   London, British Museum (IX A).

10. *Buttermere Lake, with Part of Cromack Water, Cumberland, a Shower.* R.A. 1798.
Oil on canvas;
35 × 47 in. (889 × 1,193 mm.)
London, Tate Gallery.

11. *Calais Pier, with French Poissards preparing for Sea: an English Packet arriving.* R.A. 1803.
Oil on canvas;
$67\frac{3}{4} \times 94\frac{1}{2}$ in. (1,720 × 2,400 mm.)
London, National Gallery.

12. *South View of Christ Church, &c. from the Meadows.* 1799.
Watercolour, with some pen and black ink, over pencil;
$12\frac{3}{8} \times 17\frac{3}{4}$ in. (315×451 mm.)
Oxford, Ashmolean Museum.

13. Paul Sandby, R.A.,
Windsor Castle; The Hundred Steps. c. 1790–5.
Gouache;
17¼ × 23 in. (439 × 585 mm.)
Windsor, The Royal Collection, Windsor Castle
(reproduced by gracious permission of Her
Majesty the Queen).

14. *Chepstow Castle.* 1794.
Watercolour;
8 × 11¾ in. (203 × 297 mm.)
London, Courtauld Institute of Art, University of
London.

15. Thomas Girtin,
Kirkstall Abbey, Yorkshire—Evening. c. 1800.
Watercolour;
$12 \times 20\frac{1}{8}$ in. (305 × 510 mm.)
London, Victoria and Albert Museum.

16. *Convents near Capo di Monte. c.* 1794.
    Pencil with blue and grey washes;
    $7 \times 16\frac{3}{8}$ in. (178×416 mm.)
    Manchester, Whitworth Art Gallery, University of Manchester.

17. '*Nunwell and Brading from Bembridge Mill*'. 1795.
    Pencil and watercolour;
    8 × 10⅜ in. (203 × 263 mm.)
    London, British Museum (XXIV 49).

18. *Fishermen at Sea off the Needles*. R.A. 1796.
Oil on canvas;
$36 \times 48\frac{1}{8}$ in. (915 × 1,222 mm.)
London, Tate Gallery.

19. *Transept of Ewenny Priory, Glamorganshire.* R.A. 1797.
    Watercolour;
    $15\frac{1}{2} \times 22$ in. (394 × 559 mm.)
    Cardiff, National Museum of Wales.

20. *Aeneas and the Sibyl, Lake Avernus. c.* 1798.
Oil on canvas;
$30\frac{1}{8} \times 38\frac{3}{4}$ in. (765×985 mm.)
London, Tate Gallery.

21. Richard Wilson, R.A.,
Lake Avernus and the Island of Ischia. c. 1752–7.
Oil on canvas; $18\frac{1}{2} \times 28\frac{1}{2}$ in. (470×725 mm.)
London, Tate Gallery.

23. *The Fifth Plague of Egypt* (actually the Seventh Plague). R.A. 1800.
Oil on canvas;
49 × 72 in. (1,245 × 1,830 mm.)
Indianapolis Museum of Art, Gift in memory of Evan F. Lilly.

22. *(opposite) Dolbadern Castle, North Wales.* R.A. 1800.
Oil on canvas;
47 × 35½ in. (1,193 × 902 mm.)
London, Royal Academy of Arts.

24. *The Fall of the Clyde, Lanarkshire: Noon.* R.A. 1802.
     Watercolour;
     $29\frac{3}{8} \times 41\frac{5}{8}$ in. (745 × 1,058 mm.)
     Liverpool, Walker Art Gallery.

25. *Edinburgh from St. Margaret's Loch, with Calton Hill on right.* 1801.
   Watercolour over pencil;
   $5 \times 7\frac{3}{4}$ in. (128×197 mm.) Actual size.
   London, British Museum (LV 10).

27. *Sun rising through Vapour: Fishermen cleaning and selling Fish.*
R.A. 1807.
Oil on canvas;
53 × 70½ in. (1,345 × 1,790 mm.)
London, National Gallery.

26. *Study for 'Calm'* (Sun rising through Vapour). *c.* 1805.
Black and white chalk on grey paper;
10¾ × 17⅛ in. (272 × 435 mm.)
London, British Museum (LXXXI 40).

28. *Pembroke Castle, South Wales: Thunder Storm approaching.* R.A. 1801.
Watercolour;
$26\frac{1}{2} \times 41$ in. $(673 \times 1{,}041$ mm.)
Toronto, University of Toronto.

29. *Fishermen launching a Boat in heavy Sea. c.* 1800–2.
Pen and ink and wash, on grey prepared paper;
$4\frac{1}{2} \times 7\frac{1}{8}$ in. (115 × 181 mm.) Actual size.
London, British Museum (LXVIII 3).

30. Willem van de Velde the Younger,
Vessels close-hauled. c. 1670.
Oil on canvas;
12⅞ × 15⅞ (327 × 403 mm.)
London, National Gallery.

31. *Fishermen upon a Lee-shore, in squally Weather.* R.A. 1802.
Oil on canvas;
36 × 48 in. (915 × 1,220 mm.)
London, the Iveagh Bequest, Kenwood.

32. *The Wreck of a Transport Ship. c.* 1807.
Oil on canvas;
$68\frac{1}{8} \times 95$ in. $(1,730 \times 2,410$ mm.)
Lisbon, Calouste Gulbenkian Foundation. Detail.

33. *The Thames near Walton Bridges. c.* 1807.
Oil on panel;
14⅝ × 29 in. (372 × 737 mm.)
London, Tate Gallery.

34. *Tree Tops and Sky, Guildford Castle, Evening. c.* 1807.
Oil on panel;
$10\frac{7}{8} \times 29$ in. (276×737 mm.)
London, Tate Gallery.

35. *Distant View of Lowther Castle (Park Scene)*. 1809.
Watercolour and pencil;
$8\frac{7}{8} \times 13\frac{7}{8}$ in. (224 × 352 mm.)
Oxford, Ashmolean Museum (Ruskin School Collection).

36. *(opposite) The Old Devil's
Bridge, St. Gothard*. 1802.
Watercolour and body-
colour on grey prepared
paper;
$18\frac{5}{8} \times 12\frac{3}{8}$ in. (473 × 314
mm.)
London, British Museum
(LXXV 34).

37. *The Mer de Glace, Chamonix.* 1802.
Watercolour and body-colour on grey
prepared paper.
$12\frac{3}{8} \times 18\frac{5}{8}$ in. (314×473 mm.)
London, British Museum (LXXV 22).

38. *The Mer de Glace and Source of the
Arveyron, Chamonix.* R.A. 1803.
Watercolour;
27×40 in. ($685 \times 1,015$ mm.)
United States, Mr. and Mrs. Paul
Mellon.

39. *The great Falls of the Reichenbach.* 1804. Watercolour; $39\frac{5}{8} \times 26\frac{3}{4}$ in. (1,007 × 680 mm.) Bedford, Cecil Higgins Museum.

40. *Bonneville, Savoy, with Mont Blanc.* R.A. 1803.
Oil on canvas;
36 × 48 in. (915 × 1,220 mm.)
Private Collection.

41. *(opposite)* *The Festival upon the Opening of the Vintage at Macon.* R.A. 1803.
Oil on canvas;
57 × 92 in. (1,448 × 2,338 mm.)
Sheffield, Graves Art Gallery.

42. *(opposite)* Claude Lorrain, *Landscape with Jacob and Laban.* 1654/5.
Oil on canvas;
56½ × 99 in. (1,435 × 2,515 mm.)
Petworth House, Sussex.

43. *Holy Family*. R.A. 1803.
    Oil on canvas;
    40 × 56 in. (1,016 × 1,422 mm.)
    London, Tate Gallery.

44. *The Goddess of Discord choosing the Apple of Contention in the Garden of the Hesperides.* B.I. 1806.
Oil on canvas;
61¼ × 86 in. (1,552 × 2,184 mm.)
London, Tate Gallery.

45. *Windsor Castle from the Thames. c.* 1805. Oil on canvas;
35 × 47 in. (890 × 1,194 mm.) Petworth House, Sussex.

46. *Study for 'Windsor Castle from the Thames'. c.* 1805. Watercolour and pen and ink on grey prepared paper; 5¾ × 10 in. (146 × 254 mm.) London, British Museum (xc 29a).

47. *Isleworth. c.* 1815.
    Pen and ink and wash;
    $8\frac{7}{16} \times 11\frac{1}{2}$ in. (215×292 mm.)
    London, British Museum (CXVIII I).

48. *(opposite) Isleworth c.* 1819.
Etching;
$8\frac{3}{16} \times 11\frac{1}{2}$ in. (208×292 mm.)
London, British Museum.

49. *(opposite) Isleworth.* 1819.
Mezzotint engraving by H. Dawe;
$8\frac{3}{16} \times 11\frac{7}{16}$ in. (208×290 mm.)
London, Victoria and Albert Museum.

50. *Scene on the Thames. c.* 1806–7. Watercolour over pencil;
$10\frac{1}{8} \times 14\frac{3}{8}$ in. (256 × 370 mm.) London, British Museum (xcv 46).

51. *Chevening Park, Kent. c.* 1806–7. Oil over pencil on paper; $10\frac{7}{8} \times 14\frac{7}{8}$ in. (276 × 378 mm.) London, British Museum (XCV (a) B).

52. *A country Blacksmith disputing upon the Price of Iron, and the Price charged to the Butcher for shoeing his Pony.*
R.A. 1807.
Oil on canvas;
$21\frac{5}{8} \times 30\frac{5}{8}$ in. (550×779 mm.)
London, Tate Gallery.

53. *Willows beside a Stream. c.* 1807.
Oil on canvas;
$33\frac{7}{8} \times 45\frac{3}{4}$ in. (860 × 1,165 mm.)
London, Tate Gallery.

54. *The Forest of Bere*. 1808.
    Oil on canvas;
    35 × 47 in. (890 × 1,194 mm.)
    Petworth House, Sussex.

55. P. J. de Loutherbourg, *An Avalanche in the Alps*. R.A. 1804. Oil on canvas; $43\frac{1}{4} \times 63$ in. (1,099 × 1,600 mm.) London, Tate Gallery.

56. *The Fall of an Avalanche in the Grisons.* Exhibited 1810. Oil on canvas; $35\frac{1}{2} \times 47\frac{1}{4}$ in. (902 × 1,200 mm.) London, Tate Gallery.

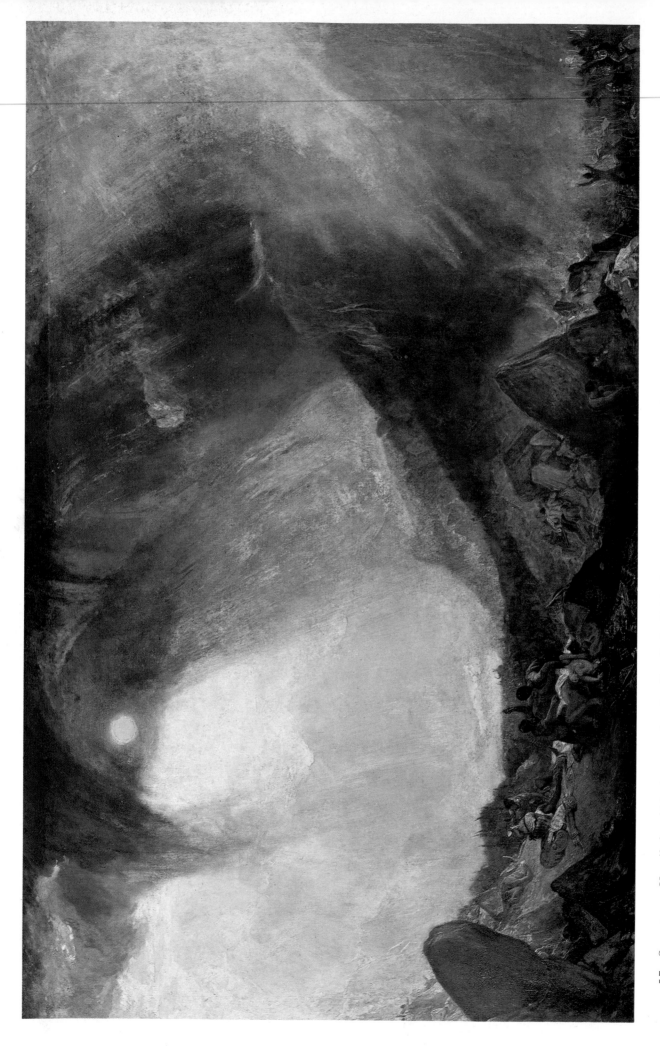

57. *Snowstorm: Hannibal and his Army crossing the Alps.* R.A. 1812. Oil on canvas; 57 × 93 in. (1,448 × 2,362 mm.) London, Tate Gallery.

58. *Frosty Morning*. R.A. 1813. Oil on canvas;
44¾ × 68¾ in. (1,137 × 1,746 mm.) London, Tate Gallery.

61. *Tabley, the Seat of Sir J. F. Leicester, Bart.: Windy Day.* R.A. 1809.
     Oil on canvas;
     36 × 47½ in. (915 × 1,206 mm.)
     Tabley House, Cheshire, Lt. Col. J. L. B. Leicester-Warren.

59. *(opposite) Falmouth Harbour.* 1813.
     Oil on paper prepared with a grey-brown ground;
     6⅛ × 9 1/16 in. (155 × 230 mm.)
     London, British Museum (CXXX C).

60. *(opposite) The Crook of Lune.* 1816–18.
     Watercolour and pen and ink;
     11 × 16⅜ in. (280 × 417 mm.)
     London, Courtauld Institute of Art, University of London.

62. *Petworth, Sussex, the Seat of the Earl of Egremont: Dewy Morning.* R.A. 1810. Oil on canvas;
35½ × 47½ in. (902 × 1,206 mm.) Petworth House, Sussex.

63. *Somer Hill, near Tunbridge.* R.A. 1811. Oil on canvas; 36 × 48⅛ in. (915 × 1,223 mm.) Edinburgh, National Gallery of Scotland.

64. Aelbert Cuyp,
    Landscape near Nijmegen.
    Oil on canvas;
    $44\frac{1}{2} \times 69\frac{1}{2}$ in. (1,130 × 1,765 mm.)
    Petworth House, Sussex.

65. *Dorchester Mead, Oxfordshire.* 1810.
Oil on canvas;
$40 \times 51\frac{1}{4}$ in. (1,016 × 1,302 mm.)
London, Tate Gallery.

66. *Whalley Bridge and Abbey, Lancashire: Dyers washing and drying Cloth.* R.A. 1811. Oil on canvas; $24\frac{1}{8} \times 36\frac{3}{8}$ in. (612 × 925 mm.) Lockinge, Berkshire, Christopher Loyd.

67. *Sunshine on the Tamar. c.* 1813. Watercolour; $8\frac{1}{2} \times 14\frac{1}{2}$ in. $(217 \times 367$ mm.) Oxford, Ashmolean Museum (Ruskin School Collection).

68. *The Junction of the Greta and Tees at Rokeby.* 1816–18. Watercolour over pencil; $11\frac{3}{8} \times 16\frac{1}{4}$ in. (290 × 414 mm.) Oxford, Ashmolean Museum (Ruskin School Collection).

69. *Leeds.* 1816. Watercolour;
$11\frac{1}{2} \times 16\frac{3}{4}$ in. (292 × 425 mm.) United States, Mr. and Mrs. Paul Mellon.

70. *Valley of the Wharfe from Caley Park. c.* 1815.
13 × 17½ in. (330 × 440 mm.) Farnley Hall, Yorkshire, G. N. Le G. Horton-Fawkes.

72. *Appulia in Search of Appulus.* B.I. 1814. Oil on canvas;
57 × 93 in. (1,448 × 2,362 mm.) London, Tate Gallery.

71. *Roslin Castle, Hawthornden.* 1818–20. Watercolour and body-colour; $6\frac{7}{8} \times 10\frac{1}{2}$ in. (175 × 267 mm.)
Indianapolis Museum of Art; Gift in Memory of Dr. and Mrs. Hugo Pantzer by their Children.

73. *Marksburg.* 1817. Watercolour; $7\frac{7}{8} \times 12\frac{1}{2}$ in. (200×318 mm.)
Indianapolis Museum of Art; Gift in Memory of Dr. and Mrs. Hugo O. Pantzer by their Children.

74. *St. Goarshausen and Katz Castle.* 1817. Watercolour, slightly heightened with white; 7⅝ × 12 in. (193 × 304 mm.) London, Courtauld Institute of Art, University of London.

John Dewey Library
Johnson State College
Johnson, Vermont 05656

75. *A Frontispiece (at Farnley Hall)*. 1815.
   Watercolour over pencil, with pen and ink;
   7×9½ in. (178×242 mm.)
   Oxford, Ashmolean Museum (Ruskin School Collection).

76. *Sketch of a Pheasant. c.* 1815.
Watercolour; $8\frac{3}{4} \times 13\frac{5}{8}$ in. (223×345 mm.)
Oxford, Ashmolean Museum (Ruskin School Collection).

77. *(overleaf) Dido building Carthage; or the Rise of the Carthaginian Empire.* R.A. 1815.
Oil on canvas;
$61\frac{1}{4} \times 91\frac{1}{4}$ in. ($1,555 \times 2,230$ mm.)
London, National Gallery.

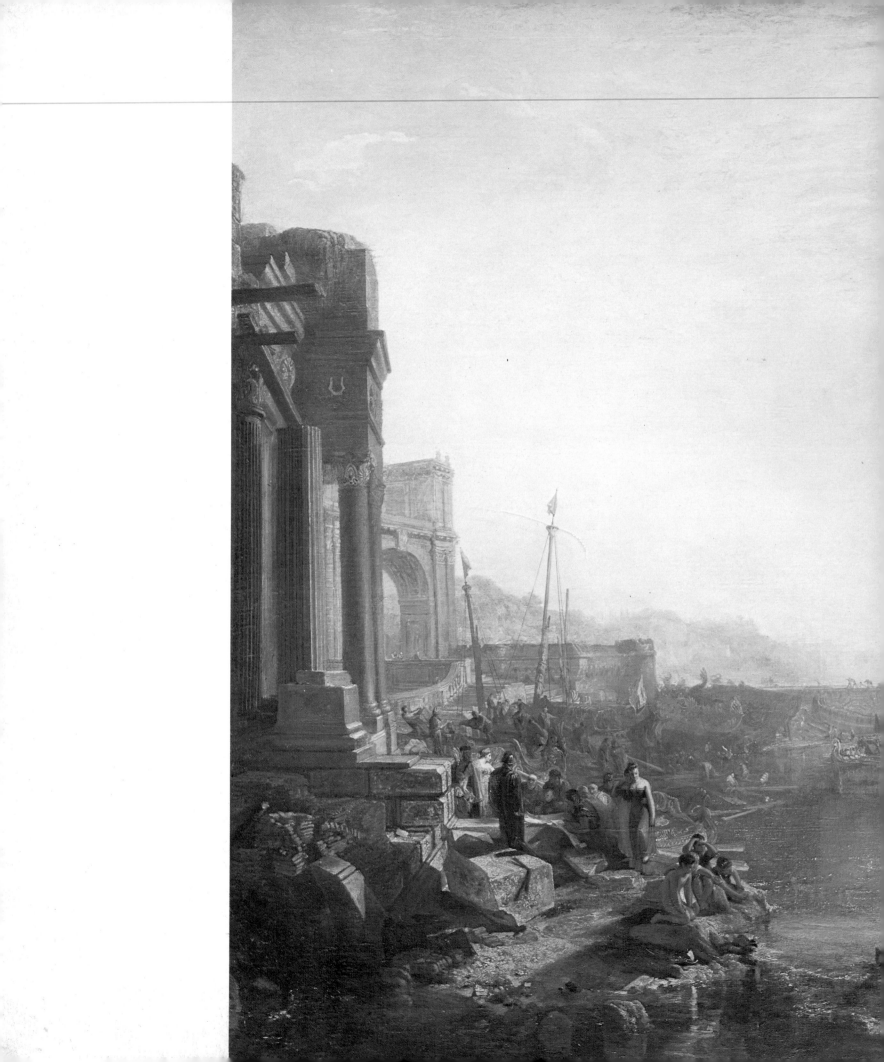

78. *Crossing the Brook*. R.A. 1815. Oil on canvas;
76 × 65 in. (1,930 × 1,651 mm.) London, Tate Gallery.

79. Claude Lorrain, *Landscape: Hagar and the Angel*. 1646. Canvas mounted on panel;
20¾ × 17¼ in. (527 × 438 mm.) London, National Gallery.

80. *A First Rate taking in Stores*. 1818.
Watercolour;
$11\frac{1}{4} \times 15\frac{5}{8}$ in. (286 × 398 mm.)
Bedford, Cecil Higgins Museum.

81. *Entrance of the Meuse: Orange-Merchant on the Bar, going to Pieces.* R.A. 1819.
Oil on canvas;
67 × 97½ in. (1,702 × 2,476 mm.)
London, Tate Gallery.

82. *View from Richmond Hill. c.* 1815. Watercolour;
$7\frac{1}{2} \times 10\frac{1}{2}$ in. (190×267 mm.) London, British Museum (CXCVII B).

84. (overleaf) *Rome from the Vatican: Raffaelle, accompanied by La Fornarina, preparing his Pictures for the Decoration of the Loggia.* R.A. 1820. Oil on canvas; $69\frac{1}{2} \times 131$ in. (1,765 × 3,332 mm.) London. Tate Gallery.

83. *England: Richmond Hill, on the Prince Regent's Birthday.* R.A. 1819. Oil on canvas; $71\frac{3}{4} \times 132$ in. (1,823 × 3,352 mm.) London, Tate Gallery.

85. Aelbert Cuyp, *View of Dordrecht*. Oil on canvas;
$38\frac{1}{2} \times 54\frac{1}{4}$ in. (978 × 1,378 mm.) London, the Iveagh Bequest, Kenwood.

86. *Dort or Dordrecht: The Dort Packet-boat from Rotterdam becalmed.* R.A. 1818. Oil on canvas; 61¾ × 93¼ in. (1,570 × 2,370 mm.) United States, Mr. and Mrs. Paul Mellon.

87. *Venice: looking east from the Giudecca: Sunrise*. 1819.
   Watercolour;
   $8\frac{3}{4} \times 11\frac{5}{16}$ in. (222 × 287 mm.)
   London, British Museum (CLXXXI 5).

88. *Venice: San Giorgio Maggiore from the Dogana.* 1819.
Watercolour;
$8\frac{13}{16} \times 11\frac{5}{16}$ in. (224 × 287 mm.)
London, British Museum (CLXXXI 4).

89. *The Bay of Baiae, with Apollo and the Sibyl*. R.A. 1823. Oil on canvas; $57\frac{1}{2} \times 93\frac{1}{2}$ in. (1,460 × 2,374 mm.) London, Tate Gallery.

90. *Ariccia?*, *Sunset*. 1828. Oil on canvas;
     23½ × 31 in. (597 × 788 mm.) London, Tate Gallery.

91. *Storm Clouds: Sunset. c.* 1825.
    Watercolour;
    $9\frac{1}{2} \times 13\frac{1}{4}$ in. (241 × 336 mm.)
    London, British Museum (CXCVII F).

92. *Scene on the Loire. c.* 1826–30.
   Body-colour and watercolour on blue-grey paper;
   $5\frac{1}{2} \times 7\frac{1}{2}$ in. (140 × 191 mm.)
   Oxford, Ashmolean Museum (Ruskin School Collection).

93. (*above*) Detail from *Harbour of Dieppe* (Plate 94).

94. *Harbour of Dieppe* (*changement de domicile*). R.A. 1825. Oil on canvas; 66¾ × 88¾ in. (1,737 × 2,254 mm.) New York, Frick Collection.

95. *Ponte di Rialto, Venice*. 1819. Pencil;
    $4\frac{3}{8} \times 7\frac{7}{16}$ in. (111×189 mm.) Actual size. London, British Museum (CLXXV 77a).

96. *Gondolas passing the Barberigo (?) Palace, Venice*. 1819. Pencil;
    $4\frac{3}{8} \times 7\frac{7}{16}$ in. (111×189 mm.) Actual size. London, British Museum (CLXXV 38).

97. *Rome, from the Vatican*. 1819. Pencil, pen and ink, heightened with white on grey paper;
$9\frac{1}{8} \times 14\frac{1}{2}$ in. (231 × 370 mm.) London, British Museum (CLXXXIX 41).

98. *View in Rome with the Basilica of Constantine and the Colosseum*. 1819. Pencil and watercolour on grey paper;
$9\frac{1}{8} \times 14\frac{1}{2}$ in. (229 × 370 mm.) London, British Museum (CLXXXIX 20).

101. *The Passage of Mont Cenis: Snowstorm.* 1820.
Watercolour;
28 × 40 in. (711 × 1,017 mm.)
Birmingham, City Art Gallery.

99. *(opposite) Naples.* 1819.
Watercolour over pencil;
$10\frac{1}{16}$ × 16 in. (255 × 406 mm.)
London, British Museum (CLXXXVII 13).

100. *(opposite) Tivoli.* 1819.
Watercolour over pencil;
$10\frac{1}{16}$ × 16 in. (255 × 406 mm.)
London, British Museum (CLXXXVII 32).

102.

Totnes, on the River Dart.
1824. Watercolour;
$6\frac{3}{8} \times 9\frac{1}{16}$ in. (162×232
mm.) London, British
Museum (CCVIII B).

103.

Totnes, on the River Dart.
Mezzotint engraving
by C. Turner; $6\frac{5}{16} \times 9$
in. (160×228 mm.)
London, British
Museum.

04. *Colchester. c.* 1827.
Watercolour,
slightly heightened
with white; $11\frac{1}{8} \times$
$15\frac{7}{8}$ in. $(283 \times 404$
mm.) London,
Courtauld Institute
of Art, University of
London.

05. *Richmond Hill and
Bridge, Surrey. c.* 1830.
Watercolour; $11\frac{1}{2} \times$
17 in. $(292 \times 432$
mm.) London,
British Museum
(R. W. Lloyd
Bequest).

106, 107. *Ulysses deriding Polyphemus*. R.A. 1829.
　　　　Oil on canvas;
　　　　52¼ × 80 in. (1,325 × 2,030 mm.)
　　　　London, National Gallery. Detail on right.

108. *Petworth Park: Tillington Church in the Distance. c.* 1828.
Oil on canvas;
$25\frac{1}{4} \times 58\frac{1}{4}$ in. ($642 \times 1,480$ mm.)
London, Tate Gallery.

109. *Chichester Canal*. *c*. 1830.
Oil on canvas;
$25\frac{1}{2} \times 52\frac{3}{4}$ in. ($647 \times 1,340$ mm.)
London, Tate Gallery.

110. *Calais Sands, low Water, Poissards collecting Bait.* R.A. 1830.
Oil on canvas;
$28\frac{1}{2} \times 42$ in. ($724 \times 1,067$ mm.)
Bury Art Gallery, Lancashire.

111. *'Santa Maria della Spina, Pisa.'* *c*. 1832.
Watercolour on buff paper;
$7\frac{1}{2} \times 6\frac{3}{4}$ in. (190×173 mm.)
Oxford, Ashmolean Museum.

112. *'Santa Maria della Spina, Pisa.'* 1832.
Steel engraving by E. Finden;
$3\frac{1}{2} \times 3\frac{1}{8}$ in. (89×80 mm.) Actual size.
London, British Museum.

113. *'Château of Amboise.'* c. 1830. Watercolour and body-colour, with pen and
black ink, on grey paper; 5⅜ × 7⅜ in. (136 × 188 mm.) Actual size.
Oxford, Ashmolean Museum.

114. *'Château of Amboise.'* 1833.
Engraving on steel by J. B. Allen;
3¹¹⁄₁₆ × 5¹¹⁄₁₆ in. (94 × 145 mm.)
Actual size.
London, British Museum.

115. *Rouen, looking down River. c.* 1830.
Body-colour and watercolour on blue paper;
5½ × 7½ in. (140 × 191 mm.) Actual size.
London, British Museum (CCLIX 108).

116. *View on the Seine. c.* 1830.
    Body-colour and watercolour, on blue paper;
    $5\frac{1}{2} \times 7\frac{1}{2}$ in. (140 × 191 mm.)
    London, British Museum (CCLIX 70).

117. *The Seat of William Moffat, Esq., at Mortlake. Early (Summer's) Morning.* R.A. 1826.
Oil on canvas;
$36\frac{5}{8} \times 48\frac{1}{2}$ in. (930 × 1,232 mm.)
New York, Frick Collection.

118. *Yacht Racing in the Solent, No.1*. 1827. Oil on canvas; 18¼ × 28½ in. (464 × 724 mm.) London, Tate Gallery.

119. *East Cowes Castle, the Seat of J. Nash, Esq.: the Regatta beating to windward.* R.A. 1828. Oil on canvas; 36¼ × 48 in. (920 × 1,220 mm.) Indianapolis Museum of Art, Gift of Mr. and Mrs. Nicholas Noyes.

121. *Between Decks.* 1827.
      Oil on canvas;
      12 × 19⅛ in. (305 × 484 mm.)
      London, Tate Gallery.

120. *(opposite) Boccaccio relating the Tale of the Birdcage.* R.A. 1828.
      Oil on canvas;
      48 × 36 in. (1,220 × 915 mm.)
      London, Tate Gallery.

122. *Palestrina*. 1828; R.A. 1830.
    Oil on canvas;
    $55\frac{1}{2} \times 98$ in. (1,410×2,481 mm.)
    London, Tate Gallery.

123. *The Lake, Petworth: Sunset, fighting Bucks. c.* 1830.
Oil on canvas;
$24\frac{1}{4} \times 57\frac{1}{2}$ in. (615 × 1,460 mm.)
Petworth House, Sussex.

124. *View of Orvieto*. 1828; R.A. 1830.
Oil on canvas;
$36 \times 48\frac{1}{2}$ in. ($915 \times 1,232$ mm.)
London, Tate Gallery.

125. *Coast Scene near Naples*. 1828.
Oil on board;
$16\frac{1}{8} \times 23\frac{1}{2}$ in. (410×597 mm.)
London, Tate Gallery.

126. *Regulus.* 1828; B.I. 1837.
    Oil on canvas;
    36 × 48 in. (915 × 1,220 mm.)
    London, Tate Gallery.

127. *Pilate washing his Hands*. R.A. 1830.
Oil on canvas;
36 × 48 in. (915 × 1,220 mm.)
London, Tate Gallery.

128. *(opposite) Jessica*. 1828, R.A. 1830.
Oil on canvas;
47 × 35 in. (1,194 × 889 mm.)
Petworth House, Sussex.

129. *Landscape at Petworth: Evening. c.* 1827–30.
Body-colour on blue paper;
5½ × 7½ in. (140 × 190 mm.) Actual size.
London, British Museum (CCXLIV 59).

130. *(opposite) The square Dining Room, Petworth. c.* 1827–30
Body-colour on blue paper;
5½ × 7½ in. (140 × 190 mm.)
London, British Museum (CCXLIV 108).

131. *(opposite) Petworth; playing Billiards. c.* 1827–30.
Body-colour on blue paper;
5½ × 7½ in. (140 × 190 mm.)
London, British Museum (CCXLIV 116).

132. *The Burning of the Houses of Parliament.* 1834. Watercolour;
$9\frac{1}{4} \times 12\frac{3}{4}$ in. (235 × 324 mm.) London, British Museum (CCLXXXIII 2).

133. *The Burning of the Houses of Lords and Commons, October 16, 1834.* R.A. 1835. Oil on canvas; 36½ × 48½ in. (927 × 1,232 mm.) Cleveland Museum of Art, Ohio.

134. *Interior at Petworth. c. 1835–7*. Oil on canvas.
35¾ × 48 in. (908 × 1,220 mm.) London, Tate Gallery.

135. *Petworth; the Artist and his Admirers. c.* 1827–30. Body-colour on blue paper; 5½ × 7½ in. (140 × 190 mm.) Actual size. London, British Museum (CCXLIV 102).

136. *Watteau Study by Fresnoy's Rules*. R.A. 1831.
Oil on panel;
$15\frac{1}{2} \times 27\frac{1}{2}$ in. (394 × 699 mm.)
London, Tate Gallery.

137. *(opposite) Music Party, Petworth. c. 1835.*
Oil on canvas;
$47\frac{3}{4} \times 35\frac{5}{8}$ in. (1,212 × 905 mm.)
London, Tate Gallery.

138. *Life-boat and Manby Apparatus going off to a stranded Vessel making Signal (blue lights) of Distress.* R.A. 1831. Oil on canvas; 36 × 48 in. (915 × 1,220 mm.) London, Victoria and Albert Museum.

139. *Staffa, Fingal's Cave.* R.A. 1832. Oil on canvas; 36 × 48 in. (915 × 1,220 mm.) Private Collection.

140. *Bridge of Sighs, Ducal Palace and Custom-house, Venice: Canaletti painting.* R.A. 1833. Oil on canvas; 20¼ × 32½ in. (515 × 825 mm.) London, Tate Gallery.

141. *(below) The Burning of the Houses of Lords and Commons, 16th of October, 1834.* B.I. 1835. Oil on canvas; $36\frac{1}{2} \times 48\frac{1}{2}$ in. (927 × 1,232 mm.) Philadelphia Museum of Art; the John H. McFadden Collection.

142. *The Parting of Hero and Leander—from the Greek of Musaeus.* R.A. 1837.
Oil on canvas;
$57\frac{1}{2} \times 93$ in. (1,461 × 2,362 mm.)
London, National Gallery.

143. *Keelmen hauling in Coals by Night.* R.A. 1835.
   Oil on canvas;
   $36\frac{1}{4} \times 48\frac{1}{4}$ in. ($923 \times 1{,}228$ mm.)
   Washington, National Gallery of Art (Widener Collection).

John Dewey Library
Johnson State College
Johnson, Vermont 05656

144. *A Fire at Sea. c.* 1835.
Oil on canvas;
$67\frac{1}{2} \times 86\frac{3}{4}$ in. ($1,715 \times 2,204$ mm.)
London, Tate Gallery.

145. *Waves breaking on a lee Shore. c.* 1835.
Oil on canvas;
$23\frac{1}{2} \times 37\frac{1}{2}$ in. (597×952 mm.)
London, Tate Gallery.

147. *Festive Lagoon Scene, Venice. c.* 1840–45.
    Oil on canvas;
    35¾ × 47¾ in. (910 × 1,212 mm.)
    London, Tate Gallery.

146. *(opposite) The Fighting 'Téméraire' tugged to her last Berth to be broken up, 1838.*
    Detail of Plate 152.

148. *Slavers throwing overboard the Dead and Dying—Typhon coming on* ('*The Slave Ship*'). R.A. 1840. Oil on canvas; 35¾ × 48 in. (910 × 1,220 mm.) Boston, Museum of Fine Arts.

149. *Heidelberg. c.* 1840. Watercolour;
$14\frac{1}{2} \times 21\frac{5}{8}$ in. (369 × 550 mm.) Edinburgh, National Gallery of Scotland.

150. *Light and Colour (Goethe's Theory) — the Morning after the Deluge — Moses writing the Book of Genesis.*
R.A. 1843. Oil on canvas; 31 × 31 in. (788 × 788 mm.) London, Tate Gallery.

151. *Shade and Darkness—the Evening of the Deluge*. R.A. 1843.
Oil on canvas;
$31 \times 30\frac{3}{4}$ in. (788 × 782 mm.)
London, Tate Gallery.

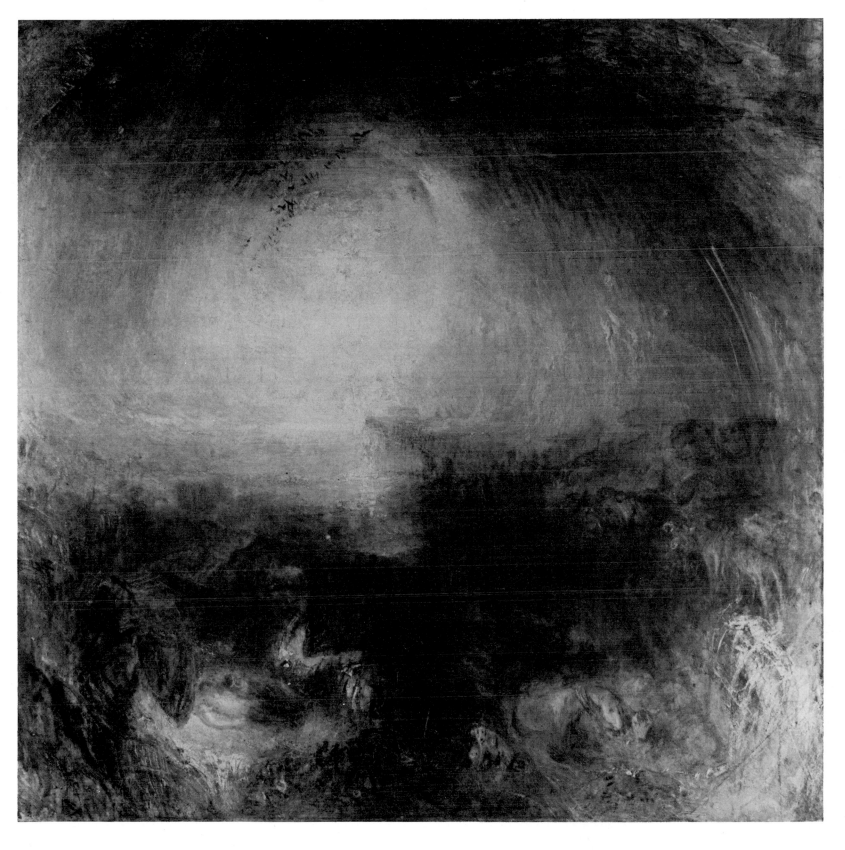

152. *The Fighting 'Téméraire' tugged to her last berth to be broken up, 1838*. R.A. 1839. Oil on canvas; 35¾ × 48 in. (910 × 1,220 mm.) London, National Gallery.

153. *Ancient Rome: Agrippina landing with the Ashes of Germanicus.* R.A. 1839. Oil on canvas; 35 × 47½ in. (889 × 1,206 mm.) London, Tate Gallery.

156. *Venice, the Piazzetta with the Ceremony of the Doge marrying the Sea. c. 1835–40.*
Oil on canvas;
36 × 47¾ in. (915 × 1,212 mm.)
London, Tate Gallery.

154. *(opposite) Modern Italy—the Pifferari. R.A. 1838.*
Oil on canvas;
36½ × 48½ in. (926 × 1,232 mm.)
Glasgow, Art Gallery.

155. *(opposite) The Ponte delle Torri, Spoleto. c. 1840.*
Oil on canvas;
36 × 48 in. (915 × 1,220 mm.)
London, Tate Gallery.

157. *Venice, from the Canale della Giudecca, Chiesa di S. Maria della Salute, &c.* R.A. 1840. Oil on Canvas; 24 × 36 in. (610 × 915 mm.) London, Victoria and Albert Museum.

158. *The Dogana, San Giorgio, Citella, from the Steps of the Europa.* R.A. 1842. Oil on canvas; 24½ × 36½ in. (622 × 926 mm.) London, Tate Gallery.

159. *Campo Santo, Venice*. R.A. 1842.
     Oil on canvas;
     $24\frac{1}{2} \times 36\frac{1}{2}$ in. $(622 \times 926$ mm.$)$
     The Toledo Museum of Art, Ohio (Gift of Edward Drummond Libbey).

160. *Schloss Rosenau, seat of H.R.H. Prince Albert of Coburg, near Coburg, Germany.* R.A. 1841.
Oil on canvas;
$38\frac{1}{4} \times 49\frac{1}{8}$ in. (970 × 1,248 mm.)
Liverpool, the Walker Art Gallery.

161. *Heidelberg Castle in the Olden Time.*
c. 1840.
Oil on canvas;
$52 \times 79\frac{1}{2}$ in. (1,320 × 2,020 mm.)
London, Tate Gallery.

162. *Venice: the Grand Canal.* 1840. Watercolour over slight pencil indications, with pen and red and blue ink, and some heightening with white; $8\frac{7}{16} \times 12\frac{3}{8}$ in. (215 × 315 mm.) Oxford, Ashmolean Museum.

163. *Venice: the Riva degli Schiavoni.* 1840. Watercolour, with pen and red and brown ink and some scraping out; $8\frac{1}{2} \times 12\frac{1}{2}$ in. (217 × 317 mm.) Oxford, Ashmolean Museum.

164. *(opposite) St. Benedetto, looking towards Fusina.* R.A. 1843. Oil on canvas; $24\frac{1}{2} \times 36\frac{1}{2}$ in. (622 × 926 mm.) London, Tate Gallery.

165. *(opposite) Venice Quay, Ducal Palace.* R.A. 1844. Oil on canvas; $23\frac{1}{2} \times 35\frac{1}{2}$ in. (597 × 902 mm.) London, Tate Gallery.

166. *River, with a Distant Castle. c.* 1845.
    Watercolour;
    $10 \times 10\frac{1}{2}$ in. (254 × 267 mm.)
    London, British Museum (CCCLXIV 148).

167. *Ehrenbreitenstein. c.* 1840.
Watercolour and pen and ink
irregular approx. $9\frac{3}{4} \times 11\frac{7}{8}$ in. (248×302 mm.)
London, British Museum (CCCLXIV 285).

168. *The Splügen Pass.* 1842. Watercolour;
11½ × 17¾ in. (292 × 451 mm.) Washington, J. Biddle.

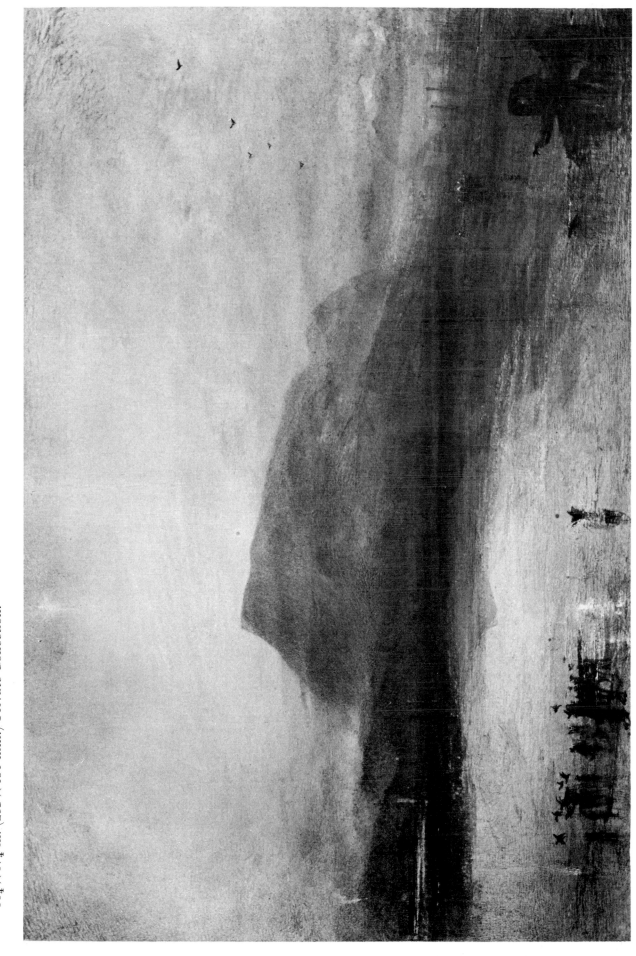

169. *Lake of Lucerne—Sunrise. The 'Blue Rigi'*. 1842. Watercolour; 11¾ × 17¾ in. (299 × 451 mm.) Private Collection.

170. *Breakers on a flat Beach. c.* 1835.
Oil on canvas;
$35\frac{1}{2} \times 47\frac{1}{2}$ in. ($902 \times 1{,}206$ mm.)
London, Tate Gallery.

171. *(opposite) Dawn after the Wreck. c.* 1840.
Watercolour and body-colour;
$9\frac{5}{8} \times 14\frac{1}{4}$ in. (254×362 mm.)
London, Courtauld Institute of Art, University of London.

172. *(opposite) Lake of Geneva. c.* 1846–8.
Watercolour;
$14\frac{1}{2} \times 21\frac{1}{4}$ in. (368×540 mm.)
Indianapolis, Mr. and Mrs. Kurt F. Pantzer.

173. *Snowstorm—Steamboat off a Harbour's Mouth.* R.A. 1842.
Oil on canvas;
36 × 48 in. (915 × 1,220 mm.)
London, Tate Gallery.

174. *Peace—Burial at Sea*. R.A. 1842.
Oil on canvas;
34¼ × 34⅛ in. (870 × 867 mm.)
London, Tate Gallery.

175. *Rain, Steam and Speed—The Great Western
      Railway*. R.A. 1844.
      Oil on canvas;
      35¾ × 48 in. (910 × 1,220 mm.)
      London, National Gallery.

176. *Whalers*. R.A. 1845.
      Oil on canvas;
      35 × 47 in. (889 × 1,194 mm.)
      London, Tate Gallery.

177. *Norham Castle, Sunrise. c.* 1840–45.
Oil on canvas;
$35\frac{3}{4} \times 48$ in. (910 × 1,220 mm.)
London, Tate Gallery.

178. *Sun setting over a Lake. c.* 1845.
Oil on canvas;
$35\frac{7}{8} \times 48\frac{1}{4}$ in. (912 × 1,225 mm.)
London, Tate Gallery.

179. *(opposite) Lucerne—Evening. c.* 1842.
Watercolour;
$9\frac{1}{4} \times 12\frac{7}{8}$ in. *(235 × 327 mm.)*
London, British Museum (CCCLXIV 324).

180. *(opposite) Lucerne by Moonlight.* 1843.
Watercolour;
$11\frac{1}{2} \times 18\frac{3}{4}$ in. (292 × 477 mm.)
London, British Museum (R. W. Lloyd Bequest).

181. *The Angel standing in the Sun.* R.A. 1846.
Oil on canvas;
31 × 31 in. (788 × 788 mm.)
London, Tate Gallery.

182. *The Visit to the Tomb*. R.A. 1850.
Oil on canvas;
36 × 48 in. (915 × 1,220 mm.)
London, Tate Gallery.

183. *The Wreck Buoy. c.* 1809 and R.A. 1849.
      Oil on canvas;
      $36\frac{1}{2} \times 48\frac{1}{2}$ in. (926 × 1,232 mm.)
      Liverpool, Walker Art Gallery.

184. *(opposite) Norham Castle.* 1797.
      Pencil;
      $8\frac{1}{4} \times 10\frac{5}{8}$ in. (210 × 270 mm.)
      London, British Museum (XXXIV 57).

185. *(opposite) Norham Castle.* 1801.
      Pencil;
      $6\frac{1}{2} \times 9$ in. (165 × 228 mm.)
      London, British Museum (LIII 44a & 45).

John Dewey Library
Johnson State College
Johnson, Vermont 0565&

186. *Study for a Picture of Norham Castle. c.* 1798. Watercolour; 26 × 32 in. (660 × 813 mm.)
London, British Museum (L B).

187. *Norham Castle, on the Tweed. c.* 1815.
Pen and ink wash;
7½ × 10¾ in. (190 × 273 mm.)
London, British Museum (CXVIII D).

188. *(opposite) Norham Castle, on the Tweed.* 1816.
Mezzotint by C. Turner;
8¼ × 11½ in. (210 × 292 mm.) London, British Museum.

NORHAM CASTLE ON THE TWEED.
the Drawing in the Possession of the late Lord Lascelles

189. *Norham Castle, on the River Tweed. c.* 1824.
Watercolour;
$6\frac{1}{8} \times 8\frac{1}{2}$ in. (155 × 216 mm.)
London, British Museum
(CCVIII O).

190. *Norham Castle, on the River Tweed.* 1824.
Mezzotint by C. Turner;
$6 \times 8\frac{1}{2}$ in. (152 × 216 mm.)
London, British Museum.

(These notes should be read in conjunction with the *Introduction*. There is not a note for every plate, and where a plate is omitted in this section the work reproduced is usually fully discussed in the *Introduction*.)

1. Painted in about 1798, when Turner was twenty-three, this is one of the few self-portraits known today. Both this, and an earlier one of about 1792, which once belonged to Ruskin, show clearly the brightness and intensity of Turner's eyes, still very much in evidence in later portraits of Turner by other artists.

2. This satirical Rembrandtesque drawing provides many clues to Turner's interest in the fashion for technical theorising and experiments, which prevailed among English artists at the turn of the century. Draft verses inscribed on the back begin with the lines, 'Pleased with his work he views it o'er & o'er/And finds fresh beauties never seen before'. The drawing is fully discussed by John Gage in *Colour in Turner*, pp. 136–8.

3. John Thomas Smith (1766–1833) was a topographical artist and antiquary. He became Keeper of Prints and Drawings at the British Museum in 1816, and was a respected figure in the London art world.

4. This telling portrayal of Turner at work at the Royal Academy on varnishing day, should be studied in conjunction with E. V. Rippingille's vivid description of a similar scene, quoted on pp. 41–2. Turner showed several square paintings at the R.A. between 1840 and 1846, but they were all smaller than the canvas on which he is seen working here.

5. Probably made at the end of his life, in about 1850, this study shows Turner in heavy and somewhat shabby clothes looking singularly out of place; this impression is reinforced by the stubble on his chin and by the fact that he is wearing slippers. Turner never took much care about what he wore, nor did he often move in 'society'; indeed he would surely much have preferred to be holding a mug of ale than the tea-cup with which he is portrayed here.

6. This is one of a set of three small compositions painted by George Jones, R.A., one of the artist's executors, soon after Turner's death. The others show his body lying in state in the Gallery, and his burial in the Crypt of St. Paul's Cathedral. George Jones was a close friend of Turner, and must have been a frequent visitor to his Gallery in Queen Ann Street West.

7. Turner bought land at Twickenham in 1807, and started building Sandycombe Lodge (first called Solus Lodge) to his own designs in 1810. The garden was looked after by Turner's father, whose declining health led to the sale of the property in 1826. The house still stands today.

8. One of eight drawings exhibited by Turner at the Royal Academy in 1795, the last year in which he showed only watercolours. This luminous drawing shows him already at the height of his powers as a topographical draughtsman in the traditional manner; it was at this exhibition that the diarist Joseph Farington, R.A. first noticed Turner's work. Turner had visited Tintern in 1792, and perhaps again in the following year; there are several early drawings of Tintern in the Turner Bequest, though none is related to the present composition, of which there is, however, a weaker version in the R.W. Lloyd Bequest at the British Museum.

9. This ambitious composition displays Turner's early mastery of the current style of architectural draughtsmanship, and his emulation of artists such as Edward Dayes in bringing the subject to life by the inclusion of action and many figures on quite a large scale. Two sketches of the ruins of the Pantheon are also in the Turner Bequest (IX B and C).

10. Exhibited in 1798, the first year in which verses were allowed in the R.A. catalogue, this was accompanied by an adaptation of six lines from Thomson's *Spring* referring to a 'grand ethereal bow'. The composition is derived from an on-the-spot watercolour made on Turner's first visit to the Lake District, in 1797 (XXXV 84), in which there is no rainbow. The painting, which has probably darkened considerably, shows the strong influence of Richard Wilson.

11. See note to Plate 32.

12. A full account of the ten Oxford Almanack drawings and of the commission for them is given in the present author's *Ruskin and Turner*, pp. 55–

63. Turner was paid ten guineas per drawing. He delivered the final drawings in 1804.

13. Paul Sandby (1730–1809), a Founder Member of the Royal Academy, was one of the most influential and successful drawing masters of his day. He exhibited watercolours and gouache drawings regularly at the R.A., and in his last years also showed work in oils.

15. Thomas Girtin (1775–1802) worked almost exclusively in watercolours, and exhibited his drawings at the Royal Academy from 1794 onwards. This drawing is a well-known example of his later panoramic compositions, in which the rendering of atmosphere is particularly effective.

16. This is a fairly close copy, in which, however, the light effect is strengthened, of a drawing in Volume V of the Beckford Sketch-Books of J. R. Cozens, now in the Whitworth Gallery, Manchester. Numerous such wash copies of Cozens drawings were made for Dr. Monro by Turner, Girtin, Edward Dayes and others, and it is always difficult to give a specific attribution to them. Turner himself purchased several lots at Dr. Monro's sale in 1833, which are included in the Turner Bequest.

17. Like the view of Chepstow (Plate 14), this unfinished drawing shows close affinities with the work of Girtin at this time, both in the detailed outline and colouring of the windmill and in the freer rendering of the distant landscape. It is probable that the pencil drawing was made on the spot, and was then partially coloured in at a later time.

18. Known as 'The Cholmeley Sea Piece', this canvas can be identified with confidence as the first oil painting exhibited by Turner at the Royal Academy, in 1796. Turner toured in the Isle of Wight in 1795, but none of the surviving sketches are connected with this painting, which relies heavily on the influence of P. J. de Loutherbourg and Joseph Wright of Derby, who both specialised in moonlight scenes. Turner's life-long interest in the depiction of light is already clearly seen here, with the striking contrast between the cold light of the moon and the warm light of the lamp in the boat.

19. A contemporary reviewer compared this dramatic interior with Rembrandt, and John Gage has suggested the influence of Piranesi. There is a slight pencil sketch of this scene in the 'Smaller South Wales' sketch-book (xxv 11), used on a tour in Wales in 1795, but this gives no indication of the light effect. The watercolour is dryly and quite thinly applied, and is brilliantly manipulated to render the shimmering effect of the light streaming in through the windows and door.

20. One of the most Wilsonian of Turner's paintings, this Italian scene precedes his first visit to Italy by many years. It is probably Turner's earliest effort in the classical tradition of historical landscape, with an historical, biblical or mythological subject as its theme. The composition is based on a drawing by Sir Richard Colt Hoare, whose part in the development of this picture is analysed by John Gage in a recent article, 'Turner and Stourhead: the Making of a Classicist?' in *The Art Quarterly*, xxxvii (1974), pp. 59–87.

21. Richard Wilson, R.A. (1713–82), was born in Wales, and, having been trained as a portrait painter, decided to devote himself almost exclusively to landscape during a lengthy visit to Italy which began late in 1750. The present canvas was painted during that visit, but Wilson continued with his Italian subjects throughout the remainder of his career. Ruskin rightly singled out Wilson as the founder of the British landscape school.

22. Exhibited at the Royal Academy in 1800, the first exhibition after Turner's election as an Associate, this was the earliest painting to be accompanied in the catalogue by some of Turner's own verses. When he was elected a full member of the Academy in 1802, Turner presented *Dolbadern Castle* as his Diploma Work, though he later tried, unsuccessfully, to exchange it for another (unidentified) painting. Thickly and solidly painted, it is typical of Turner's work under the influence of Wilson. Based on a number of drawings made during a visit to North Wales in 1798, it is already far more than a topographical or picturesque record, and has a strong romantic feeling, emphasised by the group of small figures in the manner of Salvator Rosa in the foreground.

23. When shown in 1800 this was the largest and most ambitious canvas that Turner had yet submitted to the Royal Academy, and it heralded the impact

of a new influence on the artist, that of Nicolas Poussin. Though he gave the painting the title of *The Fifth Plague of Egypt*, the lines from Exodus which accompanied it in the catalogue describe the Seventh Plague, that of thunder and hail, and these seem to be the main themes of the composition. It has been suggested that Turner gained inspiration for this painting from a storm he had experienced in the mountains of North Wales. Turner exhibited another Plague subject, *The Tenth Plague of Egypt*, in 1802 (Tate Gallery, No. 470).

24, 28. Turner exhibited a series of such exceptionally large and ambitious watercolours in the early 1800s. Their dark and heavy texture re-echoes that of his oil paintings at this time, and in this instance he was probably adapting his oil technique to watercolour rather than the other way round, which became his more usual custom.

25. Turner paid his first visit to Scotland in 1801, and spent about three weeks there, during which he used some six sketch-books, one of which was devoted to Edinburgh (LV). In this he achieves a new delicacy of touch, using a limited range of washes with greatly increased freedom and speed to suggest form and light.

26, 27. The 'Calais Pier' sketch-book (LXXXI) contains a number of studies connected with *Sun rising through Vapour*, including the one reproduced here. This sketch-book is devoted exclusively to studies connected with several of Turner's major canvases of this period, and there is no indication as to where, if anywhere, he witnessed the scene shown in the painting. This was unsold until 1818, when it was purchased by Sir John Leicester (later Lord de Tabley) for 350 guineas. At the sale following his death in 1827 Turner bought it back for 490 guineas. *Sun rising through Vapour* and *Dido building Carthage* (Plate 77) were the two paintings which Turner bequeathed specifically to the National Gallery, on condition that they were 'hung kept and placed . . . always between the two pictures painted by Claude'—the *Seaport* and '*The Mill*' from the Angerstein Collection. When the time came they were accepted on this condition, and today the two paintings by Turner are again to be seen next to the two by Claude.

9, 31. This composition was preceded by an exceptional number of preliminary studies and sketches. The initial source was probably a series of rapid studies, in various media on pink prepared paper, of waves breaking on a shore. These are in the 'Dunbar' sketch-book (LIV), one of those used on the Scottish tour of 1801. Two much slimmer sketch-books (LXVII and LXVIII) are largely devoted to studies of fishing boats in surf, such as Plate 29, more directly connected with *Fishermen upon a Lee-Shore* and another marine subject painted for the same patron, Samuel Dobree.

32, 11. Such dramatic and majestic marine subjects on a monumental scale played an important part in establishing Turner's reputation in the first decade of the nineteenth century. From the great variety of comment about the *Calais Pier* (see Plate 11) reported by Joseph Farington in his *Diary* it is clear that Turner's exhibits were already a focal point of interest among artists and those interested in the arts. The bold and free technique aroused much criticism, and a writer in *The Sun* saw in it 'a lamentable proof of genius losing itself in affectation and absurdity'. Modern critics have tended to see the earliest signs of Turner's mature genius in these marine paintings.

33, 34. See note to Plate 50.

35. Lowther Castle, Westmorland, was built for the 1st Earl of Lonsdale between 1806 and 1811 in Gothic style by Robert Smirke; it is a ruin today. Turner showed his pair of paintings of the house (which still belong to the Lonsdale family) at the Royal Academy in 1810. The evening scene is closely related to one of the three drawings of Lowther in the Ashmolean, and it also features a detailed study of a thistle in the foreground. The view of Petworth (Plate 62) was Turner's only other R.A. exhibit in 1810.

36, 39. The immediate impact of the Alps on Turner is best seen in the coloured drawings in the 'St. Gothard and Mont Blanc' sketch-book (LXXV), two of which are reproduced here. These are executed with the same freedom as the watercolours in the 'Edinburgh' sketch-book of the previous year, and in the same rather muted colours. Most of the large exhibition watercolours of Swiss subjects which Turner executed after his return to England are variants rather than direct adaptations of the on-the-spot studies. This applies to the two reproduced here, which were both acquired by Walter Fawkes. It has been plausibly suggested by recent research that Fawkes may have accompanied Turner on his first Continental tour (David Brown, 'J. M. W. Turner in Switzerland,' 1973, unpublished B. A. dissertation, University of Leicester).

40. The evolution of this canvas and its companion view of Bonneville, also shown in the 1803 exhibition, was fully described and illustrated by Evelyn Joll in a pamphlet accompanying the exhibition of the latter at Thos. Agnew and Sons in July, 1974.

41, Claude's *Landscape with Jacob and Laban* is dated
42. 1654, and was acquired by its first English owner within about twenty years of that date. It was bought by the sixth Duke of Somerset for Petworth House in 1686, and it must be presumed that Turner had seen it before painting the closely related *Macon*. This does, however, also record a visit to that area in 1802. Having declined an offer of 250 guineas from Sir John Leicester during the R.A. exhibition, Turner sold it to the Earl of Yarborough for 400 guineas in the following year. The painting had been received with the usual mixture of praise and criticism. Among the most fulsome praise was that of the critic of the *British Press*, who referred to it as 'the First landscape of the kind that has been executed since the time of Claude Lorrain, on whose works, indeed, Mr. Turner has evidently and usefully fixed his eye; and we are bold to say, that he has even surpassed that master in the richness and forms of some parts of his pictures'.

43. Several drawings in the 'Calais Pier' sketch-book (LXXXI) are connected with the evolution of this unwonted composition, which borrows heavily from Titian's *Holy Family and a Shepherd*, formerly part of the W. Y. Ottley Collection sold in London in 1801 and now in the National Gallery. One of the sketch-book drawings shows the figures in an upright composition, in the landscape setting of Titian's famous *St. Peter Martyr*, which Turner studied in the Louvre in 1802; it had been removed from Venice by Napoleon. The Titian was well known in England through engravings, and it was particularly admired by both Turner and Constable, who each eulogised and analysed it in lectures.

44. In this somewhat theatrical composition even the rocks and mountains have an air of artificiality, as do the carefully posed figures. The actual subject of the painting is confused, and John Gage has suggested that it illustrates Turner's current interest in alchemy, probably under the influence of De Loutherbourg (*Colour in Turner*, pp. 136–9).

45, This canvas, which may have been included by
46. Turner in one of the first exhibitions in his own gallery, is reminiscent both in style and technique of the two Bonneville subjects of 1803. As in these the application of the paint is rather dry and flat, and this makes the influence of Poussin all the more apparent. The same dryness of technique is to be found in the watercolour study for this composition.

47– In 1804 Turner was living at Sion Ferry House,
49. Isleworth, a house situated behind the group of trees seen on the right of this composition. Turner designated the subject of this plate as 'Epic Pastoral'. The Ionic 'temple' on the River's bank is a shooting lodge built by Robert Mylne for the second Duke of Northumberland; it still stands today. Four of the five subjects issued as the thirteenth part of the *Liber Studiorum* feature a river; one of them is derived from the painting of Bonneville reproduced here as Plate 40.

50, Turner did not resume his annual sketching tours
51; after his first journey abroad in 1802, and for the
33, next few years most of the places he visited were
34. within easy reach of London. At this period his on-the-spot studies in watercolour and oils are unusually naturalistic for him, in keeping with the practice of several of the younger landscape artists of the day. Turner may well have decided to concentrate his sketching on scenery which he knew well in order to achieve this naturalism more easily. Despite their naturalism, the majority of these sketches, both in oils and watercolour, achieve a balanced pictorial composition, something which probably came instinctively to Turner.

52. Turner was probably fired to paint and exhibit this genre scene in the manner of Teniers by the great success the year before of the young David Wilkie's first exhibit at the Royal Academy, *Village Politicians* (Private Collection), which is also reminiscent of Teniers. In 1807 Wilkie showed another interior, *The Blind Fiddler* (Tate Gallery), and Farington records in his *Diary* (8 May) that

when Sir John Leicester enquired the price of the *Blacksmith*, 'Turner answered that He understood Wilkie was to have 100 guineas for His *Blind Fiddler* & He should not rate His picture at a less price'. Turner got his price, and himself paid 140 guineas for the canvas when he bought it back at the Leicester sale in 1827. The *Country Blacksmith* was Turner's most ambitious and successful interior with figures in a conventional manner.

53. This wonderfully fluent study belongs to a group of seventeen large oil sketches in the Turner Bequest of subjects on or near the Thames, which are all very freely and thinly painted on a whiteish ground. It is possible that some can be identified as the canvases referred to by the son of Turner's friend the Rev. H. S. Trimmer, in a reminiscence printed by Thornbury; Turner 'had a boat at Richmond. . . . From this he painted on a large canvas direct from Nature. Till you have seen these sketches, you know nothing of Turner's powers. There are about two score of these large subjects, rolled up, and now national property.'

54. For long known as 'Evening—the Drinking Pool', this evocative scene shows the strong influence of Rubens and Gainsborough, and emulates particularly their use of figures. The men on the left are barking chestnut trees for caulking or tanning.

55, Both versions of De Loutherbourg's *Avalanche in the*
56. *Alps* were owned by patrons of Turner—that reproduced here by Sir John Leicester and the other (still at Petworth) by Lord Egremont—and thus he would have been familiar with both. There can be little doubt about the connection between De Loutherbourg's and Turner's treatment of the subject, though it seems that, despite being neighbours in Hammersmith, the two artists were not on friendly terms. Turner did not visit the Grisons on his Swiss tour in 1802, nor could he have witnessed an avalanche, as he was there in September and October. However, the authenticity of the scene is based on his close observation of other parts of the Alps.

57. This was the first of Turner's great vortex-like compositions, and he was particularly concerned that it should be hung low in the Academy exhibition. It was also the first of Turner's paintings to illustrate the struggle between Carthage and Rome, and John Gage has suggested that he saw this as a parallel to the conflict between England and Napoleonic France.

58. Turner's extensive studies from nature in the years around 1810 come to fruition in this canvas, which ignores all picturesque or topographical content and concentrates simply on an actual scene of countrymen at work early on a winter's morning. When exhibited it was accompanied by one line from Thomson's *Winter*: 'The rigid hoar frost melts before his beam'.

59. In a reminiscence quoted by Thornbury, Sir Charles Eastlake described 'a small portable painting-box, containing some prepared paper for oil sketches, as well as other necessary materials', which a Mr. Johns prepared for Turner's use while he was touring in Devonshire. He also records that 'one of the sketches was done in less than half an hour'.

60. See note to Plate 68.

61. Tradition (recorded by Farington) has it that Turner spent much of his time fishing in the lake while staying at Tabley in 1808. The folly-like round water-tower as well as a 'Gothic' boathouse still stand by the lake today. The pair to this view of Tabley House was bought by Lord Egremont at the Leicester sale, and is at Petworth.

63. Nothing is known of the early history of this painting, which does not seem to have been executed as a commission. It is based on a drawing in the 'Vale of Heathfield' sketch-book (CXXXVII, 3 and 4).

64– Aelbert Cuyp (1620–91) was the most popular
66. Dutch landscape painter among British collectors and connoisseurs in the later eighteenth and nineteenth centuries. His mellow treatment of water and his depiction of calm sunlight were especially influential on Turner in the years around 1810. This was remarked upon by many critics of the day and can be clearly seen in some of the country house 'portraits' reproduced here, and in *Dorchester Mead* and *Whalley Bridge and Abbey*. The former has only recently been identified as the painting of that title exhibited in Turner's Gallery in 1810; it was for long known as 'Abingdon, Berkshire, with a View of the Thames—Morning'.

67. Ruskin thought very highly of this drawing and often referred to it. In the catalogue of the 1878 Exhibition of his Turner drawings at the Fine Art Society he wrote, 'it shows already one of Turner's specially English (in the humiliating sense) points of character—that, like Bewick, he could draw *pigs* better than any other animal. There is also some trace of Turner's constant feeling afterwards. Sunshine, and rivers, and sweet hills; yes, and who is there to see or care for them?—Only the pigs.'

68, Turner had already provided illustrations for
69; several books by the antiquarian, Dr. Whitaker,
60. when he was commissioned to illustrate that author's *History of Richmondshire*, published in parts by Longman's between 1819 and 1823. Turner was paid twenty-five guineas for each of his twenty drawings, and they were sold by the publishers, soon after the work was completed, for about the same sum. Plates 60 and 68 belong to this series, while Plate 69, though dated 1816, was only used in 1823, when it was lithographed by J. D. Harding for a new edition of Whitaker's *History of Leeds*. Plates 68 and 69 belonged to Ruskin, who tried unsuccessfully to persuade Oxford University to purchase Plate 60 in 1884; his failure was a contributory factor in deciding Ruskin to resign the Slade Professorship.

70, These three drawings are all connected with
75, Walter Fawkes and Farnley Hall in Yorkshire.
76. Turner's friendship with Fawkes and the latter's patronage of Turner is discussed in the *Introduction* (pp. 22ff). Among the Turner drawings still at Farnley today are a series of the interior of the house, drawn in some detail in body-colours. One of these shows the *Dort* (Plate 86) hanging over the fireplace in the drawing room.

71. This drawing was engraved by W. R. Smith and the plate was published in 1822. Several other artists provided illustrations for *The Provincial Antiquities of Scotland*, including A. W. Callcott and the Rev. J Thomson. The exceptional success of this book has been attributed to Sir Walter Scott's text, rather than to the illustrations, of which twelve are after Turner.

72. This vast canvas is inscribed at the bottom left, 'Appulia in Search of Appulus learns from the Swain the Cause of his Metamorphosis'. Character-istically Turner has illustrated his own variant of Ovid's tale, to which he referred in the British Institution catalogue; Appulia is his own invention. However, the composition is not original, for it is closely based on the Petworth Claude, *Landscape with Jacob and Laban* (Plate 42), which Turner knew well. The somewhat Neo-Classical *Empire* figures were thought even worse than Claude's by William Hazlitt.

73, The Rhine had been popular with British travellers
74. and artists in the later years of the eighteenth century, and the romance and picturesqueness of the castles caught their imagination. Turner was the first recorded British artist to sketch on the Rhine after the Napoleonic wars. For him the chief subject-matter lay in the landscape and light of the great river rather than in the castles, which he usually integrated as relatively minor features in his compositions.

77. Inscribed with the title on a wall on the extreme left of the picture and signed *J. M. W. Turner 1815*, this work was one of Turner's own favourites. Tradition has it that he planned to be buried wrapped up in it, but it was, in fact, one of the two canvases which he bequeathed specifically to the National Gallery (see note to Plate 27).

78, Much has been made of the importance for
79. Constable of Sir George Beaumont's small Claude *Landscape: Hagar and the Angel* (Plate 79), which the baronet is said always to have taken with him on his travels. *Crossing the Brook* could well also be a derivation from this beautifully balanced composition, but adapted by Turner in reverse. It may be this fact that led Sir George to be so highly critical of Turner's canvas.

81. Though far less obviously than the *Dort* (Plate 86) this canvas also shows the influences of Cuyp's luminous treatment of sea and sky, and of Turner's own experience of Dutch light during his tour of 1817. The full title of the painting names a specific location. 'Brill Church bearing S.E. by S., Massensluys E. by S.' The figures in the boats in the foreground are particularly clumsy in execution, but play an important role in the balance of this open composition.

82, Turner made many drawings of the extensive view
83. from Richmond Hill, one of the most spectacular

to be found in and around London. The earliest of these dates from about 1795 (Turner Bequest XXVII K). Turner may have felt that he could not do full justice to this great view except on the monumental scale of *Richmond Hill*, the largest painting he exhibited. As in his other R.A. exhibit of 1819 (Plate 81), the figures play a vital role in the composition. These fashionable ladies, with their sloping shoulders and long necks, lend credence to the idea that Turner made use of dummies for some of his depictions of figures. However, the influence of Watteau's figure painting can also be cited. Whatever the source of such figure groups they leave little doubt that Turner had difficulty in painting them.

84. This important canvas was most successfully cleaned for the Turner Bi-Centenary Exhibition at the Royal Academy. As a result the delicate beauty of the distant view of Rome re-appeared as an essential element of this ambitious composition. The didactic and biographical character of the work has been fully discussed by John Gage (*Colour in Turner*, pp. 92–5), who considers it an 'art-historical picture', in which Turner reveals his admiration for Raphael and his attempts to compare himself with that 'universal' artist. The landscape canvas in the centre foreground is inscribed *Casa di Raffaello* and the plan near it *Pianta del Vaticano*. Thus Turner illustrates not only Raphael's range as a painter but also his activities as an architect.

89. This is inscribed on the stone at bottom left, *Liquidae Placuere Baiae*, a quotation from Horace alluding to the delight of the waters of Baiae. Turner visited this lovely spot from Naples and made numerous drawings there. When exhibited the painting was catalogued with the line 'Waft me to sunny Baiae's shore', but the mythological subject depicted and the symbolic white rabbit and snake all lead to a rather gloomy interpretation of Turner's intentions, which have been discussed by John Gage and others. The descriptive adjective most commonly used by contemporary critics of this much-praised canvas was 'gorgeous'.

93, 94. Turner made a number of sketches connected with the *Dieppe* during his brief visit to France in the early autumn of 1821. (Turner Bequest CCXI and CCLVIII, mistakenly dated in the *Inventory* 1824 and 1830 respectively.) In 1826 Turner exhibited a

companion to the *Dieppe*, which is now also in the Frick Collection in New York. Entitled *Cologne, the Arrival of the Packet-Boat: Evening*, this, like the *Dort* of 1818 (Plate 86), is indebted to the harbour scenes of Cuyp.

95– 101. Turner's first visit to Italy was the most extensive sketching tour that he ever undertook; it is discussed above in the *Introduction* (pp. 26–30). The pencil, ink and watercolour drawings reproduced here illustrate the great variety of drawing techniques which he used to record what he saw. He made full use of his thirty years' sketching experience to assemble a reference collection of Italian subjects sufficiently wide in its scope to last him for the rest of his life. (As a result he spent relatively little time actually sketching on his subsequent visits to Italy.) The success of this undertaking is demonstrated by the fact that Turner had not re-visited Venice when he began his great series of exhibited Venetian oils in 1833. The high point of his sketching in 1819 can be seen in the small series of Venetian watercolours (Plates 87, 88), which lend weight to the argument that some of the coloured drawings were executed out-of-doors.

102 105. The large number of finished watercolours which Turner executed for British topographical engravings in the 1820s have been unjustly neglected in recent decades, though in the early years of this century they were, correctly, considered to be among Turner's outstanding achievements in that medium. Again and again they demonstrate his total mastery of technique and composition. That Turner was well served by his engravers can be seen when comparing the drawing (Plate 102) and the mezzotint (Plate 103) of *Totnes*.

107. The subject is from Book IX of Homer's *Odyssey*, and, as Ruskin noted, Turner closely followed Pope's translation of the text in details of the light and sea. However, most of the critics were upset by the strong colours of this canvas. One (*Morning Herald*, 5 May, 1829) described it as 'a specimen of *colouring run mad*—positive vermilion—positive indigo, and all the most glaring tints of green, yellow, and purple contend for mastery of the canvas, with all the vehement contrasts of a kaleidoscope or Persian carpet'.

108,109; Researches in the Petworth papers and records
123. have not led to any fuller information concerning

Lord Egremont's patronage of Turner, and the artist's visits to Petworth. It has been suggested that after the death of his father Turner spent several Christmases at Petworth. It is to be hoped that John Gage's discovery of the descriptive passage in the Creevey Correspondence (see p. 34 above), and of Lord Egremont's interests in the Chichester Canal (Plate 109) and the Chain Pier at Brighton (the subject of the fourth canvas in this series) will be followed by the finding of more such evidence.

110. The figures are related to a drawing in the 'Rivers Meuse and Moselle' sketch-book (CCXVI 227), inscribed *Fisherwomen looking for bait*. Turner's accuracy of observation is evident here, for when figures are seen in a strong light walking or standing on wet sand they appear unnaturally tall, as in this painting.

111, Though described as based on the sketch of another
112. artist, W. Page, this view of the chapel at Pisa is closely related to a drawing in the 'Genoa and Florence' sketch-book (CCXXXIII 55), which Turner made when he visited Pisa in 1828. Turner produced twenty-six illustrations for Murray's edition of Byron (1832–4), and as he never visited Greece or the Near East the majority of the plates had to be based on drawings made on the spot by others.

113– Two of the *Rivers of France* drawings reproduced
116; here (Plates 92, 114) belonged to Ruskin, who
92. considered his group from this series a focal point of his own collection and then of his gift to Oxford. How Ruskin had acquired his twenty-seven *Rivers of France* drawings in 1858 was long something of a mystery, until it was discovered that the Mrs. Hannah Cooper from whom he purchased them in two lots was the niece of Charles Stokes, friend, stockbroker and patron of Turner. Stokes had bought twenty-four of these drawings from Turner through Mr. Griffith of Norwood in 1850 for 600 guineas. Ruskin paid 1500 guineas for these and three additional ones. It is ironical that Turner had apparently offered Ruskin the whole series for 25 guineas a piece, but his father thought that Ruskin 'was mad to want them', and declined to buy them. (See Luke Herrmann, *Ruskin and Turner*, passim, and 'Ruskin and Turner: A riddle resolved' in *Burlington Magazine*, CXII, 1970, pp. 696–9.)

117. This, like its companion piece, a morning scene shown in the following year (1827), was painted for William Moffatt. There are numerous studies connected with the two paintings in the 'Mortlake and Pulborough' sketch-book (CCXIII), which Turner used in 1825. The drawing on ff. 10–11 is a direct study for the present composition.

118– These works and others connected with Turner's
121. stay on the Isle of Wight as the guest of John Nash are discussed and illustrated by Graham Reynolds in a recent article ('Turner and East Cowes Castle' in *Victoria and Albert Museum Yearbook*, 1969, pp. 67–79). This influential visit was also well illustrated in the Turner Bi-Centenary Exhibition at the Royal Academy (Cat. Nos. 311–322).

122. It is not known why Lord Egremont declined the *Palestrina*, which Turner had painted specifically for him as a companion to the Petworth Claude (Plate 42). It was ultimately bought by Elhanan Bicknell, one of Turner's major patrons in his later years.

124, Turner re-worked all his Roman exhibits when they
126. were shown again in London. The third painting definitely exhibited in Rome was the *Vision of Medea* (Tate Gallery, No. 513), which was shown at the R.A. in 1831. The strong criticisms that these canvases received in Rome may well have been one reason for Turner's subsequent stand against the recently formed British Academy in Rome. It was a grave blow for the British artists living in Rome when the Royal Academy re-imposed the rule that its own members must be resident in Britain, and it was largely Turner who enforced that decision.

127. This scene illustrates the passage from Matthew, XXVII, 24, and clearly shows Turner's debt to Rembrandt. The Angerstein Collection, purchased as the initiation of the National Gallery in 1824, included two biblical interiors by Rembrandt, one of which, *The Woman taken in Adultery* (No. 45), features a similar concentration of light on the central figures.

128. Exhibited with a line from Shakespeare's *Merchant of Venice*: SHYLOCK: Jessica, shut the window, I say', and painted with Rembrandt's Jewish subjects much in mind. However, the dark and almost monochrome character of Rembrandt's

treatments of such subjects is replaced here by strong and glowing colours, among which red predominates.

129– The series of 116 body-colour drawings listed by
131, Finberg under the title 'Petworth Water Colours'
134, (CCXLIV) has long been recognised as one of the
135, most spontaneous and confident by Turner. They
137. range from highly detailed interiors such as Plate 130 to the most economical of impressions, as in *Teasing the Donkey* (CCXLIV 97). Reflecting the ease and spaciousness of life in the great house, they provide a very personal record of Turner's re-actions to it: as Lord Clark has written so aptly, 'he set down in every scene, exactly what had touched or amused him, and nothing more' ('Turner at Petworth' in *The Ambassador*, August 1949). The paintings of Petworth interiors are just as personal, and it has been suggested that the *Interior at Petworth* (Plate 134) was painted by Turner in reaction to the news of Lord Egremont's death in 1837.

136. For a full discussion of the didactic qualities of this panel and of Turner's debt to Watteau see John Gage, *Colour in Turner*, pp. 91–2.

138. This work was probably painted for the architect John Nash, and was certainly in the sale of his pictures in 1835, when it was bought on behalf of John Sheepshanks. It is fully discussed by Graham Reynolds in 'Turner at East Cowes Castle' in *Victoria and Albert Yearbook*, 1969, pp. 75–8.

140. Graham Reynolds has suggested that this Venetian scene may have been inspired by those of Boning-ton, who had died in 1828 (*Turner*, 1969, pp. 158–60). It was recorded at the time of its exhibition that Turner's Venetian scene was painted in rivalry with the much younger William Clarkson Stanfield's *Venice from the Dogana*, also shown at the Royal Academy in 1833 and purchased by Lord Lansdowne.

142. The study connected with the *Hero and Leander* is on f. 57 of the 'Calais Pier' sketch-book (LXXXI), which Turner was using around 1802, and which includes studies for several other compositions such as the *Macon* (Plate 41) and *Hannibal* (Plate 57). Turner's prolonged use of this sketch-book is but one example of how essential his 'library' of sketch-books was for his painting.

143. The scene of this painting is on the Tyne. According to its first owner, Henry McConnell, it was painted at his suggestion as a contrasting companion to the Venetian scene which he had purchased at the Academy in the previous year. This was very pro-bably the *Venice; Dogana and San Giorgio Maggiore*, now also in Washington (repr., Butlin and Rothenstein, *Turner*, pl. 98).

144. We know from Ruskin that this work was included in the first selection of paintings from the Turner Bequest temporarily exhibited at the National Gallery in 1857 (*Works*, XIII, p. 310). It was one of the very few paintings not exhibited during Turner's lifetime which was selected on that occasion. It is most instructive to compare this canvas with some of the great sea-pieces (such as Plates 11 and 32) of about thirty years earlier.

147, The Turner Bequest includes a number of un-
156. exhibited and incomplete Venetian compositions, among them two very faint impressions which were shown for the first time at the Turner Bi-Centenary Exhibition (Tate Gallery Nos 5487 and 5488).

148. In August 1869 Ruskin was appointed the first Slade Professor of Fine Art at Oxford. Some months previously he had sold some of his Turner drawings at Christie's, but had failed to sell *The Slave Ship*, which he now found 'too painful to live with'. However, in 1872 it was sold in America.

149, The romantic University city of Heidelberg, on
161. the Neckar, provided Turner with material for numerous drawings, several finished watercolours, and this canvas. In the finished works festive groups of figures play an important role, and it seems possible that Turner witnessed a carnival or other festival on one of his visits. In Plate 161 Turner has restored the castle which was partially destroyed in 1689, and the costumes suggest a seventeenth-century scene.

150, Much has been made of the symbolism, and re-
151. levance in Turner's philosophy, of this pair of canvases, which were both accompanied by melancholy lines from Turner's *Fallacies of Hope*. These points and the importance of Goethe's colour theories for Turner have been fully discussed by John Gage (*Colour in Turner*, pp. 173–88).

154. The large plates (each measuring 17 × 24 ins.) of *Ancient Italy* and *Modern Italy* were published in

1842, engraved by J. T. Willmore and W. Miller respectively. The story of these plates, in which Turner took a very active interest, is fully recounted by W. G. Rawlinson (*The Engraved Work of J.M.W. Turner*, Vol. II, pp. 338–41).

155. The location of this scene has only been identified in the last few years; it was previously known as *Bridge and Tower*.

158. Turner stayed at the Hotel Europa during his last visit to Venice, in 1840 and possibly also on his earlier visits. The Turner Bequest includes many drawings and watercolours made from the hotel.

162, 163. There are still many unresolved questions in connection with the large number of Turner's later Venetian watercolour and body-colour studies in the Turner Bequest and in other collections. The problems have been succinctly summed up by Andrew Wilton on pp. 154–5 of the *Catalogue* of the Turner Bi-Centenary Exhibition. Ruskin was probably correct in suggesting that such drawings as those reproduced here were made on the spot, though Finberg believed that this applied only to the pencil outlines, which were coloured later.

168, 169, 180. Ruskin recounted his memories of the origin and execution of the 1842 and 1843 Swiss watercolours in the 'Epilogue' to the *Notes by Mr. Ruskin on his Drawings by the late J. M. W. Turner, R.A.*, published in connection with the exhibition of his collection at the Fine Art Society, New Bond Street, in March 1878. The 'Epilogue' did not appear until the third edition of this booklet, for Ruskin suffered his first attack of insanity in February 1878, and was unable to complete it in time for the opening of the exhibition. The 'Epilogue' was revised for the sixth edition. The fascinating and complex bibliographical story of these *Notes* and the 'Epilogue' is fully outlined in Volume XIII of the *Works* (pp. 393–402), where the text and all its variants are given on pp. 403–536. In view of the conditions under which the 'Epilogue' was written its reliability should perhaps be accepted with caution.

173. One of Turner's greatest vortex compositions, this canvas emphasises the hopelessness of man's struggle in face of the brute force of nature. It also demonstrates once again Turner's determination to record nature at first hand. In this instance he may have been deliberately emulating the example of the French painter Claude-Joseph Vernet, whose grandson, Horace Vernet, exhibited at the Salon of 1822 a large canvas showing his grandfather (sketch-book in hand) lashed to the mast of a ship to observe a storm. This episode in Joseph Vernet's life was first recorded in 1789, the year of his death. (The information about Vernet was communicated in an unpublished lecture by Philip Conisbee.)

174. Wilkie died on board the *Oriental* on 1 June 1841, and was buried at sea off Gibraltar at 8.30 that evening. *Peace—Burial at Sea* was painted in friendly rivalry with George Jones, R.A., whose own rendering of this melancholy scene was also shown at the R.A. in 1842, but is now known only in a watercolour version in the Brinsley Ford Collection.

175. This famous painting is the subject of John Gage's 'Art in Context' volume, *Turner: Rain, Steam and Speed*, published in 1972. Here the well-known account by Lady Simon of a train journey in wild weather when 'an elderly gentleman, short and stout, with a red face and a curious, prominent nose. . . jumping up to open the window [of a railway carriage], craning his neck out, and finally calling to her to come and observe a curious effect of light', is given little credence. The place recorded in the painting is the Maidenhead railway bridge, built to Brunel's design between 1837 and 1839, the subject of some controversy as it was considered unsafe by critics of the Great Western Railway. The chief railway event of 1844 was the opening of the Bristol and Exeter extension of the G.W.R., which more or less coincided with the opening of that year's summer exhibition at the Royal Academy. These and several other points show how very up-to-date Turner was in this famous 'document' of the railway age.

176. Three of the whaling pictures are in the Tate Gallery and one is in the Metropolitan Museum, New York. There are several studies related to these compositions in general terms in the 'Whalers' sketch-book (CCCLIII). John Gage has pointed out (Turner Bi-Centenary Exhibition *Catalogue*, B 109) that Turner's interest in whaling may have arisen as a result of his contacts with Elhanan Bicknell, one of the major patrons of his later years, who was a whaling entrepreneur.

177; 184-190. The village of Norham is pleasantly situated in the meadows on a bend of the River Tweed. At the far end of the main street rise the splendid ruins of the Castle, once the chief northern stronghold of the Bishops of Durham. The steep bank of the river is to the north and west, and a deep ravine lies to the east. Turner first visited Norham during his Northern tour in the summer of 1797, when he made the rapid pencil study (Plate 184) in the 'North of England' sketch-book. He used this drawing in connection with the large watercolour study reproduced as Plate 186, which is very experimental in its use of washes and wiping out, and then executed two finished watercolours with similar compositions, of which one was shown at the Royal Academy in 1798 (No. 43), with a quotation from Thomson's *Seasons*. These two drawings are now in British private collections. Turner saw Norham again in 1801, when he passed through on his way to Scotland. On this occasion he made ten pencil studies of the castle, including Plate 185, in the 'Helmsley' sketch-book. Comparison of Plates 184 and 185 shows how simplified the later drawing has become; it concentrates on the outline of the castle against the sky, which is the principal feature in Turner's *Liber Studiorum* rendering of this scene (Plates 187 and 188). There is no evidence that Turner took up Norham between 1801 and his work on the *Liber* drawing in about 1815, and he certainly did not re-visit Norham between these dates. Nor had he been to Norham again before his next development of the subject, the glowing watercolour of Plate 189, which was engraved in mezzotint by Charles Turner in 1824 for *The Rivers of England* (Plate 190). In this drawing and plate the monochrome sombreness of the *Liber* version is replaced by brilliant colour and light. Turner was at Norham again in 1831, and

there are drawings of the castle in the 'Abbotsford' sketch-book (CCLXVII). One of Turner's illustrations for Cadell's edition of Scott's *Prose Works* was *Norham Castle—Moonrise*, engraved in 1834 by William Miller (Rawlinson, No. 522); this is the only finished view of Norham in which the sun does not appear. The sun is an essential element in the two or three 'Colour Beginnings' in the Turner Bequest identified as being of Norham, and sunlight is, of course, the main theme of *Norham Castle, Sunrise* (Plate 177). This delicate and glowing canvas is the climax of all Turner's renderings of Norham Castle. It is usually dated *c*. 1835–40, but the later date suggested here seems more likely, for it was only in his final years that Turner achieved such total understanding of the qualities of colour and light.

180. Accompanied in the catalogue by two verses from Revelations, XIX, beginning: 'And I saw an Angel standing in the sun; and he cried with a loud voice'. The companion to Plate 180 in the 1846 Exhibition was entitled *Undine giving the Ring to Masaniello, Fisherman of Naples* (Tate Gallery, No. 549). Masaniello was a Neapolitan revolutionary, and it is difficult to find a link between the two pictures.

183. Originally painted in about 1809, *The Wreck Buoy* was sent down to London from Scotland by Mr. Munro of Novar, so that Turner could show it at the Royal Academy in 1849. When he saw it again Turner was dissatisfied with it, and anxiously watched by Munro, he re-painted it, though exactly to what extent is hard to determine. Turner did not alter his other R.A. exhibit of this year, the Titianesque *Venus and Adonis*, painted in about 1803 and also lent to him by Munro of Novar.

Bibliography

Many books about Turner have been published, but sadly few of these have added greatly to our knowledge of his art and life. A selection of the most valuable books and catalogues is listed here in chronological order of publication.

John Ruskin, *Modern Painters*, 5 vols., London 1843–60.
A classic, which, especially in its first volume, provides valuable insight into the work of Turner. It is included as volumes III to VII in the *Library Edition* of *The Works of Ruskin*, 39 vols., London 1903–12, which contains all his writings on Turner.

Walter Thornbury, *The Life of J. M. W. Turner, R.A.*, 2 vols. London 1862; 2nd edition, 1 vol., London 1877.
The first full-length biography of Turner. Though based partly on many contemporary reminiscences of the artist, this work has become notorious for its inaccuracies and distortions, which greatly influenced subsequent opinion on Turner.

Samuel and Richard Redgrave, *A Century of British Painters*, 2 vols., London 1866; 2nd edition, 1890; Phaidon Press edition, 1947.
Includes an excellent chapter on Turner, and is a mine of information about his contemporaries by an artist and a writer on art who knew them.

P. G. Hamerton, *The Life of J. M. W. Turner, R.A.*, London 1879.
A serious biography by a leading later nineteenth-century critic, now almost forgotten.

C. F. Bell, *The Exhibited Works of J. M. W. Turner, R.A.*, London 1901.
The first, rather dry, work of 'modern' research, which contains useful descriptions of works and details of provenance.

Sir Walter Armstrong, *Turner*, London 1902.
A huge and luxurious volume, which has a balanced text, useful illustrations, and list of works, still valuable though now out of date.

W. G. Rawlinson, *Turner's Liber Studiorum, a Description and a Catalogue*, London 1906; *The Engraved Work of J. M. W. Turner*, R.A., 2 vols., London 1908 and 1913.
These comprehensive reference books provide the groundwork for the study of all the engraved work by and after Turner.

A. J. Finberg, *A Complete Inventory of the Drawings of the Turner Bequest*, 2 vols., London 1909.
An essential, though now sadly outdated, tool for working among the Turner Bequest drawings in the British Museum. Since its publication all references to these thousands of drawings follow the numeration established in the *Inventory*.

A. J. Finberg, *Turner's Sketches and Drawings*, London 1910.
The most scholarly of several contemporary illustrated publications.

National Gallery, Millbank (Tate Gallery), *Catalogue—Turner Collection*, London 1920.
A largely descriptive catalogue of the majority of the oil paintings in the Turner Bequest, and other paintings by Turner in the National Collections, and a list (based on Finberg's *Inventory*) of several hundred exhibited drawings and watercolours.

A. J. Finberg, *The History of Turner's Liber Studiorum with a new Catalogue Raisonné*, London 1924.
A handsome volume in which each plate is well illustrated in several states. It gives ample material for the study of the *Liber*.

A. J. Finberg, *In Venice with Turner*, London 1930.
Though now superseded in many of its conclusions this book contains useful illustrations and lists.

Bernard Falk, *Turner the painter: his Hidden Life:* London 1938.
Described as 'a frank and revealing biography' it is largely fictional, but includes a list of the books that Turner had in his own library.

A. J. Finberg, *The Life of J. M. W. Turner, R.A.*, Oxford 1939; 2nd edition, 1961.
The only full and reliable biography of Turner, based on the author's life-long study of the artist. It includes a good bibliography and a valuable list of Turner's exhibited works. The 2nd edition was revised by the author's widow, and has a supplement to the list of exhibited works.

Sir Martin Davies, *National Gallery Catalogues; British School*, London 1946; 2nd edition 1959.
The first edition includes full entries for over 100 paintings by Turner; the second for only 15.

Kenneth Clark, *Landscape into Art*, London 1949.
A stimulating book with a most sensitive appraisal of Turner.

Exhibition Catalogue, *J. M. W. Turner, R.A.*, Whitechapel Art Gallery, London, 1953.
The first major post-war exhibition. The catalogue includes a very useful chronological list of 'Turner's Travels in Great Britain and Europe'.

Martin Butlin, *Turner Watercolours*, London and Basel 1962.
A selection of thirty-two fine reproductions, supported by an informative introduction and excellent notes.

John Rothenstein and Martin Butlin, *Turner*, London 1964.
A succinct survey of Turner's career, based on a comprehensive selection of plates.

Mary Chamot, *The Early Works of J. M. W. Turner*, London (Tate Gallery) 1965.
Martin Butlin, *The Later Works of J. M. W. Turner*, London (Tate Gallery) 1965.
Two small picture books providing useful introductory texts and a selection of 30 reproductions each.

Lawrence Gowing, *Turner: Imagination and Reality*, New York 1966.
The well-illustrated catalogue, with a provocative text, of an exhibition devoted to Turner's late work held at the Museum of Modern Art.

Jack Lindsay, *J. M. W. Turner—His Life and Work*, London 1966.
Described as 'a critical biography' this presents Turner from a modern, and rather psychological, point of view. It is good on the part that literature and poetry played in Turner's work, on which the same author's *The Sunset Ship—The Poems of J. M. W. Turner* (Lowestoft 1966) is also useful.

Exhibition Catalogue, *Loan Exhibition of Paintings and Watercolours by J. M. W. Turner, R.A.*, Messrs. Thos. Agnew & Sons, London, 1967.
An outstanding exhibition held to mark the 150th Anniversary of Agnew's, the leading dealers in the works of Turner for over a century. Full catalogue entries compiled by Evelyn Joll.

Martin Butlin, *Watercolours from the Turner Bequest*, London (Tate Gallery) 1968.
A selection of 24 colour reproductions with a brief supporting text in English, German and French.

Luke Herrmann, *Ruskin and Turner*, London 1968.
A fully illustrated *catalogue raisonné* of the Turner drawings in the Ashmolean Museum, Oxford, with introductory chapters on 'Ruskin as a Collector of Turner Drawings' and 'Turner as a Draughtsman'.

John Gage, *Colour in Turner—Poetry and Truth*, London 1969.
A compilation of several studies in depth of various aspects of Turner's work, this is a book which provides much new material and thinking.

Graham Reynolds, *Turner*, London 1969.
A readable, balanced and well-illustrated account of the artist's life and work.

John Gage, *Turner: Rain, Steam and Speed*, London 1972.
An illuminating and scholarly study of this well-known masterpiece, in the 'Art in Context' series.

Exhibition Catalogue, *J. M. W. Turner*, Nationalgalerie, Berlin, 1972.
The standard foreign capital loan exhibition of paintings and drawings from the Turner Bequest enriched by a few loans from other sources.

Gerald Wilkinson, *The Sketches of Turner, R.A. 1802–20: genius of the Romantic*, London 1974.

A personal selection from Turner's early sketch-books in the British Museum, with numerous, sadly misleading, reproductions.

A.G.H. Bachrach, *Turner and Rotterdam*, Rotterdam 1974.
Devoted to the reproduction of the sketchbook studies of Rotterdam of 1817, 1825 and 1841, many identified in detail for the first time. The introduction makes a good case for a re-evaluation of the Netherlands' place in Turner's work.

Gerald Wilkinson, *The Sketches of Turner, R.A. 1802–20: genius of the Romantic*, London 1974.
A sequel to *Turner's early sketch-books*; there is no improvement in the standard of reproduction.

Exhibition Catalogue, *Turner 1775–1851*, The Royal Academy, London, 1974–5.
Helpful introductory essay and comments by Martin Butlin, John Gage and Andrew Wilson. Some very full catalogue entries, especially for the paintings, with new information and ideas.

Index

INDEX OF TURNER'S WORKS

INDEX OF NAMES

DATE D

Q759.2 T854 DH436tc2   AAO-1748
Turner, J. M. W.   060101 000
Turner : paintings, watercolor

0 00003 0196784 0
Johnson State College